W9-CMU-828

Existentialism and
Phenomenology in
Education:
Collected Essays

Existentialism and Phenomenology in Education

Collected Essays

David E. Denton
Editor

Teachers College Press

Teachers College, Columbia University
New York and London

Copyright © 1974 by Teachers College, Columbia University
Library of Congress Catalog Card Number: 73-85246

Library of Congress Cataloging in Publication Data
Main entry under title:

Existentialism and phenomenology in education.

    Includes bibliographical references.
    1. Education–Philosophy–Addresses, essays,
lectures. 2. Existentialism–Addresses, essays,
lectures. 3. Phenomenology–Addresses, essays,
lectures. I. Denton, David E., ed.
LB41.E953   370.1   73-85246
ISBN-0-8077-2514-5

Manufactured in the United States of America

Acknowledgements

The preparation of a volume of essays requires much cooperation from many persons, and certain of those should be identified and thanked: the writers themselves, the directors of the University of Kentucky Research Foundation, Carol Holt, secretary *par excellence*, Kathryn O'Malley, editorial assistant, *provocateur*, and calmer of the editor's storms, and the editorial staff of Teachers College Press.

Appreciation is expressed to the following for permission to quote from the works cited:

Addison-Wesley. J. Soltis, *An Introduction to the Analysis of Educational Concepts*, 1968.

Antioch Review. H. Kallen, "Individuality, Individualism, and John Dewey," *Antioch Review*, Fall 1959.

Beacon Press. M. Scheler, *Man's Place in Nature*, 1961.

Cornelius Berry. "The Concept of Self in John Dewey and John Macmurry: A Summary Critique," unpublished dissertation, Columbia University, 1971.

Bobbs-Merrill. R. Zaner, *The Way of Phenomenology*, 1970.

Clarendon Press. J. L. Austin, *Philosophical Papers*, 2nd ed., 1970.

J. M. Dent and the estate of Joseph Conrad. J. Conrad, *Heart of Darkness*, 1950. Conrad, *The Nigger of the 'Narcissus'*, 1929.

Dial Press. F. Dostoevsky, *The Short Novels of Dostoevsky*, C. Garnett, tr., 1945.

Doubleday and Company. W. Barrett, *Irrational Man: A Study of Existential Philosophy*, 1958. J. Barth, *End of the Road*, 1958. J. Kockelmans, ed., *Phenomenology: The Philosophy of Edmund Husserl and Its Interpretation*, 1967.

Duquesne University Press. A. Dondeyne, *Contemporary European Thought and Christian Faith*, 1963. S. Strasser, *Phenomenology and the Human Sciences*, 1963.

Educational Theory. N. Roseman, "Self Realization and the Experimentalist Theory of Education," *Educational Theory*, January 1963.

Fordham University Press. Q. Lauer, *The Triumph of Subjectivity*, 1958.

Harcourt Brace Jovanovich. R. Wellek and A. Warren, *Theory of Literature*, 1956.

Harper & Row. A. Hofstadter and R. Kuhns, eds., *Philosophies of Art and Beauty*, 1964. S. Kierkegaard, *The Point of View for My Work as an Author: A Report to History*, W. Lowrie, tr., 1962. Kierkegaard, *The Present Age*, A. Dru, tr., 1962. Kierkegaard, *Purity of Heart Is To Will One Thing*, D. Steere, tr., 1938.

Holt, Rinehart and Winston. R. Beck, *Perspectives in Philosophy*, 1961. J.

Dewey, *Creative Intelligence*, 1917. J. Dewey, *Human Nature and Conduct*, 1922. J. Dewey, *Logic: The Theory of Inquiry*, 1938. J. Dewey and J. Tuffs, *Ethics*, 1956.

Humanities Press. E. Husserl, *Ideas: General Introduction to Pure Phenomenology*, 1969, W. Boyce, tr.

Kappa Delta Pi. J. Dewey, "Experience and Education," The Kappa Delta Pi Lecture Series, 1938.

Alfred A. Knopf. A. Camus, *The Plague*, 1948. S. Gilbert, tr.

Macmillan. H. Horne, *The Democratic Philosophy of Education*, 1932.

New Directions. J. Sartre, *Nausea*, L. Alexander, tr., 1959.

Martinus Nijhoff. E. Husserl, *Cartesian Meditations*, D. Cairns, tr., 1964. Husserl, *The Idea of Phenomenology*, W. Alston and G. Nakhinian, trs., 1964. M. Natanson, *Literature, Philosophy and the Social Science: Essays in Existential Phenomenology*, 1962. Natanson, ed., *The Problems of Social Reality*, 1962. H. Spiegelberg, *The Phenomenological Movement*, I, 1969.

Northwestern University Press. M. Merleau-Ponty, *Sense and Non-Sense*, H. and P. Dreyfus, trs., 1964. P. Ricoeur, *Husserl: An Analysis of His Phenomenology*, 1967. A. Schütz, *The Phenomenology of the Social World*, G. Walsh and F. Lehnert, trs., 1967. C. Schrag, *Existence and Freedom*, 1961.

Ohio State University Press. K. Winetrout, *F.C.S. Schiller and the Dimension of Pragmatism*, 1967.

Open Court. P. Schilpp, *The Philosophy of John Dewey*, 1959.

Philosophical Library. J. Sartre, *Being and Nothingness*, H. Barnes, tr., 1956. Sartre, *Literature and Existentialism (What is Literature?)*, B. Frechtman, tr., 1965.

Philosophy of Education Society. E. F. Kaelin, "The Existential Ground for Aesthetic Education," *Philosophy of Education*, 1966. P. Phenix, "Unamuno, Love and Pedagogy," *Philosophy of Education*, 1968.

Princeton University Press. R. Bretall, *A Kierkegaard Anthology*, 1946. S. Kierkegaard, *Fear and Trembling and Sickness Unto Death*, 1941.

Quadrangle Books. P. Thévenaz, *What is Phenomenology?*, 1962.

Random House. A. Malraux, *Man's Fate*, H. Chevalier, tr., 1936.

Joseph Ratner, *Intelligence in the Modern World*, 1939.

Routledge and Kegan Paul. M. Merleau-Ponty, *Phenomenology of Perception*, 1962.

Schocken Books. F. Kafka, *The Great Wall of China: Stories and Reflections*, W. and E. Muir, trs., 1960.

Israel Scheffler, *The Language of Education*, 1968.

Charles Scribner's Sons, Jonathan Cape, and the executors of the Ernest Hemingway Estate, *A Farewell to Arms*, 1952.

Viking Press. W. Kaufmann, ed., *The Portable Nietzsche*, 1954.

W. W. Norton. R. Rilke, *Duino Elegies*, J. Leishman and S. Spender, trs., 1963.

World. W. Kaufmann, *Existentialism from Dostoevsky to Sartre*, 1970.

Yale University Press. P. Tillich, *The Courage to Be*, 1952.

Contents

ASPECT A

1 | The Terrane

DAVID E. DENTON

ORIGIN AND PURPOSE

At the end of the 1971 meeting of the Philosophy of Education Society, a group of philosophers of education met to discuss the status of existentialism and phenomenology in educational thought. Recent studies and translations were discussed; the history of efforts of existentialists and phenomenologists in education was reviewed; the new climate of acceptance and the sense of intellectual maturity were noted; and possible consequences of recent work by existentialists and phenomenologists on educational thought were examined. During a perusal of the literature. it became apparent that although several new and specialized works had either recently been published or were in press, no single work comprehended the leading edge of existential and phenomenological thought. From two considerations, that there was much new material to be presented and that no single work embodied the results of recent investigations, came the impetus for this book. It was to consist primarily of original essays,[1] the topics of which were to be assigned by the editor to persons in philosophy of education who had already achieved recognition for being leading thinkers in particular areas.

It was quickly agreed that we could no longer speak simplistically of some unitary entity called existentialism in education, or phenomenology in education, or even of existential phenomenology in education. What is now required is the patient and frequently technical explication of a variety of educational topics, explications to be done in the mode of existential and/or phenomenological analysis. But even that, the method and meaning of the analysis, must also be carefully explicated. The reader should note that definitions throughout this book emerge from contexts provided by each essayist. Similarly, the book's purpose has emerged from a context, an historical one, in which educational issues and new philosophical insights converged in a temporal setting. Our goal in these essays is to provide the general readership in philosophy of education access to the most recent investigations by leading existentialists and phenomenologists in education.

BACKGROUND

The background discussed here is not that of existentialism and phenomenology in general. Where historical connections are needed in the explication of an educational situation, each essayist makes his own. Friedman's *The Worlds of Existentialism*[2] and Luijpen's *Existential Phenomenology*[3] are still among the best general introductions. Our concern is with existentialism and phenomenology in educational thought.

A 1968[4] summary of the literature stated that only two book-length treatments of existentialism and education had been written, the first of these by George Kneller in 1958,[5] and the second by Van Cleve Morris in 1966.[6] A few articles had been published before 1958, and the National Society for the Study of Education, in its *Yearbook* of 1956,[7] had recognized this new area in philosophy of education, but for approximately a decade, 1955-1965, the number of publications remained relatively small, and little attention was given to original work. Attention was instead directed toward finding implications for educational practice. Kneller and Morris, pushing against the social adjustment aims of progressive educationists on one hand, and resisting the new dominance of those interested only in analyzing theory and language on the other, called for an emphasis on meaning and authenticity and for an education which would foster that sort of inquiry. Kneller focused on the authenticity of the teacher as the ground for such an education and treated the topics of death, anguish, commitment, and the awareness of these, in developing that teacher. Morris did attempt more specific guidelines, finding in the "Socratic Paradigm" the model for the existentialist teacher. Working independently of each other, Morris and Kneller both asked a persistent question: "Where are you other philosophers of education allowing, in your respective theories, for the subjectivity, for the authenticity of individual students?" Earlier, Ralph Harper had asked philosophers of education a similar question: "Why avoid the typical serious experiences of life in which even young people are already involved?"[8]

The nature of these two questions points to something of an early identity crisis for existentialism in education. It became identified almost exclusively as a moral doctrine. The writings of Harper, Kneller, and Morris were not completely responsible for that identification, however. Titles of three articles typical of that decade, written by different persons, illustrate how accepted that identification had become: "Viktor E. Frankl and 'The Responsible Self' ";[9] "Buber: Philosopher of the I-Thou Dialogue";[10] and "Albert Camus: Philosopher of Moral Concern."[11] In retrospect, it is easy to be harsh in one's criticisms, but the historical situation must not be forgotten; the context of the writings must be remembered. The struggle of ideas was between those who emphasized social adjustment and those who would leave behind the problems of human relations for the problems of language. The early existentialists in education struggled to call attention to that which was being left out of consideration.

This intense engagement, although quite appropriate in that historical situation, generated two problems, problems which consumed much of the time and energy of existentialists and phenomenologists in education in the 1960's. These were the problem of implication and the problem of scholarship. In regard to the first, the early existentialists, in the struggle of their time, did not see the radical nature of their own philosophy. Although there were critiques of objectivity, little effort was given to generalizing those critiques to the logic of explanation or to the logic of implication; thus, there was still a search for the "principles" of an existentialist educational theory, and the acceptance of a deductive form of implication. Three recent books by Chamberlin,[12] Denton,[13] and Vandenberg[14] have addressed themselves in part to these and related problems. Certain essays in this work go beyond even those three books in respect to the problems of explanation and implication, with the emphasis being on constructive alternatives rather than on criticism.

The question of adequate scholarship began to be raised in the mid-1960's with the arrival on the scene of a new intellectual generation. Attention was given to a larger number of existentialist thinkers; the literature of phenomenology became an important source, and, with the works of Leroy Troutner and Donald Vandenberg, Heidegger's influence increased. Further, systematic critiques began to be made of the writings of the early existentialists in education. Among the first such criticisms was that of Vandenberg,[15] who charged Kneller with having misconstrued the meaning of several of Heidegger's points, especially Heidegger's notion of death. DeSoto's[16] rather heated response, in which he called Vandenberg a "dedicated flaw-picker," illustrates the sensitivities of the period. Other critiques were to follow, and the exchange of ideas had its own effect, changing the emphasis from doing battle with those outside the camp to intensive dialogue among fellow existentialists and phenomenologists.

This book of essays is one outcome of that recent dialogue. Another, and perhaps the most significant development within the period covered by this brief historical narrative, is the attempt to do original explications of educational situations. No longer is there an attempt to derive implications from statements in the literature which, in the past, appeared to have propositional status; rather, we begin in the concrete situations of the world of educating and, using the methods of existentialism and phenomenology, describe and explicate those situations. This is not a simple task, and it raises certain old questions, as well as a variety of new ones. Those questions are not ignored in this volume, but are faced and grappled with in all their complexity. Over the past twenty years, we have moved from a search for implications, through a period of growth in scholarship, to the present moment of renewed confidence in our task, a moment from which original explications of the lived-world of educating are now emerging.

Although the terms "existentialism" and "phenomenology" are used in the title of this book, the use is loose and historical, not taxonomic. It is true that Kierkegaard, the founder of existentialism, was no phenomenologist, and that Husserl, who launched the phenomenological movement, was no existentialist, but, since the publication of Heidegger's *Sein und Zeit* in 1927, a simple distinction between the two is no longer possible. In that work, Heidegger brought Kierkegaard's question of man and Husserl's question of knowledge into a new synthesis, one which is sometimes called existential phenomenology. But whatever it is called, it provides the ground for a philosophical anthropology which avoids the pitfalls of idealism on the one hand and positivism on the other.

The two terms "existentialism" and "phenomenology" are both in this book's title because there are thinkers included here who have influenced certain philosophers of education, although they have either ignored or rejected Heidegger's work. Marcel, Jaspers, Unamuno, and Camus are among that group of existentialists who continue to work in the tradition of Kierkegaard, while Alfred Schütz represents those who work from the Husserlian tradition, rejecting Heidegger's treatment of Husserlian phenomenology.

ORGANIZATION OF THE WORK

What we have, therefore, is not a taxonomy but the interrelated surfaces or aspects of a single configuration; to be true to that configuration, both terms are maintained in the title, and the contents of the work itself are grouped by aspects. Aspect A locates the configuration in the larger context of American educational thought. Aspect B reflects those contours of the configuration which are most readily identifiable with existentialism, although the phenomenological influences are quite obvious; Aspect C deals with phenomenological concerns. Aspect D focuses on other areas by bringing the materials and methods of both existentialism and phenomenology to bear on two specific questions, those of temporality and educational research.

REFERENCES

1. All essays, with the exception of those by Professors Kaelin and Phenix, have been written for original publication in this volume.
2. M. Friedman (ed.), *The Worlds of Existentialism: A Critical Reader* (New York: Random House, 1964).
3. W. Luijpen, *Existential Phenomenology* (Pittsburgh: Duquesne University Press, 1969; 1st ed., 1960).

4. D. Denton, "Existentialism in American Educational Philosophy," *International Review of Education,* XIV (1968), 97-102.

5. G. Kneller, *Existentialism and Education* (New York: Philosophical Library, 1958).

6. V. Morris, *Existentialism in Education* (New York: Harper and Row, 1966).

7. R. Harper, in *Modern Philosophies of Education: Fifty-Fourth Yearbook* (Chicago: University of Chicago Press, 1956).

8. *Ibid.,* pp. 222-223.

9. A. Wirth, "Victor E. Frankl and 'The Responsible Self,' " *Educational Theory,* XII (October 1962), 241-246.

10. K. Winetrout, "Buber: Philosopher of the I-Thou Dialogue," *Educational Theory,* XIII (January 1963), 53-57.

11. D. Denton, "Albert Camus: Philosopher of Moral Concern," *Educational Theory,* XIV (April 1964), 99-102.

12. J. Chamberlin, *Toward a Phenomenology of Education* (Philadelphia: Westminster Press, 1969).

13. D. Denton, *The Language of Ordinary Experience* (New York: Philosophical Library, 1970).

14. D. Vandenberg, *Being and Education* (Englewood Cliffs, N.J.: Prentice-Hall, 1971).

15. D. Vandenberg, "Kneller, Heidegger, and Death," *Educational Theory,* XV (July 1965), 217-221.

16. A. DeSoto, "Heidegger, Kneller, and Vandenberg," *Educational Theory,* XVI (July 1966), 239-241.

Leroy Troutner's essay locates existential phenomenology in relation to the central figure of American educational thought, John Dewey. Troutner does not merely catalogue similarities and differences, but carefully develops a new thesis, namely, that educational philosophy needs both Dewey and Heidegger. He argues for a philosophical anthropology of education and demonstrates the contributions of both Dewey and Heidegger toward that end. He also indicates where there are genuine contradictions and lacks in each, and where the thinking of both must be supplemented by the specific works of others.

2 | John Dewey and the Existential Phenomenologist

LEROY F. TROUTNER

The image of man as an earth-bound and time-bound creature permeates Dewey's writings as it does that of the Existentialists—up to a point. Beyond that point he moves in a direction that is the very opposite of Existentialism. What Dewey never calls into question is the thing he labels Intelligence, which in his last writings came to mean simply Scientific Method. Dewey places the human person securely within his biological and social context, but he never goes past this context into that deepest center of the human person where fear and trembling start. Any examination of inner experience—really inner experience—would have seemed to Dewey to take the philosopher too far away from nature in the direction of the theological.

William Barrett, *Irrational Man:
A Study in Existentialist Philosophy*

When I first started writing about existential thought and education, I always felt compelled to try to persuade my readers of the respectability of this radically different European philosophy called existential phenomenology. The reception given this movement by American philosophers, from the late 1940's when it was introduced until well into the '60's, was anything but cordial. It was for the most part rejected, often without serious study, "as sensationalism or mere 'psychologizing,' a literary attitude, postwar despair, nihilism, or heaven knows what besides."[1] Today the situation is much improved. Recently, while researching the topic of time, which is one of the favorite themes of the existentialist, I was amazed by the number of dissertations that have been written in the last two or three years on the phenomenology of time, the first analysis of which was made by Martin Heidegger in 1927.[2] This, of course, is only one topic among many that Heidegger opened up with his historic analysis in *Being and Time*; and if we were to multiply these temporality studies by ten we would probably get a more accurate picture of the impact of the Freiburg Professor upon graduate education in American philosophy today. And Heidegger is only one, albeit probably the most substantive, of contemporary existential phenomenologists.

In conjunction with this increased respect and understanding we can also see developing an increasing interest in the relationship between existential thought and that most American of philosophies—pragmatism. Many philosophers are now asking, "What is the connection between the two?" What, if anything, do they have in common and what are their major differences? As long ago as 1962, James Edie was suggesting that the future of American philosophy "may lie in the direction of an existential pragmatism."[3] At the time he was thinking primarily of the Jamesian variety of pragmatism. Since then a number of analyses have indicated a close connection between James' philosophical position and existential phenomenology, particularly the close resemblance of many of James' and Husserl's ideas.[4] More recently we see Kenneth Winetrout writing a book whose major thesis is "that pragmatism is made up of three concerns—the analytic as with Peirce, the reformist as with Dewey, and the existentialist as with James and Schiller."[5] And as recently as 1971 we saw Professor Mathur trying to make a case for calling Dewey's methods "phenomenological."[6] With this kind of discussion going on within philosophy itself, an investigation into these two philosophical perspectives with a special concern for implications for educational theory seems to be warranted.

There are other reasons that suggest the appropriateness of such an analysis and comparison at this time. Although many educators may be unaware of it, these two philosophical perspectives are being used extensively in much contemporary educational writing. Only a few years ago historians were describing the demise of progressive education, but today Dewey's ideas are far from dead. He is in fact enjoying what might be described as a quiet renaissance. From the specific methodology of "inquiry training" to the general but exceedingly vague ideology of the counter-culture one can find, if one goes deep enough, a number of Dewey's ideas. In addition, any in-depth analysis of the ideas behind the Educational Romantics and the Free School Movement would reveal both Deweyan and existential ideas, sometimes in the most curious and seemingly inextricable mixture. Paul Goodman, for example, apparently relied heavily on Dewey's ideas for much of his educational philosophising,[7] and George Dennison's writings, particularly his *Lives of Children,* provide an excellent illustration of the kind of confusing mixture of the Deweyan and the Existential that we find in so many of the modern romantic critics of education.[8]

Also, there is a sound pedagogical reason for such a comparison—a reason, incidentally, that is reflected in the placement of this analysis early in the anthology. There are still a large number of educators who are familiar with Dewey's ideas but know little about existential thought and what implications it may have for education. With this comparison many should find it easier to make the transition from the more familiar Deweyan landscape to the rather strange existential scene. Hopefully the contrast between the two will help the educator find his way in the new terrane.

The final argument for the appropriateness of this discussion brings us to one of the central features of our analysis. In any comparison between the two positions one is forced to come to grips with the contrast between their respective conceptions of the human. Since one of the major concerns of the existential phenomenologist is to describe the basic structure of human existence, and since experience is the primary category of Dewey's formulation, their respective conceptualizations of man seem central to both positions. This focusing on the respective conceptions of the human, and particularly the difference between the two, is very important to this study for a number of reasons. It brings to our attention the importance of philosophical anthropology to educational theory. In these days any viable theory of education seems to require a strong, healthy conception of man as an integral part of that theory. It highlights one of the primary contributions of existential thought to education, viz., the carefully delineated description of the basic structure of human existence. This analysis also helps to point up some of the weaknesses of Dewey's conception, particularly his formulation of the self. As a result of the above findings the comparison also suggests the need for a working partnership between Dewey and the existentialists. When thinking about educational theory, Dewey's weakness will prove to be the existentialists' strength and vice versa.

The major purpose of this essay is: to see education in its widest possible framework, that is, to realize a view of education which includes both the traditional view of schooling and the becoming of a person, while at the same time gaining some leverage on the process. To do this will require both the Deweyan and the existential perspectives in some sort of working partnership. When referring to the two perspectives we are, at the same time, including the two methods, the empirical and the phenomenological.

THE IMPORTANCE OF
PHILOSOPHICAL ANTHROPOLOGY IN EDUCATION

One of the important assumptions in this analysis is that education is a many-faceted phenomenon and that when trying to develop a theory of education, philosophers of education, at least ideally, should try to incorporate as many dimensions in their theorizing as possible. Just as philosophers of the past asked "What is it *all* about?" so educational theorists today should try to deal with the full range of educational meaning. Comprehensiveness and universality are still philosophical virtues. To realize this ideal we must include, to the greatest possible extent, a spectrum of meaning all the way from the traditional, conservative view of education as the transmission of knowledge, through the liberal perspective of John Dewey, in which education is seen more as a transaction which occurs between the human organism and his environment, to the radical view which sees education primarily as a "letting be" or "allowing process" whereby the child or the adult simply becomes who he is. The range of educational meaning extant twenty years ago could have been accommodated in the conservative and liberal perspectives. Today, however, the radical or free school orientation which sees education more in terms of "human becoming" must also be included in any comprehensive consideration of education. This means that Kierkegaard's definition must now be included in any discussion of the educational process. When asked, "What is education?" he replied:

> I should suppose that education was the curriculum one had to run through in order to catch up with oneself, and he who will not pass through this curriculum is helped very little by the fact that he was born in the most enlightened age.[9]

By reformulating this concern for inclusiveness into philosophical questions that the educational philosopher can address himself to, we might get something like the following. The conservative educator asks, "What knowledge should be taught?" and "What is teaching?"; the liberal educator asks, in addition to the conservative questions, "What is knowledge?" and "What are the best environmental conditions for learning?"; while the radical educator asks, in addition to the liberal questions, "Who is man?" and "What are his basic modes of being?" Much has been written about knowledge, teaching, and learning environments, but little attention has been given to the important connection between philosophical anthropology and education. One of the major purposes of this essay is to correct this oversight.

The time has come when we, as philosophers of education, must concentrate our energies and insights on man himself. How have we, how do we, and how should we conceptualize man? When discussing education we must ask, "What is your anthropological ground? What is your conception of the human when you talk about education? Is it Skinnerian man beyond freedom and human dignity? Is it Aristotle's 'rational animal'? Is it Marx's or Freud's conception of man that is implied in your educational thinking? Or is it Dewey's or Heidegger's conception?" In the past philosophers of education have concentrated on epistemology, value theory and metaphysics; today we must focus on philosophical anthropology. "Who is man?" and "What is his relation to the world?" are the persistent questions of the day. Max Scheler describes the central problematic of twentieth-century man as follows:

> In the ten thousand years of history, we are the first age in which man has become utterly and unconditionally 'problematic' to himself, in which he no longer knows who he is, but at the same time *knows that* he does not know. It is only by a firm resolution to wipe the canvas clean of all traditional answers . . . and to look upon man with a radical, methodological alienation and astonishment that we can again hope to gain some valid insights.[10]

Any theory of education today that seeks to persuade teachers and public alike should be grounded in a healthy, substantial, well articulated conception of the human. Today the vast majority of American youth, as well as many adults, find themselves in a desperate struggle "for the preservation of the person, for the self-affirmation of the self, in a situation in which the self is more and more lost in its world."[11] Although a few, like Skinner who has tried to reduce man to a "technology of behavior," have given up, most people continue the struggle. It is no wonder that the radical educator, who never seems to tire of repeating the dehumanization argument when criticizing the public schools, currently enjoys such appeal. With students being continually bombarded in and out of the classroom by mounting evidence of an ever-increasing rationalization of society, with increasing numbers of thinkers, including most students, accepting the argument that contemporary man is in grave danger of losing his ground and meaning in existence, primarily because of the technological, mass producing, controlling society in which he finds himself involved, and with so many being convinced that modern industrial-technological society transforms people into things, "into pieces of reality which pure science can manipulate and technical science can control,"[12] any philosophy of education that claims to reflect American society in the 1970's and/or hopes to persuade the thinking public, must include a pivotally positioned, vibrant conception of the human. The philosophy of existential phenomenology can provide such a conception, while Dewey's experimentalism, contrary to what is popularly believed, cannot and does not.

This is one of the primary reasons that we argue for a working partnership of both Deweyan and the existential perspectives in our theorizing about education: Dewey's conception of man does not accommodate the radical idea of education as a becoming. At least this seems to be the case when

Dewey's formulation is compared with the existential view of man. When compared with the scholastic conception of man, which was the customary contrast until a few years ago, Dewey's description appeared in a much better light. His characterization of man as an "agent of doing" or as "a psychobiological problem-solving organism" seemed much more concrete and active than the scholastic's "rational animal." But compared with the existentialists' description of the self, Dewey's conception appears emaciated, and some would even say nonexistent. There is no room for the "inwardness" so dear to existentialists' hearts, in Dewey's house of objectivity, natural objects, and the scientific method.

There are a number of philosophers of education who would disagree with this conclusion that Dewey's conception is inadequate.They feel that Dewey's philosophising about self-realization and individuality represents one of the strongest facets of his whole formulations. And it is true that in his educational writings, particularly, he does seem to place the development of individuality in a central position. So we must present our case as forcefully, but also as carefully and accurately, as we can.*

HISTORY OF THE CONTROVERSY

Criticism of Dewey's conception of the self goes back many years. As early as 1932 we find Professor Horne criticizing Dewey's concept of mind and self:

> the individual mind is more than an agent of reorganization. It is a conscious center of existence; it is a private self; it is a responsible being; it is a moral agent; it is a source of aesthetic enjoyment. *Dr. Dewey's view is depersonalizing; it denies the private personal self* [13] [italics mine].

In 1962 I attempted an analysis of Dewey's conception and found it to be weak and inadequate, particularly when compared with the existential description.[14] Other commentators, however, have taken the opposite position. Also in 1962, Father Robert J. Roth came out with his book on *John Dewey and Self-Realization* in which he claimed that the dominant theme of Dewey's philosophy was self-realization, or the development of the human personality according to its capacities and energies.[15] While admitting that Dewey is not very precise as to what this development would entail, Roth definitely claims that Dewey's idea of self-realization is not only pivotal to his whole philosophy but that it permeates all of his writings. Since then there have appeared a number of other studies on the topic. For example, Norman Roseman concludes:

*This has always been somewhat difficult for me because of a long-held prejudice in favor of the existential phenomenological position.

The question as to the validity of the concept of self-realization in experimental theory, which must ultimately be answered by the experimentalist in terms of stable personality structure, cannot be so answered because *it has no personal referent, no self that is intrinsic to its own nature, and no end that is not a function of the confronting situation*[16] [italics mine].

Kallen, on the other hand, describes Dewey's conception of the individual as ambivalent.

It has seemed to me these many years that Dewey's philosophy so far as it is concerned with the individuality of individuals, is ambivalent. On the one hand, individuality . . . gets reduced to a procession of behaviors in the courses of a more rather than less propitious nature. On the other hand, Dewey's specifications of a design for living, his theory and practice of education, of social change, of pursuing knowledge and confirming belief, postulate individuality, with its liberation and growth, as the initiation and consummation of the human enterprise.[17]

Thus we see that the question of the adequacy of Dewey's philosophical anthropology is a controversial one that needs further discussion and clarification. This is particularly important since so many educators continue to see the individual as central to Dewey's formulation.

Fortunately, a study was published in 1971 that throws considerable light on the many ambiguities and confusions to be found in Dewey's position vis-à-vis man. C. O. Berry's *The Concept of the Self in John Dewey and John MacMurray: A Summary Critique,* which far surpasses all previously mentioned analyses in depth, range, and clarity of understanding, has been a great help to me in rethinking and rearticulating Dewey's conception of man.[18] In the analysis that follows I have relied extensively upon Berry for confirmation of many ideas I have long held concerning Dewey, as well as for many new insights and arguments regarding Dewey's position.

The analysis is organized around three major considerations: the influence of Darwin; the social dimension of Dewey's conception; and the importance of intelligence to his conception. After discussing each topic, a contrast with the existential phenomenological position is offered. Finally, a plan for a partnership between Dewey and the existentialists is suggested.

THE INFLUENCE OF DARWIN

In his sweeping attempt to reconstruct philosophy, which meant among other things a thoroughgoing criticism of the rationalist tradition all the way from the Greeks down through Descartes and Hegel, Dewey found it necessary to attack the rationalist's conception of the self, whether it be called a thinking thing, an epistemological subject, a mind, a transcendent spirit or whatever. Being the naturalist that he was, Dewey could not suffer any form of separation between man and nature. And one of the pervading ideas (with its long history of dominance in the thinking patterns of western man) that had to be overcome was the idea of a substantial self, i.e., a self that could of its own volition make of itself an object to itself, a self being separate from or having an independent existence vis-à-vis the natural environment. Many of the ills of contemporary philosophy, according to Dewey, could be traced to this mistaken conception of the human which assumes "that experience centers in, or gathers about, or proceeds from *a center or subject which is outside the course of natural existence,* and set over against it" [italics mine]. It makes no difference whether the subject is termed "soul, or spirit, or mind, or ego, or consciousness, or just knower or knowing subject."[19] Dewey was convinced that if philosophy were to progress in the twentieth century, it would have to go beyond this way of viewing man. How did he hope to undercut this bifurcation of man and nature? More specifically, how did he hope to demolish the substantial soul? Quite simply, by placing his whole philosophical schema within the context of the Darwinian world. Berry explains:

> Dewey sought to smash the rationalistic view of human nature by putting human experience within the Darwinian setting of nature. Man is not a transcendent spirit, a rational substance, an epistemological subject. He is an animal, an intelligent animal, to be sure, but an animal involved in all the processes of nature seeking what all other animals seek—a successful and harmonious adjustment to the natural (and in man, social) environment. Man is essentially a doer, not a thinker; practical, not theoretical. Man is continuous with natural processes and his 'mind' is basically an instrument to help him in meeting problems and securing a better adaptation to his environment. Mind, consciousness, soul—what Dewey calls 'wholesale' words—are not independent entities, things in themselves, but adverbial descriptions of how man interacts with his natural and social environment. Dewey follows James in wanting to 'loosen up' the block universe of the rationalists.[20]

"Human is as human does,"[21] and the full meaning of human life is explainable and understandable in the ways we act and react in and on the societal and natural environment. "Life is a self-renewing process through action on the environment."[22]

Any and all understanding of human life must be visualized in this larger biological evolutionary setting.* The human, who is different not in kind but

---

*In an article written late in his life, Dewey states: "For many years I have consistently—and rather persistently—maintained that the key to a philosophic theory of experience must proceed from initially linking it with the processes and functions of life as the latter are disclosed in biological science." (Dewey, "Experience, Knowledge and Value: A Rejoinder," in *The Philosophy of John Dewey,* P.A. Schilpp, ed. [Evanston and Chicago: Northwestern University Press, 1939].)

only in degree from the nonhuman, is seen by Dewey as part of and continuous with nature; man is completely and totally a child of nature, born both within and of nature. It is man's existence in nature that is the fundamental reality, because "the facts of man [are] continuous with those of the rest of nature."[23] This human biological existence, moreover, is to be seen as an organism which is continually seeking a successful adjustment with its environment.

Life as disclosed in the biological sciences also implies a particular metaphysical world view. The world in which the organism interacts with its environment is not a world of fixed forms with specific histories of origins, as the term "species" was usually used prior to Darwin. Dewey sees a world characterized throughout by process and change, a precarious world, incomplete and indeterminate. No longer is the future an unfolding of a reality already antecedently complete. It is an open, unfinished world where everything must be understood as in the making and not as once for all finished or made. It is a world in which the book of Genesis is still being written, a world in which we ourselves can lend a hand in the writing. This is possible because Dewey's world of process and change is not only characterized by the precarious and the indeterminate, but also by stability and continuity. In Dewey's open, incomplete universe, with its inextricable mixture of the stable and the precarious, man, by virtue of his intelligence, which means using the method of science, is not only capable of extending the stable over the precarious but should continually try to gain greater and greater control in order to realize a more satisfying life for all. To behave otherwise would be "incredibly flippant."[24]

The principles that define the basic orientation of naturalism are: "(1) nature is all there is; there is no supernatural being, realm, or entity, and (2) scientific method is the most reliable means of inquiry for men to use in exploring nature."[25] Dewey's perspective of man and the world is naturalistic; and most of his key categories are borrowed outright from the natural sciences. Dewey sees man as a natural object, "one existing thing in the world—one 'object' among other objects whose distinguishing traits are to be learned by inquiry,"[26] but a natural object that whenever and wherever situated was always to be found in an environment. The relationship between the organism and the environment, which is pivotal to Dewey's perspective, was first called an interaction. In fact even in his later writings on many occasions he still refers to this primary relationship with this term. But since "interaction" suggests the putting together of two entities that were antecedently separate, and since Dewey wanted to convey the idea that the relationship between organism and environment itself represented the given, he later favored the term "transaction." But whether "interaction" or "transaction," the two constituent elements of Dewey's basic formulation are the organism and the environment. In his own words: "The structure of whatever is had by way of immediate qualitative presences is found in the recurrent modes of interaction taking place between what we term organism, on one side, and environment, on the other. This interaction is the primary fact, and it constitutes a transaction."[27] The organism-environment interaction/transaction is the primary fact of experimentalism, and the *lumen naturale,* as we shall see later, is intelligence, which means using the method of science.*

HABIT REPLACES
THE TRADITIONAL CONCEPT OF SELF

In this world of the precarious and the stable, of transactional events and the scientific method, human experience is seen as "a matter of function and habits, of active adjustments and re-adjustments, of co-ordinations and activities, rather than of states of consciousness."[28] One of the keys to understanding Dewey's description of human experience is to be found in his notion of habit, for the closest that Dewey comes to anything like a concept of enduring self-identity is in this concept. Habit is his term for that "centered organization of energies" which is selfhood.[29]

Habit is both an organic and a dynamic concept, and should not be confused with the ordinary connotation of the term which sees it as a lazy, passive, automatic following of routine and custom. "The nature of habit is to be assertive, insistent, self-perpetuating."[30] It operates within the human organism as an "organized disposition to act" in certain ways. "Our actions not only lead up to other actions which follow as their effects but they also leave an enduring impress on the one who performs them, strengthening and weakening permanent tendencies to act. This fact is familiar to us in the existence of habit."[31] Moreover, this activity as habit is an organic process through which the human organism seeks to accommodate the environment. To Dewey the self or subject is a human organism reacting to an environment.

*Every philosophy starts out with a basic premise, a central reference point from which all philosophising emerges and to which all must return. It is the given, the primary, irreducible, original datum that constitutes the heart and center of a particular philosophy. Albert Dondeyne calls this central intuition the primitive fact. But the primitive fact of any given philosophy represents more than the starting point or given. It also represents the *lumen naturale,* the primary source of the meaningful the consequence of which results in a particular way of looking at the relationship between man and the world. Dondeyne describes it as follows: "This intuition is not necessarily a conceptual evidence. . . . It may just as well be—in fact, it will much more often be—an 'existential' experience, a certain manner of grasping our 'presence-to-the-world' on the basis of a particular sensitivity towards some fundamental value, in consequence of which the world is viewed in a certain way. What we mean here by a 'central intuition' is not an idea nor an isolated fact, but a first intelligible or meaningful moment which is primitive, central, all-embracing, the source of universal intelligibility. It confers a certain intelligible clarity on all things and permits us to situate them, each in its place, in the totality of the real." (A. Dondeyne, *Contemporary European Thought and Christian Faith* [Pittsburgh: Duquesne University Press, 1963], p. 25-26.)

It is an "agent of doing" not a knower, mind, or consciousness, and the basic apparatus of this "agent of doing" is habit. It is the medium through which the *execution* of an idea or intention occurs. But it is much more. Habit is also the medium through which the *conception* and *formulation* of ideas occur. "The medium of habit filters all the material that reaches our perception and thought."[32] In fact man is his habits.

> When we are honest with ourselves we acknowledge that a habit has this power because it is so intimately a part of ourselves. It has a hold upon us because we are the habit.
>
> . . . a predisposition formed by a number of specific acts is an immensely more intimate and fundamental part of ourselves than are vague, general, conscious choices. . . . They [habits] form our effective desires and they furnish us with our working capacities. They rule our thoughts, determining which shall appear and be strong and which shall pass from light into obscurity.[33]

What we would normally conceive of as a conscious or mental act has been reinterpreted here by Dewey in terms of "biologically conceived patterns of behavior-habits."[34]

It should be stressed that for Dewey, habit functions in the same way as any other organic process in a given environment. All organisms, when finding themselves out of balance in a given environment, attempt to redistribute and reorganize the energy field so as to redress the imbalance and again realize a harmony with the environment. And so it is with habit. It is continually in need of, and works toward, modifications and revisions when faced with new situations. Habit should not be seen as responding passively to external stimuli but rather dynamically trying to redistribute and reorganize the situational field. In fact, habit, like all other natural processes, possesses the dual characteristics of stability and precariousness: it must be conceived of in terms of its dependable, regular, and stable aspects as well as its continual attempts at modification and revision. Berry summarizes:

> Clearly then, to conceive of a free will or transcendent self apart from the network of habits whereby a person is related to an environment and has built up specific organic adjustments and patterns of thought and behavior is, for Dewey, to tear asunder what nature has joined together. And if we can give up the old notion of habit as passive routine and conceive it in such a way as to express this dynamic relation we need not import alien concepts to grasp the nature of human behavior.[35]

By casting his entire philosophy into the Darwinian world of organism-environment transactions and reinterpreting the transcendent self in terms of habits, Dewey has laid the foundation for a perspective that is free from any troublesome substantial soul. In this Deweyan context we can see "the essential unity of the self and its acts."[36] Man is what he does: he is an "agent of doing" who responds to the stimuli of the environment.

The Existentialist Position

While Dewey is trying to get rid of the substantial self, the existential thinker is trying to describe the lived reality of this same transcendent, substantial self. Moreover, it is precisely that feature of the self that Dewey is attempting to deny, i.e., the ability of the self to get above itself through reflection, that the existentialist finds constitutes the self. Kierkegaard, in his historic analysis, writes:

> Man is spirit. But what is spirit? Spirit is the self. But what is the self? The self is a relation which relates itself to its own self, or it is that in the relation [which accounts for it] that the relation relates itself to its own self; the self is not the relation but [consists in the fact] that the relation relates itself to its own self.[37]

It is this reflexive nature of selfhood, i.e., wherein the self relates itself to itself, that makes possible knowledge of oneself.* The self can transcend itself, make of itself an object, judge itself, appraise itself, feel guilty about itself. It can ask "Who am I?" With this ability to get out of itself the self can gain knowledge of itself. "To be a self is to be able to look at one's self, love one's self, become estranged from one's self, be anxious about one's self, and evaluate one's self. The self can have knowledge of itself through becoming 'objective' to itself."[38] And it is precisely this characteristic of reflexivity, which Dewey is anxious to deny, that constitutes selfhood.

This existential concern for the world of the transcendent self, which the existential thinker calls the *Eigenwelt,* however, is only one facet of the major thrust of the existential phenomenologist, which is to describe the basic structure of all of lived experience. There are two other primary worlds or horizons: the *Mitwelt,* which is the world of other people, and the *Umwelt,* which is the world of the surrounding environment. Together these horizons constitute human existence. In fact, in his analysis the existential thinker does not start with the self at all. Rather, he concentrates on a description of the many different modes of the being of man, of which the reflexivity of the self is one.

Another feature of the existentialist analysis that needs to be noted here is that the existential thinker does not assume, as Dewey apparently does, that if one conceives of a transcendent self it necessarily has to be thought of as being "outside the course of natural existence." We recall that Dewey is highly critical of any view of man that assumes that "experience centers in, or gathers about, or proceeds from a center or subject *which is outside the*

*As far as I know Dewey never speaks of this knowledge of oneself.

course of natural existence, and set over against it"[39] [italics mine] . But so also is the existential phenomenologist. He too is interested in healing the breach between subject and object. However, the existential phenomenologist is convinced that he can realize a conception of the transcendent self that can be included within the course of natural existence. This is where Dewey and the existentialist disagree. Hence, it is the way in which Dewey and the existentialist propose to bring philosophy down to earth from the aery abstractions of the idealist-intellectual perspective* and heal the break between subject and object that they differ. Moreover, it is this difference in approach which will give us an important clue to one of the basic differences between these two philosophies. Dewey turns to the natural sciences for a solution while the existentialist turns to immediate experience.

Dewey undercuts the subject-object split by placing his whole formulation in the Darwinian world of "organism-environment transactions." The existential phenomenologist, on the other hand, does not propose to undercut the dichotomy by positing another theory of man and the world, as Dewey does. Rather, he goes directly to man's lived reality and illustrates, through a careful description of the basic structure of immediate experience, how the real scandal of philosophy is that anyone would ever seriously believe a break between man and the world to exist in the first place. In lived reality it is a pseudo-problem. Anyone who is aware of and reflects upon immediate experience knows that only the most abstract thinkers believe it necessary to question the existence of an external world. Ever since Descartes, this has been a problem with philosophers. How does one prove the existence of an external world? How does one get the subject and object together in a meaningful accord? Dewey does it by casting all experience into events which, when analyzed, are seen to be organism-environment trans-actions. The existentialist, on the other hand, in effect goes back to the pre-Cartesian world, before the pseudo-problem was even perpetrated, and

---

*Both the existentialist and the experimentalist are critical of the idealist position which gives the primacy to knowledge, more particularly, to reflective and philosophical knowledge. Existential phenomenology introduced the concepts of "existence" and "intentional consciousness" specifically in order to challenge this alleged primacy of knowledge and reflection. They introduced lived experience in the concrete here and now as the original datum rather than some aery abstractions about man and the world. Dewey introduced the idea of experience as his primary category with the same purpose in mind. He vehemently rejects any interpretation of experience as primarily a knowledge affair. There is more to experience than knowing. Philosophers of the past have failed to give proper attention to the basic structure of ordinary experience which, for the most part, according to Dewey, is non-cognitive. Things "are objects to be treated, used, acted upon and with, enjoyed and endured, even more than things to be known. They are things had before they are things cognized." (Dewey, *Experience and Nature*, p. 21.) Experience "indicates that *being* and *having* things in ways other than knowing them . . . are pre-conditions of reflection and knowledge. . . . All cognitive experience must start from and must terminate in being and having things." (Dewey, *Experience and Nature* [1st ed.], pp. 18-19.) Although using different language the existentialist would agree completely with this criticism of the idealist position.

makes a phenomenological analysis of immediate experience. When one analyzes immediate experience phenomenologically, i.e., by accepting only that phenomenon which reveals itself to consciousness, one knows that the world is always given. Wherever man is in his lived reality, there is also the world. In immediate experience the world is always present; in fact human existence is being-in-the-world.

While Dewey goes to a biological theory in his attempts to undercut the subject-object opposition, the existential thinker goes to the deeper precognitive level of immediate experience. In keying on this original datum, the existential thinker finds that theorizing about reality is a derivative kind of knowledge, i.e., it is not the primary mode of knowing, but is derived from, although contemporaneous with, a more primordial precognitive understanding. The *lumen naturale* of the existentialist is not a hypothetical construct, like Dewey's organism-environment transaction model which is open to the scientific method, but existence itself, which is prior to theoretical predication. The primitive fact of the existentialist is the human life-world (being-in-the-world) that each of us experiences immediately, an experience which is prior to all explanations and theories.

Thus, fundamental to any contrast between Dewey and the existential phenomenologist is an analysis and comparison of their respective primitive facts: the organism-environment transaction and being-in-the-world.* Each formulation represents the basic irreducible beginning of that particular philosophy. Such an analysis should help to point up a number of the similarities and differences between these two perspectives.

THE BASIC EXISTENTIAL-EXPERIMENTAL COMPARISON

In any comparison between the two formulations, one of the first things we notice is that both Dewey's organism-environment-transaction and Heidegger's being-in-the-world, as the hyphens indicate, are all of a piece. One cannot take an organism and an environment and put them together into an organism-environment transaction, because the given is the transaction itself. It is the starting point of Dewey's experimentalism. This is the irreducible, primordial beginning. (As we will see later, however, Dewey is not always consistent on this point.) The same is to be said for Heidegger's primitive fact. One cannot take a human being and a world and put them together into being-in-the-world, because man is a being who is always already in-a-world. So being-in-the-world is also all of a piece. Neither formulation starts out with

*The central intuition of existential philosophy goes by many names. The most common term is "existence," a name that was originally coined by Kierkegaard. Buber sometimes refers to it as "man in his wholeness." Husserl referred to it as the *Lebenswelt,* the human life-world, while Heidegger conceptualizes it in terms of being-in-the-world. It is this latter formulation that we will be using in our contrast.

discrete entities; both would agree with Buber: "In the beginning is relation."[40] This similarity, however, is somewhat misleading, because the commonality is to be found only in the structure of the two formulations, not in the content; it is in the content of the two that we see the major difference.

We have already seen that each philosophy focuses on a different level of human experience. The primitive fact of the pragmatic construction represents a second-level construction of the human mind, the primary purpose of which is to explain a particular biological relationship between man and the environment; the central intuition of the existentialist refers to a deeper, more primordial level where man and his world meet in a precognitive, antepredicative understanding. This is the heart of the difference between the existential and experimental perspectives. Dewey's perspective represents an explanation or theory about man, as well as other natural objects, and their relationship to the environment, while Heidegger's perspective represents a description of human experience as lived. Moreover, Dewey's explanation focuses on both man and nature, as the scientist does, while Heidegger's description focuses on man's lived experience as he-intends-the-world. Dewey's organism-environment transaction is a naturalistic, biological conception that refers to all natural objects including man. Experience is "of as well as *in* nature . . . [it] reaches down into nature; it has depth."[41] There is no break between the human and the nonhuman. This gives the Deweyan conception considerable scope and inclusiveness. Heidegger's formulation, on the other hand, assumes a basic difference between *Dasein,* or human existence, and non-*Dasein.* This makes the existential conception appear to be much more exclusive and particular in its emphasis. In the *Dasein* analysis the focus appears always detailed, incisive, almost microscopic as the Freiburg Professor methodically reveals his articulation of being-in-the-world. In Dewey's writings, on the other hand, the focus seems much more Olympian, even telescopic as he tries to include a broader range in his conceptualization and articulation of experience.

One should be careful, however, not to overdraw this contrast, because it is possible to argue the opposite case with almost equal plausibility. One could say, for example, that it is Heidegger's philosophy, with its overriding concern for an understanding of all that is, that is really Olympian. Heidegger repeatedly insists that his primary philosophical purpose is not to describe the structure of existence but to reopen the question of the meaning of being. Dewey, on the other hand, has been criticized by many, in particular Santayana, for not giving sufficient attention to nature in its more inclusive sense and for being too narrowly preoccupied with "the dominance of the foreground."[42] Given his point of view that "things are what they are experienced as," it is not difficult to understand such criticism.[43] What one can say, however, is that the kind and range of data acceptable in each case which, after all, is a function of the method, varies considerably. The scientific method, Dewey insists, can accept all kinds of data. It can handle all kinds of problems, both human and nonhuman, and it is in this sense that the experimentalist perspective is broadly gauged. The phenomenological method, on the other hand, is much narrower in that it will only accept that phenomenon which reveals itself to consciousness.

This difference in focus is also reflected in the fact that the connotation of "world," in each perspective of man and the world, is somewhat different. When Dewey insists that man should always be seen as continuous with "nature" or "world," he seems to be thinking, for the most part, in terms of scientific, objective categories, while the existentialist understands the world in an antepredicative preobjective sense before scientific naming. Moreover, as long as one thinks of the world in objective, cosmological categories, the immediate experience of the world which the existentialist is trying to catch will remain concealed. If one asks, "*What* is the world?" or "*What* is nature?", as so many philosophers since Descartes have done, one has already preconditioned the answer to be forthcoming in objective, scientific terms. The existential thinker is careful not to ask the "what" question of the world because he knows that the existential meaning of the world will only be disclosed when the "how" question is asked. "How do I live in the world?" is the existential question. To reveal immediate experience in all its psychic density and particularity, one must always ask the existential "How do I live?" question: "How do I live time, space, death, the other, choice, body, etc.?" One of the things we have already noted in answer to the "How do I live in the world?" question, is that in lived reality I always live-the-world-as-being-present. In immediate experience I am always being-in-the-world.

Dewey does not ask the existential question; but neither does he ask the single "What is nature?" question. Instead, Dewey asks: "What is experience?" and after analysis, finds that the question involves posing both a "what" and a "how" question simultaneously. "How does man experience?" and "What does man experience?"

> it [experience] includes *what* men do and suffer, *what* they strive for, love, believe and endure, and also *how* men act and are acted upon, the ways in which they do and suffer, desire and enjoy, see, believe, imagine. . . . 'Experience' denotes the planted field, the sowed seeds, the reaped harvest, the changes in night and day, spring and autumn, wet and dry, heat and cold, that are observed, feared, longed for; it also denotes the one who plants and reaps, who works and rejoices, hopes, fears, plans, invokes magic or chemistry to aid him, who is downcast or triumphant. *It is 'double-barrelled' in that it recognizes in its primary integrity no division between act and material, subject and object, but contains them both in an unanalyzed totality* . . . . Life denotes a function, a comprehensive activity, in which organism and environment are included[44] [italics mine].

In realizing the continuity of man and nature through his organism-environment formulation Dewey does include both the how of man's living in the world and the what of the world in which he lives, but this is only after analysis. In its primary and basic integrity, experience is an "unanalyzed totality." "It is 'double-barrelled' in that it recognizes in its primary integrity no division between act and material, subject and object." The relationship, not the two terms that go into the relationship, is the given.

When discussing Dewey's philosophy, however, sometimes it seems necessary to ask "Which Dewey?" Sometimes he seems to be talking about the human organism and the environment as givens which together "produce" an experience. For example, he writes, "the things of experience are produced, as they are according to my theory, by an interaction of organism and environment."[45] This confusion, which is never satisfactorily resolved in Dewey, often can be found in his educational writings where, at least on occasion, he seems to focus almost entirely upon the "how" question, i.e., "How does *an individual* live in an environment?" And when, in this way, he concentrates on the interaction between the two principle features of the relationship and how the interaction of the two produces an experience, Dewey's analysis seems to come close to the existential analysis, as in the following statement in *Experience and Education*:

> The statement that individuals live in a world means, in the concrete, that they live in a series of situations. And when it is said that they live *in* these situations, the meaning of the word "in" is different from its meaning when it is said that pennies are "in" a pocket or paint is "in" a can. It means, once more, that interaction is going on between an individual and objects and other persons.[46]

It should be noted, however, that here Dewey is not going to immediate experience for an answer to his question. Although he often comes close, to my knowledge he never asks the existential question: "How do I (John Dewey) live in (in the sense of experience) the world?" He always sticks to the objective, natural science model: "How does an individual live in the world?" Dewey is concerned with showing how an individual in general lives in the world, while the existentialist is concerned with describing not man in general, but how *this man that I am* experiences the world. Dewey always insists that:

> In the first instance and intent, it is not exact nor relevant to say "I experience" or "I think." "It" experiences or is experienced, "it" thinks or is thought, is a juster phrase. Experience, a serial course of affairs with their own characteristic properties and relationships, occurs, happens, and is what it is. Among and within these occurrences, not outside of them nor underlying them, are those events which are denominated selves.[47]

The "Being-in" Contrast

In answer to his question Dewey replies: An individual lives in a world, "not as pennies are in a pocket," but in the sense of living "in a series of situations." In *Human Nature and Conduct* he varies the analogy somewhat but makes the same point. "Human nature exists and operates in an environment. And it is not 'in' that environment as coins are in a box, but as a plant is in the sunlight and soil."[48] What Dewey is pointing to here is the particular kind of relationship that obtains between the plant and the soil and sunshine that is not to be found between the coin and the box. The coin and the box can be separated and still be a coin and a box; but the plant and the soil cannot: the plant, soil, and sunlight depend upon each other in a way in which the coin and the box do not. In this sense, Dewey's human can never be viewed as discrete or alone. "Everything that exists insofar as it is known and knowable is in interaction with other things. . . . Man is nothing save the ties that bind him to others."[49] *

Compare this analysis with Heidegger's description of how the being-in of being-in-the-world differs from the being-in of both the plant in the soil and sunshine and the coin in the box. (We should keep in mind that Heidegger is asking a somewhat different question, not "How does an individual live in the world?" but "How do I experience the world?"). Whereas Dewey's perspective naturally and logically leads him to a description of the similarity between man and other biological life, the existential phenomenological perspective leads in the opposite direction of indicating how human existence is unlike other biological life. Existence, claims the existentialist, should not be confused with life. Only man exists. Only man is a becoming, choosing, transcending being who discloses truth, temporalizes time, and distances himself spacially. Only man is anxious and alienated. Only man asks himself "Who am I?" Only man is a being-unto-death. All of these modes of being are unique to man.

"How do I live in (experience) the world?" The "being-in" of man's being-in-the-world, in Heidegger's analysis, refers to the touching, manipulating, dealing with, meeting, encountering, in short, caring for people and things in a familiar world. The key to these modes of being is reflected in the term "concern.† Man's being-in-the-world can be seen as a field of concern, suffused with vectoral meanings going out to other people and things. The

*All of which, in a sense, brings us back to where we started in our basic comparison when we noted the structural similarity in both formulations. You cannot have one part of the relationship without the other; however, it is not only organism and environment but also existence and world that are correlative terms. Nevertheless, as we have noted, this similarity in structure turns into a difference in content providing Dewey is consistent and holds to the idea that the formulation is a transaction.

†More specifically, and accurately, the key term in man's involvement with things, according to Heidegger, is *concern,* while *solicitude* characterizes his involvement with people.

being-in of existence entails going out to that which is other than itself and in a way that is different from the way a plant goes out to the soil and sunshine. "Why do I hurt when my son hurts or feel proud when he excels?" Because my son is included in-my-world. He is a part of my zone-of-concern which extends over other people and things. When father announces to the children that mother, who has just returned from a long siege in the hospital, is now in-the-kitchen, the being-in of mother is distinctly different, both spacially and temporally, from the being-in of the chair in the kitchen or the plant in the soil and sunshine. This difference between the respective conceptions of being-in, which in turn reflects a difference in content, clearly illustrates one of the major differences between the two perspectives. Again we see Dewey going to biology while the existentialist goes to immediate experience.

So far we have tried in a general way to compare Dewey's view of the connection between man and the world with how the existentialist sees the connection.* Now we want to sharpen the focus somewhat and contrast Dewey's environment with Heidegger's world.

The basic difference, of course, is that Heidegger's world necessarily entails human existence while Dewey's environment does not. It is only in human consciousness that man experiences being-in-the-world; it is only the human being in his lived, precognitive experience who always finds himself in-a-world. In fact, without *Dasein* there is no world.[50] *Dasein* represents the site of the wording of the world. Dewey's environment, on the other hand, refers to that against which and through which the organism—human and otherwise—acts and reacts. "Life (i.e., both human and the non-human) is a self renewing process through action on the environment."[51] From Dewey's naturalistic, scientific perspective the human environment as such is not different from other biological environments. One may be more complex than the other, but the environments are not basically dissimilar. In order to generalize about environments in this manner, Dewey must use theoretical constructs that are one stage removed from lived experience. In a sense, "organism" and "environment" have been objectified and neutralized for science. From the perspective of lived experience, however, man does not find himself as an organism-environment transaction at all. On this primordial, antepredicative level man finds himself all-of-a-piece, in-a-world. The moment the human organism becomes existentially concrete the environment becomes a world.

*Before leaving this topic, however, it should be pointed out that when Heidegger analyzes the "world" of being-in-the-world he explicitly states that he is not talking about the world as nature, i.e., as that which signifies the totality of things in the world (Martin Heidegger, *Being and Time,* p. 93), as apparently Dewey does in at least some of his writing. But when Dewey talks about environments and organisms the focus sharpens. Dewey speaks of a "natural world that exists independently of the organism" but then goes on to say that "this world is environment only as it enters directly and indirectly into life functions. The organism . . . exists as organism only in active connections with its environment." (Dewey, *Logic: The Theory of Inquiry* [New York: Henry Holt, 1938], p. 33, as quoted in Berry, p. 52.)

Another way of saying the same thing is to say that only the-human-being-intends-a-world. Only the human being provides the site for world as meaning. The key to the difference between environment and world is that in the Deweyan perspective the transaction occurs out-there between two natural objects: an organism and an environment which may or may not be human; whereas in the existential phenomenological perspective the transaction is between the *noesis,* which is the way the subject intentionally orients himself toward that which is other than consciousness, and the *noema,* which is the object correlate of the intentional consciousness. *Noesis* and *noema* correspond to the subjective and objective side of intentional consciousness. It points to the juncture where consciousness meets the natural world. This transaction, which is an ever-present reality in the lived experience of the person, in Heidegger's analysis becomes being-in-the-world. Moreover, it all occurs within consciousness on a preconceptual level before the abstractions "organism" and "environment" have been constructed.

Another facet of the contrast can be seen when one analyzes the relationship between the constituent parts of the two formulations. Again there is an apparent similarity, but a similarity with a difference. In both formulations the interaction between the two constituent elements is correlative. In the organism-environment transaction each interpenetrates the other, and it is often difficult to know the precise contribution of each to the transaction. Since the two constituent elements that make up the transaction are both natural objects, the interaction is basically bilateral. The contribution of each to the transaction, which incidentally can be determined by the scientific method, will vary depending upon the context. On the other hand, the noetic and noematical correlates of the intentionality of consciousness also continually interpenetrate each other in a correlative action. The meaning of one points to the meaning of the other; in order to describe one element one must bring in the other. However, in this latter case there is a significant difference, because in the noetic-noematic structure we find a definite and constant direction to the interaction. In the description of the intentionality of consciousness, which is the philosophical principle that makes the conception being-in-the-world possible, all conscious acts "have a fundamentally directional character." That is to say, as Natanson explains it:

> they point toward some object, whether objectively real or not. Thus, all thinking is thinking *of* or about something, all remembering is remembering *of* something, all imagining is imagining *of* something, all willing is willing *of* something. Consciousness is intentional in the sense that it has as its essential character this projective or directional activity.[52]

The interaction found in both conceptions is correlative; however, because of the difference in content, being-in-the-world has a definite directional character, while the organism-environment transaction which refers to the natural world out-there does not. This is yet another significant way in which Heidegger's description of lived reality differs from Dewey's description and explanation of "scientific" reality.

Both Dewey and Heidegger are concerned with human experience, but when they look at man and the world they see different phenomena. One of the primary reasons for this is that they use different conceptual equipment. For the most part we see only what our concepts allow us to see. Dewey sees man and the world as a natural scientist does, i.e., as reality objectified as natural objects out-there; Heidegger sees man and the world as a phenomenologist does, i.e., from the perspective of human consciousness. Both attempt to abandon the primacy of cognitive knowledge in their theorizing by refocusing on human experience, but Dewey focuses not on the person who is experiencing, but upon the process of experiencing. Heidegger is concerned with describing human existence as lived; moreover, he is able to describe lived experience by using the method and perspective of phenomenology, which sees consciousness as intentional. Dewey is also concerned with human experience, seeing not a being-who-is-intending-a-world, but a process of transaction between an organism and an environment.

THE SOCIAL DIMENSION OF DEWEY'S CONCEPTION

We have discussed the biological character of Dewey's conception of the human and noted the importance of his notion of habit as a substitute for the traditional substantial self. But this is only part of the explanation of Dewey's conception, because man is not only a biological organism but, even more importantly, a social being. By far the greatest influence on the development of the self is the social or cultural. According to Dewey the relationship between the individual and society is a transaction, not an interaction. "Individual-in-society" is one word; one cannot have one without the other. Just as Dewey inveighs against any theory that understands man apart from nature, he is also critical of any suggestion of a break between the individual and society.

Dewey conceived of the social as the most fruitful way of interpreting man's experience in and with nature because it not only includes within it all of the qualities of the physical and physiological, but the mental as well. The latter is described by Dewey in his analysis of language and communication in which he takes pains to show how "the facts concerning the development of language and discourse, the realm of meanings, require that mind and self be understood as a social (therefore natural) transaction." [53] "Of all affairs, communication is the most wonderful." With communication "events turn into objects, things with a meaning." [54] This is all made possible through language, "which is the greatest single discovery of man." [55] The heart of language is not an expression of something antecedent, but rather, as a form of action, it is itself communication, "the establishment of cooperation in an activity in which there are partners, and in which the activity of each is modified and regulated by partnership."[56] Moreover, there is no mode of action as fulfilling and as rewarding as this cooperative activity.[57] Finally, communication, language, and meaning are basically public and objective. "Primarily meaning is intent, and intent is not personal in a private and exclusive sense."[58] The "truth of classic philosophy in assigning objectivity to meanings, essences, ideas remains unassailable. It is heresy to conceive meanings to be private, a property of ghostly psychic existence."[59]

In its widest sense, however, the social is seen as culture, or, as Dewey describes it, custom. Dewey was one of the first to realize the power of culture over one's life: human beings "are what in anthropological jargon are called acculturated organisms."[60] It is culture that gives shape, direction, and meaning to life; for to be human is to be encultured in a human environment. Without the human environment of associated life, man is nothing. Moreover, what man is to become will be determined, to a large extent, by the human environment into which he is thrown. Dewey, who rarely uses extravagant language, pulls out all the stops when describing the power of culture.

> The greatest educational power, the greatest force in shaping the dispositions and attitudes of individuals, is the social medium in which they live.[61]

> ... apart from unconditioned reflexes like the knee jerk it may be questioned whether there is a single human activity or experience which is not profoundly affected by the social and cultural environment.[62]

In a very simplified interpretation, culture channels native tendencies or impulses into habits. So the direction comes from the culture, not any native tendencies in man. To Dewey, man is not only his habits, but even more directly his culture. "Human beings are, at any given time, the organic unity and totality of what their experiences, biological and social, have been."[63] It is almost impossible to overemphasize the importance of this insight for education. As we will see later, the organism-environment model is particularly well suited to handle this new notion of the human as an organism interacting in a cultural-social environment. And in terms of the development of a human being, there is probably no other conceptual structure available to man at the present time that is more powerful. This, in my judgment, is one of Dewey's greatest contributions and one that must be incorporated in any workable theory of education. We will have more to say about this later. At the present time, however, we want to contrast Dewey's predominantly social interpretation of man with the existentialist's predominantly individual interpretation of man.

The Existential Perspective of the Social

The soft underbelly of the existentialist position, many would argue, is the apparent radical individualism of the philosophy. To abstract the single, discrete individual from the social context and neglect the communal character of · existence does violence to the meaning and immediate experience of human life. It is undoubtedly true that some existential thinkers, notably Kierkegaard and Sartre, seem to advocate an almost solipsistic individualism that largely neglects the social dimension, but any comprehensive study of the broader sweep will indicate that this is not necessarily the case with existential phenomenologists. They simply see the social dimension from a different vantage point. In fact, the "individual" and the "social" are not existential categories but pragmatic concepts. From Dewey's Olympian vantage point he sees an individual transacting in a social medium. From the existential perspective, which is that of lived experience, something quite different is seen. When the existential thinker tries to come to grips with the so-called social dimension he asks: "How do I live my being-with-others?" And the answer discloses that being-with-others involves a double status and import: it is both a sustaining force and an easy way to escape from authentic living.

First of all, argues the existentialist, the "other" is very important in my life. Basically I live in a state of being-with; the *Mitwelt,* or being-with-others, is equiprimordial with the *Eigenwelt,* or being-myself. "Communality," explains Schrag, "belongs to the very Being of Dasein insofar as his world is always a world that he shares with others. To exist is always to exist in interdependence with other selves." [64] Having recognized that the "we-world" is the primordial axis of life and that it nourishes and sustains my being in the world, however, is to have only partly answered the existential question, "How do I live my being-with-others?"

Heidegger claims that this dimension of being-with evidences a positive as well as a deficient mode. My being-with others not only involves a positive, solicitous concern for the other,* but at the same time it also involves an indifference to the other as well as an ever-present temptation to disburden myself from my responsibility for my own becoming. Moreover, for the most part, my being-with is lived in the deficient mode.

For the most part, in average everydayness I treat the other as a thing or a unit in the crowd: I view the other in terms of his function—where he fits into the larger context of things. Is he higher or lower, more or less influential in terms of the great average of which I am a part? Where does he fit into the big public world? In this way I classify and stereotype the other for purposes of use. Man is his function.

*Many scholars have evidenced annoyance that Heidegger takes barely a page to analyze this positive, authentic solicitude that man has for others. Annoyance or not, one cannot disregard the fact that he does recognize this mode as a basic possibility of *Dasein.*

At the same time, in average everydayness, I also tend to view myself in this same indifferent mode. At least this is a constant temptation. Most of the time I objectify my being and see myself as a functioning unit in the larger whole. In this sense I allow the world of the other to take over my life, thus disburdening myself of the responsibility for my own becoming. "Why do I do that?" "Because everybody does that." This is the easy, pleasant way of losing my single self in the "they world" of conformity and busyness. This is the easy way of succumbing to the tempting call of the "they," a call that constantly beckons to a cozy busyness with people and things. It is easy to disperse the singularity and responsibility of my single self into the busyness of my "they" self. I thus find it easy to hide from my essential responsibility: that I can choose, that I can be.

There is, of course, a close connection between the radical individualism of the existentialist and seeing society as the tempting "crowd" or "they" that must be resisted. Douglas V. Steere describes the radical individualism of Kierkegaard as well as his indictment against the deficient mode of being-with:

> Kierkegaard conceived it his function as a writer to strip men of their disguises, to compel them to see evasions for what they are, to label blind alleys, to cut off men's retreats, to tear down the niggardly roofs they continue to build over their precious sun-dials, to isolate men from the crowd, to enforce self-examination, and to bring them solitary and alone before the Eternal. Here he left them. For here that in man which makes him a responsible individual must itself act or it must take flight. No other can make this decision. Only when man is alone can he face the Eternal. And the act that is called for at this point is not one of mere noetic recognition. When all is known that can be known, the responsible core of the will in the man has still to yield. He must act, he must choose, he must risk, he must make the leap.

> All attempts at mass prescription, all things attainable in the mass as such, in fact the very notion of the crowd, of the mass, drew the most violent invective Kierkegaard had at his command. For he believed the crowd, the mass, to be a hiding-place in which the individual may abdicate his true quest for inward intensity and responsibility. The crowd is a sink of cowardice in which individuals are relieved of individual responsibility and will commit acts they would never dare to do alone. When a man is to be executed by shooting, not one executioner shoots, but several. When the noble Caius Marius was seized, no individual soldier dared touch him, but a crowd of them had no such restraint. "Take the highest of all, think of Christ—and think of the whole human race, all that have been born and will be born. Now the situation is one where Christ is alone, so that someone as an individual alone with Christ stepped up to Him and spat upon

Him: the man was never born and will never be born, who possesses the courage or the audacity to do this: that is the truth. As they became a crowd, however, they had the courage to do it—oh, terrible falsity." The mass flatters, the mass excuses, the mass condemns, the mass counts heads, the mass pronounces on truth, and in all these things, the mass, for Kierkegaard, is that which is both false and debasing.[65]

My being-with is distinguished by two features. It is essential to my being-in-the-world. The life-world is first and primordially the we-world. At the same time there lurks within being-with the constant temptation to forfeit my responsibility for my own becoming.

The Importance of Intelligence and Choice

No description of Dewey's conception of the human is complete without a consideration of the role of intelligence in human experience; for although he carried on a vigorous attack against "intellectualism," few thinkers in the annals of philosophy have been accorded a higher place in human affairs to intelligence. Intelligence to Dewey, in the last analysis, means using the methods of science, which he often referred to as "organized co-operative inquiry." Empirical science is the key to all solvable human problems. Dewey possesses a remarkable faith that just as physics, chemistry, biology, and the other physical and natural sciences have been and will continue to be capable of solving problems appropriate to their disciplines, so also are sociology, psychology, anthropology, and the other human sciences capable of solving problems that deal with society and the individual. Since human experience is continuous with nature and since the scientific method, in principle, will work just as effectively with human as with physical problems, the day will come, if man perseveres with his intelligence, when the subject matter of psychology and sociology will be solving such problems as war, unemployment, ignorance, racism, delinquency, just as the subject matters of physics and chemistry now solve problems of matter.

Here we can see a direct contrast with the existential viewpoint regarding method. Instead of claiming that there is one method applicable to all problems, the existentialist generally accepts the European idea that the subject matter of the human sciences is so radically different that a different method is called for. Most European thinkers made a distinction between the human and nonhuman sciences, and maintain that the empirical method is only appropriate for the latter sciences. The existential thinker is persuaded that human problems, because of their essentially different nature, i.e., the impossibility of effectively separating the data being investigated from the investigator, are not in principle solvable as technical problems are. In other words, the European existential phenomenologist takes the "anthropological dilemma" seriously. Gunnar Myrdal, many years after writing *The American Dilemma,* was asked, "Has America solved the Negro problem?" and is reported to have answered, "To social problems there are no solutions."[66] In any case, the scientific method and the results of the method represent the *lumen naturale* of experimentalism. Therefore, in order to understand Dewey's conception of the human, we need to look at the pivotal role that intelligence plays (or should play) in human life.

It should be pointed out right at the outset that in my judgment, it is Dewey's strategic positioning of the scientific method within his formulation more than anything else that prevents him from realizing an adequate conception of the human. More specifically, it is the need to cast all experience into objective, public fact and the need to cast "individual mind" ultimately into "objective mind"—both conditions of course being necessary for the proper functioning of the scientific method—that so militates against any viable conception of the human.

In order to cast all experience into objective, public fact, Dewey finds it necessary to position the problematic situation, not the individual man, at the center of his formulation. Experience to Dewey is not only life biologically conceived; it is also method. The organism-environment paradigm serves a double function: it describes biological life and it provides us with a conceptual structure that is made to order for the method of science. Dewey's experience, described variously as an "unanalyzed totality," "simultaneous doings and sufferings," a "serial course of affairs," and an "undifferentiated flow of events and occasions," constitutes the ideal subject-matter to which the scientific method can be applied. It is inclusive of all natural objects. It is neutral, objective, and free of all troublesome separations. Moreover, the advantage is mutually operative. Experience is not only ideal subject matter for science, but the scientific method is the only method that can do justice to this "inclusive integrity of experience." "It alone takes this integrated unity as the starting point for philosophic thought."[67] In all classical philosophies which posit the "self" and the "world" as given originally, the primary problem is how to get the subject and object back together again. The problem of an empirical method whose subject matter is an undivided experience is vastly different:

> Its problem is to note how and why the whole is distinguished into subject and object, nature and mental operations. Having done this, it is in a position to see to what effect the distinction is made; how the distinguished factors function in the further control and enrichment of the subject-matters of crude but total experience.[68]

In one masterful stroke Dewey has eliminated the subjects and objects as given, and has recast the entire structure in terms of a continuum of events and occasions, thus making the method of science applicable to all life including man. Now Dewey does not have to worry about the "my" in "my experience" swallowing up "experience" and thereby interdicting the method.[69] The "my" is to be understood only as derived or inferred. By so constructing his philosophical formulation Dewey has made it possible for the method of science to become the "winnowing fan,"[70] the directing force in the "doing and undergoing" which is experience.

No one would deny that Dewey was a great liberal, a true democrat who believed in the dignity and integrity of the individual, but according to his philosophy the individual is not positioned at the center of his lived experience. Instead, in pursuing his major concern of showing how best to provide the proper conditions which will enable man to realize a more satisfying life, Dewey positions the problematic event, which is amenable to scientific treatment, at the center of his formulation. We must never forget that to Dewey the living of a human life can best be described in terms of a process of interaction with an environment; and, to a large extent, the quality of the life as well as the kind of human being who will develop in the future will depend upon the conditions through which he interacts. Consequently, Dewey says, "Let us work on the conditions as effectively and efficiently as possible." It is true that the ultimate purpose of all his philosophising is to maximize man's fulfillment and satisfaction; Dewey is a humanist in the best sense of the word. But as he focuses on the "how" of realizing the proper conditions, Dewey's conception of man is forced to fit into the Procrustean bounds of his larger concern. One cannot combine being human, with all the psychic density of that condition, and the scientific method, with all its objectivity, without badly distorting one or the other. In this case it is man who is pushed out of shape.

This strategic positioning of the problematic event with its accessibility to the method of science has had significant consequences for Dewey's conception of man. For one thing, as we have already seen, it has purged Dewey's perspective of the personal dimension of human experience. We quote again a key point in Dewey's position. "In the first instance and intent, it is not exact nor relevant to say 'I experience' or 'I think.' 'It' experiences or is experienced, 'it' thinks or is thought, is a juster phrase."[71] To Dewey, "What experience suggests about itself is a *genuinely objective world* which enters into the actions and sufferings of men and undergoes modification through their responses."[72] In the experimentalist's world of experience, meaning is objective, knowledge is objective, habits are objective, values are objective, motives are objective, emotions are objective, and intelligence is objective.

The strategic positioning of objective intelligence, sometimes referred to as freed intelligence or organized cooperative inquiry, is particularly troublesome to the development of a consistent theory of a self. Here we find Dewey's problematic situation both nourishing the development of a self and, at the same time, depriving the self of its personality, because the individual mind must ultimately become the objective mind.

Dewey sees the self as developing from the conflict that is inherent in any imbalance in the organism's interactions with the environment. When the organism and the environment are out of adjustment, when the normal habits and ways of doing things are blocked, the individual or "intermediate" mind is born by reconstituting and redirecting the objects in the environment. But it must never be forgotten that the resolution of all problematic situations involves the use of the scientific method. This means disinterested inquiry in which the proclivities and predispositions of the self must be neutralized. For the method to function properly, the projections and biases of the self cannot be allowed to impinge upon the data. Berry describes this paradoxical situation as follows:

> The self arises out of conflict being marked by frustrated desire and emotion which puts it in "partial and temporary" opposition to its environment. Reflective thought arises out of this situation. "Empirically, it [subjective mind] is an agency of novel reconstruction of a preexisting order." However, in accomplishing its task of reconstructing the problematic situation, the self must eliminate from the cognitive task those feelings and emotions which the situation aroused and which, in some sense, constitute the very meaning of selfhood. In short, the self as individual mind must be capable of becoming objective mind.[73]

Dewey, unlike the existentialist, does not take the anthropological dilemma seriously. The crucial problem in any empirical human science, such as Dewey visualized, can be expressed in the following question: How can man as a person make man as a person the object of an empirical inquiry?[74] How can the sociologist or psychologist analyze and describe the human problematic situation when they themselves are involved in the situation? "How can there be a real science," Strasser asks, "of something as changeable, as ephemeral, as difficult to grasp as an inclination, an evaluation, a motive, a decision, a project?"[75] As Kluckhohn points out, "The scientist of human affairs needs to know as much about the eye that sees as the object seen."[76] Dewey apparently was aware of the anthropological dilemma but, obviously, he did not find it a serious obstacle in his attempt to create an empirical human science. What Dewey was unaware of was the price he would have to pay for the strategic positioning of this new science. When all events must be cast in public objective fact and when individual mind must be transformed into objective disinterested intelligence, there is little left over with which to conceptualize a warm, alive human being. As Professor John E. Smith has observed:

> Dewey went so far in the direction of behaviorism or the translation

of experience into external, public fact and function that the individual experiencer becomes insignificant.

The fact that an individual self is always the locus of experience, that experience, as William James puts it, is always somebody's experience, somewhere and somewhen, is not taken seriously; as either overt behavior or impersonal public fact, experience virtually closes with nature, and the individual is forced to abscond into the realm of art.[77]

In his house of science and natural objects Dewey finds it very difficult, if not impossible, to accommodate that ever present variable in human experience called *my* experience, *my* life, *my* death, *my* meaning. He seems always concerned lest the "my" of "my experience" swallow up experience and thus interdict the method.

Freedom and Choice

The implications of the strategic positioning of the problematic situation and also of the insistence upon the use of the scientific method with its objective "freed intelligence" in the resolution of all problems can also be seen in Dewey's discussion of freedom and choice—two topics dear to the existentialist's heart. In a general sense Dewey's articulation of freedom and choice places him in the great tradition of rational freedom where one's moral obligation to be rational and intelligent is emphasized.[78]

Dewey distinguishes between natural and positive freedom in explaining his concept. Berry explains this distinction as follows:

In Dewey's view what he calls "natural freedom" whereby nature allows for contingency and innovation is integrated with "positive freedom" which is a human achievement. Natural freedom is at the mercy of accident and caprice. Positive freedom is the work of intelligence as it permits us "freedom in and among events, not apart from them." What man requires to be truly free is not an isolated self cherishing some metaphysical free will "mysteriously cooped up" in the personality, but freedom which is the fruit of a knowledge of natural forces and energies operant.[79]

What we need is a kind of individual freedom that is general and shared and that has the backing and guidance of "socially organized intelligent control." Intelligence and control of future consequences are the keys to positive freedom. But reliable intelligence, tested and verified knowledge, is not an individual affair. It is organized cooperative inquiry. It is science, or rather the scientific method. To the degree, therefore, that organized cooperative inquiry becomes effective in guiding the life of society, the problem of freedom and order, individual innovation and social control, diminishes. For the method of science is precisely the method of testing individual claims by treating them as hypotheses that need to be validated in the public arena of intersubjective agreement. In fact this is what democracy is all about. In this context what happens to choice?

Choice is a very important feature of Dewey's formulation, because without it, growth, which is the one absolute moral good, would be impossible. But choice, which is individual, actualizes the possibility for growth and change by an intelligent foresight into the consequences. Again the key to real freedom of choice is intelligent appraisal of conditions and consequences. With the problematic situation as central, making a particular choice is closely tied in with the problem-solving process, which is turn involves the scientific method with its operational cause-effect (antecedent-consequence) relationship principle. Under these circumstances the accent is not so much on decisive choice as it is on making an intelligent appraisal of consequences. Here one hypothesizes a plan of action based upon the evidence and a very careful regard for the probable consequences. Moreover, this kind of decision must be treated hypothetically until freed cooperative inquiry has reached a judgment, that is, until it has been validated in the public arena. If one's first hypothesis proves to be unwise, then the intelligent thing to do is to choose another one. The pragmatist's conception of freedom of choice as individual judgment, which ultimately is based upon the settled outcome of inquiry, is a far cry from the existentialist's conception, in which the focus is upon the self as it wills and risks itself in choice. The essential ingredient of experimental choice is disinterested organized cooperative inquiry, while the key to existential choice is the individual will.

It is the conviction of all existentialists, who of course position human existence as being-in-the-world at the center of their formulation, that man exists in the mode of radical freedom. This freedom, however, entails certain limits. In fact, freedom is impossible without limits. Dewey and the existentialists should agree that freedom is always found in a situation, but to the existentialist, it is man-in(tending)-the-situation, not the situation that is focal. To the existentialist, man is basically an ambiguous creature who is both free and determined. He is free to choose within the limits and determinations of conditioning and the situations into which he is thrown. We do not choose our parents or the culture in which we are reared, nor do we choose the conditioning to which we are subjected when young or many of the situations we are thrown into, but within the limits and determinations in which we find ourselves we do have the power to choose. But it is more than just having a capacity or ability. To be human is to choose; it is to risk oneself in choice, and it is to commit oneself to one's choices and to the consequences of one's choices. Without risk there is no choice, at least the kind of choice that makes a difference to the self.

The prototype of the existentialist's conception of choice is Kierkegaard's "leap of faith" in which man commits his life to an idea that is contrary to reason. To choose Christ as one's personal savior, a man of lowly birth who befriended publicans and sinners and claimed to be the son of God, is to choose the absurd. It is to choose that wnich is contrary to reason. (Here Kierkegaard is asking one to respond to the person of Christ rather than to the dogma, doctrine, and rationalizations about Christ that have developed.) Notice that to Kierkegaard the "absurd" is a very important category; without it there would be no need for the "leap." If believing in Christ were not absurd but rational and logical, there would be no need for the kind of personal risk and commitment that is so essential to both the development of the self and the becoming of a Christian. One does not make a decisive existential choice by carefully weighing the probable consequences and then relying upon the final judgment of organized cooperative inquiry. Becoming a Christian involves a decisive choice based not upon knowledge and understanding ("knowledge demolishes Jesus Christ"), but upon willing one thing. Dewey's idea of choice is only meaningful when it is closely tied in with and guided by the method and results of intelligent inquiry; Kierkegaard's choice is described as a "leap of faith" which results in "fear and trembling," precisely because one does not have reason as one's guide.

THE PLAN FOR PARTNERSHIP

Both the pragmatic and the existential perspectives are needed in order to come to grips with American education in the latter part of the twentieth century. Both perspectives, biological life and immediate experience, the individual and the social dimensions of human life, intelligent searching for consequences and awareness of the importance of risk in the development of the self—all should be incorporated in any viable theory of education today. But before beginning a discussion and illustration of the proposed partnership, we must clear the way by facing up to two pragmatic principles that cannot be reconciled with existential thought.

It is impossible to realize a partnership between the pragmatist and the existentialist as long as the pragmatist insists that there is only one method—that of empirical science—with which to approach all problems. This addiction to the scientific method to the exclusion of all other approaches must be repudiated if we are to develop a philosophy of education that encompasses the full range of educational meaning. By placing so much emphasis on the method, the key concepts become objectivity and intersubjective agreement. This leaves little room for that discrete sense of the personal which is also a very important part of human experience. Empirical thinking must be fructified by existential thinking. Schrag comments trenchantly on the dangers involved in subscribing to any absolutism in methodology:

The existentialists have repeatedly pointed out the danger of losing one's self in methodological analysis at the expense of never arriving at the data themselves. A continual preoccupation with methodology leads to philosophical sterility. Heidegger calls our attention to a classic quotation appearing in Lotze's *Metaphysics*: "The continual sharpening of the knife is tedious, if there is nothing to cut." Also, a preconceived method may distort rather than disclose a given subject matter through an imposition of an arbitrary and unwarranted restriction on the breadth, range, and richness of human experience. Scientism affords a clear cut instance of such an imperialism of methodology. Applied to human existence, the scientific method, which is an objectification of experience, discloses this human existence only by converting it into an object and thus distorting it. This does not mean that the scientific method has no validity when applied to its proper sphere of knowledge, which may include certain levels of human existence, but it does mean that when stretched beyond its elastic limits the scientific method conceals as readily as it reveals. Scientific absolutism leads to methodolatry. A method becomes an idol—an idol which later is found to have feet of clay.[80]

There is still another guiding principle in Dewey's philosophy that also must be rejected if partnership is to be realized. Any experimentalist interested in effecting a partnership with existential thought will have to give up attempting to rid philosophy of the transcendent self. The reflexive self, i.e., that self which is capable of objectifying itself and gaining knowledge of itself, is as much a part of human experience as is the external behavioral manifestation. There is both an inside and an outside to man. As any authentic empiricist knows, man is more than his acts, more than an agent of doing. The *Eigenwelt* is equiprimordial with the *Umwelt* and the *Mitwelt*.

Now, what are the possibilities for a partnership between the two philosophies? Going from the more specific to the more general, there are at least three areas where we can see possibilities for a partnership. Certainly any explanation and/or description of choice, particularly as it relates to the educational process, must include both the major features that have been described by the two philosophies. The existentialist obviously is not talking about taking risks for the sake of risk or thrill. This is foolishness. Kierkegaard is talking about risking oneself for an idea, or ideal, that is larger than oneself and the psychological importance of this phenomenon for the development of the self; Heidegger describes choice more as a projection which can be lived authentically or inauthentically. Human existence, or *Dasein,* always projects itself into the future and understands itself in terms of the future. This is one of the constituent elements of being human, a mode of being that can be exercised through one's own self or through the instrumentality of one's "they" self. Affirmation of self, i.e., authenticity and being true to oneself, is, at least on some occasions, more important than a "wise" choice based upon an intelligent appraisal of consequences. Today, as in every age, we not only need the cautious, rational type who always weighs the consequences, but we also need heroes who will take a stand against the majority if necessary. Clearly both features of choice should be included in any modern theory of education.

In order to be able to understand and explain the full range of educational meaning extant today we also need to include both Dewey's social emphasis and the existentialists' individual emphasis. Education includes both the transmission of culture and the becoming of an individual. A consideration of both the importance of society to human life and the empirical fact of the "crowd" as temptation should be included in any comprehensive thinking about education today. To leave out either one impoverishes our understanding of what education is all about. In a more general sense both the existential and the pragmatic perspective—immediate experience and evolutionary, biological life—are needed to come to grips with the contemporary educational scene.

In order to see education in its widest possible context, one needs to be able to see it as it is lived through in human existence by the student. This is where the existential perspective is called upon to play its major role in the partnership.

As we have already mentioned, human existence, as being-in-the-world, consists of three primary horizons or worlds, two of which seem to follow directly from the existential phenomenological principle of the intentionality of consciousness. Man experiences his world as a surrounding environment (*Umwelt*), which one should always be careful to distinguish from Dewey's environment,* and as a communal world that he always shares with others (*Mitwelt*). Human consciousness is essentially an openness toward what is

---

*The difference between Heidegger's *Umwelt* and Dewey's environment again illustrates two of the basic differences between their respective primitive facts: Heidegger's description is of lived experience while Dewey's is not; and Heidegger's formulation has a directional character while Dewey's is strictly bilateral. The environmental world of Heidegger is indissolubly linked with man's existential projects. It is *Dasein's* surrounding environment as he lives his life precognitively that constitutes the *Umwelt*. Notice, on the other hand, Dewey's description of experience which he says is characterized by focus and content. "The word which I have just written is momentarily focal; around it there shade off into vagueness my typewriter, the desk, the room, the building, the campus, the town, and so on. *In* the experience, and in it in such a way as to *qualify* even what is shiningly apparent, *are all the physical features of the environment extending out into space no one can say how far, and all the basics and interests extending backward and forward in time, of the organism which uses the typewriter* and which notes written form of the word only as temporary focus in a vast and changing scene" [italics mine]. (Dewey, *Essays in Experimental Logic,* p. 6.) Dewey's description is not of lived experience as the person is typing the word but of theoretically "having an experience" where the experiencing has been neutralized and objectified, in short, made ready for mediation by the methods of science. In the lived reality of typing a word one does not experience "the building, the campus, the town, and so on," or "all the physical features of the environment extending out into space no one can say how far, and all the habits and interests extending backward and forward in time, of the organism which uses the typewriter."

other than itself; man is able to realize himself as an interiority with consciousness and freedom only by going outside himself. The to-beness of man, i.e., his existence, always involves being-outside-himself-in-a-world of surrounding environment (*Umwelt*) and other people (*Mitwelt*). The third horizon of human existence is the world in which man becomes aware of himself as a reflexive being capable of asking himself "Who am I?" (*Eigenwelt*). In this latter world of self-relatedness, he apprehends himself as a being capable of becoming himself, in all of his particularity and uniqueness, through choice. All three horizons of being-in-the-world, neither one of which is prior to the other, continually interpenetrate and disclose themselves simultaneously in lived experience.

This description of being-in-the-world, with its attendant horizons, is the basic structure of the student's world, as well as that of every human being. He lives in a world of things—books, cars, classrooms, pencils—not as things, but as a context of relationships that constitute a surrounding environment; he lives in a world of other people—family, friends, peer-groups, and teachers. He also lives in his own inner world of possibilities, feelings and moods, doubts, certainties. He is a reflexive being who is concerned about his own uniqueness as a person, about how he responds to life and death and the good; but at the same time, his being-in-the-world, as a zone of concern, extends over other people and things. The student is a becoming, temporalizing being who is concerned about himself, but who is also at the same time transcending himself through projected possibilities.

The strength of the existential phenomenological perspective can be seen in its power to reveal this lived reality. For the first time philosophers have considered an analysis and description of the human life-world as a matter of central importance. This very strength, however, exposes a weakness—at least when we are looking at education. When the perspective is human existence as lived through in all of its immediacy and psychic density, it is very difficult, if not impossible, to see and incorporate those environmental factors that influence our lives which we do not consciously experience in lived reality, but which, nonetheless, are extremely important as far as our education is concerned. I am referring to those influences in the natural and man-made environment which, since they are not readily apparent in lived experience, cannot be revealed in a phenomenological analysis such as Heidegger uses in *Being and Time*. When young we are not conscious of imitating the values and mannerisms of our parents, older siblings, and teachers; nor are we consciously aware of the fact that we continually incorporate into our personality structures, not only when we are very young but throughout our entire lives, the values and attitudes of our culture; yet this social-cultural environment, as Dewey and many others have pointed out, works the most profound influence upon the development of our character. The effect of the environment upon our becoming is cumulative; it occurs over a long period of time and is imperceptible to immediate conscious experience. Hence it cannot be described phenomenologically because it does not reveal itself to consciousness.* It can only be seen through reflection, i.e., inference and explanation.

This inability to accommodate the influences of the natural and social environment upon man's becoming represents one of the major weaknesses of the existential perspective for education. But this existential weakness is Dewey's strength. Dewey's organism-environment transaction perspective, which is one step removed from immediate experience, is tailored to reveal these environmental influences, and, moreover, his perspective as method is also designed specifically to help man to gain some leverage on these same environmental forces that shape man.

So we can see that we not only need both conceptual models, but both methods. In order to see education in its totality we must be able to take into account both the lived experience of the student, which can be revealed through a phenomenological method, and those important environmental forces which can be best handled through the empirical method of science. In order to illustrate this point, let us now look at the man-culture relationship.

There is probably no single idea that packs more explanatory power for education than the idea of culture.† Enculturation as a process involves both the human organism and the environment, each interpenetrating the other in a reciprocal relation. Man creates culture, but at the same time man is created by culture: he is both creator and creature. Again, Dewey's statement comes to mind: "Life is a self-renewing process through action on the environment." To effect changes in man, it is necessary to work through the institutions and culture of which he is a part.

What happens when we think about concrete man in his lived experience? If man is created by culture, how can he in turn create culture? How can he get outside the vicious circle? How can he get above the gravitational pull of his culture in order first to recognize it for what it is and then to try to improve and create culture through the process of critical thinking? When we thus go a little deeper into the man-culture relationship, by using the existential perspective, we can see that it is much more problematic than the organism-environment transaction theory would lead us to believe. It is one

---

*The battle cry of the phenomenologist is "back to the things themselves." The "things" referred to here are the "phenomena," that is, those things that manifest themselves in consciousness. This manifestation "is grasped in an intuition that precedes any reflexion or any judgment. It has only to be allowed to show itself, to manifest itself; the phenomenon is that which gives itself (*Selbstgebung*)." (P. Thévenaz, *What is Phenomenology? Four Basic Essays* [Chicago: Quadrangle Books, 1962].)

†In any discussion of culture it is important to know whether one is using the term as a purely theoretical or ontological construct. Here we will be using it in the latter sense, since man as a culture builder is an important part of our analysis. (See A. J. Newman, "Sociologistic Concepts of Culture: Some Inadequacies," *Educational Theory*, XXI [Summer 1971].)

thing to understand in a theoretical way how a human organism out-there experiences the process of transaction with a particular cultural environment and how one of the most effective ways of educating and changing man is through working on the environment of which he is a part; but it is quite another thing to realize in an existential way the nature of the relationship between a self and his culture.

Professor Hocking has stated that the purpose of education is to transmit the type and provide for growth beyond the type. As teachers we have the responsibility of transmitting the culture to future generations, but we must also nurture and instruct the child in such a way as to help him transcend the culture in order to criticize it and help improve it. But because it is so close to him, getting outside his culture to criticize it is a very difficult feat.

In trying to teach students the significance of the relationship between education and the man-culture relationship, the largely theoretical approach of John Dewey needs to be supplemented by the more personal approach of the existentialists. First, in order to realize how man is the creature of culture, the student must become aware of the power of culture in his own life and then, after recognizing what culture is, he must be able to distance himself from it in order to criticize it and thereby help create it by changing it. The student must ask himself the questions: "Am I sensitive to the influence and power of culture in my own life?" and "Have I ever gotten on top of my culture and seen it for what it is?" If he can answer these two questions in the affirmative then he is in a position to ask: "To what extent am I my culture and to what extent can I become more than my culture through objectification, criticism, and choice?" Knowledge of self is basic to any in-depth understanding of the man-culture problematic.

One of the most effective strategies that a teacher can use to help the student understand his culture in order to get a handle on the man-culture problematic is to have him consider the identity question. It is in working with the "Who am I?" question, however, that Dewey's perspective is weakest, for the organism-environment perspective cannot accommodate the *Eigenwelt* horizon in which man in his self-relatedness experiences his world as distinctly and uniquely his own. As we have seen in Dewey's frame of reference, the self is a derivative, a function of the larger process of experiencing; it has no personal referent that is intrinsic to its own nature. The Dewey human would either not ask the identity question or, if he did, would realize that such a question is meaningless. For the most part the discrete and particular "Who am I?" identity question, in the experimentalist framework, is transformed into the social engineering question "What can *we* make of ourselves?"* By working on the social-culture environment we can

---

*In this connection Professor Thomas explains the Deweyan position as follows: "The Experimentalist does not ask, 'What is the purpose of life?' but rather 'In view of our knowledge of conditions and possibilities to date, what shall *we make* the purpose of life?' " (L. G. Thomas, "The Faith of an Experimentalist," *Harvard Educational Review.* XIII [1948], 156.)

effect the future of the human organism as a social being. Man creates culture, and culture creates man. But to the identity question, which the existential-phenomenologist would hasten to claim is the more primordial of the two, Dewey would simply reply: "Man is nothing apart from the ties that bind him to others."[81] Dewey placed his faith in the "miracle" of the shared life.

The existential thinker, on the other hand, is interested in analyzing and describing the "inner" man and his world. As a result there are a number of existential-phenomenological questions (which it is difficult to see how Dewey's naturalistic, biological, scientific world view could handle) that can be very helpful for anyone with an identity crisis. For example: "*Who am I in relation to my* body? Do I neglect and waste my body in profligate living, or am I fussy and worried about my body as though it were the temple of my soul? Do I costume and parade my body as an object to be desired? What does it mean to have a body?" Other important questions are: "*Who am I in relation to the Other*? How important is the Other in my life? Have I developed a sense of autonomy, or do I always need the omnipresent Other for meaning and sustenance? Am I always concerned about how the Other sees me? Do I always get my clues for action from the Other? Can I relate to the Other? How do I relate to the Other? Is it an "I-Thou" or an "I-It" relationship? *Who am I in relation to the Transcendent Other*? Do I need someone or something larger than myself in order to realize myself? Who is my God—the God of Abraham, the god of ambition, wealth, self-improvement, or the God of the Trinity? Time and death are also relevant in any identity quest. *Who am I in relation to time?* Is my time, for the most part, clock time, or does my time transcend objective time? What is my attitude toward the past? Is it a part of who I am at present or is it just so much excess baggage that should be jettisoned as soon as possible? Do I feel imprisoned by my past? How do I view the future? What is my existential temporal configuration? Does the question 'How much time do I have left?' plague me? *Who am I in relation to my death*? Am I continually preoccupied with my death? Am I always willing, even eager, to talk about other peoples' death but never my own? Do I mask my death or have I incorporated it into my life?" Then there are the important questions of self-relatedness and my becoming. "*Who am I in relation to myself*? Do I know myself? Do I like myself? Am I honest with myself or do I just play games? Finally, *Who am I in relation to choice*? Am I happy with my manner of choosing as well as with the choices I have made? Am I making satisfactory progress in my becoming?"

These are some of the existential questions, analyzed and elucidated by Heidegger's analysis of being-in-the-world,* that can be used as guideposts for

*The question "Who am I in relation to my body?" is barely mentioned in *Being and Time*. It is Merleau-Ponty and Gabriel Marcel who have made extensive analyses of this topic.

anyone interested in the identity question. They point to certain dimensions of human existence that one must become aware of, and, if possible, understand, if the identity quest is taken seriously. But this type of question will take one only so far. After the structural description of human existence has been reflected upon, and one understands some of the basic conditions of human life such as finitude, freedom, transcendence, and choice, sooner or later another question will gradually but ineluctably insinuate itself upon one's consciousness. And that question is *"Why?"* Why am I the way I am? Why am I who I am in relation to myself? Why am I who I am in relation to the Other, including the Transcendent Other? Why do I continue to believe in a secular world of non-belief? This will immediately catapult us back to the cultural-social, has had a powerful effect upon my becoming. I can transcend of the answer. It is true that I am free to choose and that, in a sense, I become my choices; but it is also true that these choices must be made within the context and limits of who I am. I did not choose my parents or the culture into which I was thrown when born; nor did I choose my conditioning when young. *Why* have I become who I am? Here Dewey has the explanation; because I am a human organism that interacts with an environment and this environment, which includes both the natural and the cultural-social, has had a powerful effect upon my becoming. I can transcend my culture in choice, but only to a limited extent. This same choosing must take place within a valuational context which, for the most part, I have appropriated from my culture. The existential phenomenologist describes the conditions of existence which includes the power to choose within the limits of "thrownness" or "facticity"; the experimentalist explains the how of our becoming by the organism-environment interaction perspective. Both the who and the why of man are important in any identity search; this requires a partnership of the existential and the experimental points of view.

We have repeatedly seen in this last illustration that Dewey's strength is the existentialist's weakness and Dewey's weakness the existentialist's strength. It is not a case of either/or. Dewey, in thinking about experience, primarily in terms of the process of experiencing, has seen the value of casting experience and nature into an organism-environment transaction. For sheer explanatory power this formulation has few equals. This is especially true, as we have seen, when thinking about education. It makes it possible to reflect upon, explain, and to make judgments about many facets of life and nature, about many experiences of the world. All would admit to the value of such a view; but this is only part of the picture. Besides being able to reflect, explain, and make judgments about our experiences of the world, it is also important to understand the pre-predicative, pre-conceptual relationship of man to his world which is "the source or the conditions of the possibility of any experience of the world." As Edie explains it, "While reflexive, judging consciousness is important, we must first turn to the pre-reflexive, pre-conceptual, pre-logical structures which are at the origin of experience, prior to any thought *about* experience."[82] This is precisely what Heidegger does in his analysis of the basic structure of human existence as being-in-the-world. In order to see education in its widest possible context it is necessary to include both thinking about experience, with all its explanations, mediations, and inferences, and experiencing experience, with all of its moods, frustrations, and satisfactions. This is why we need a perspectival partnership of both Dewey and the existentialists if we are to develop a workable theory of education. In order to encompass the full range of educational meaning extant today both Dewey's primarily explanatory analyses of experience grasped by reflection as they are known by scientific reason and the existentialists' descriptive analyses of experience grasped by reflection as they are lived are required.

REFERENCES

1. W. Barrett, *Irrational Man: A Study in Existential Philosophy* (Garden City, N.Y.: Doubleday, 1958), p. 8.
2. M. Heidegger, *Being and Time* (New York: Harper & Row, 1962).
3. P. Thévenaz, *What is Phenomenology?*, edited with an Introduction by James M. Edie (Chicago: Quadrangle Books, 1962), p. 36.
4. See, for example, J. Wild, *The Radical Empiricism of William James* (Garden City, N.Y.: Doubleday, 1969).
5. K. Winetrout, *F. C. S. Schiller and the Dimensions of Pragmatism* (Columbus: Ohio State University Press, 1967), p. 68.
6. D. C. Mathur, *Naturalistic Philosophies of Experience: Studies in James, Dewey and Farber Against the Background of Husserl's Phenomenology* (St. Louis: Warren H. Green, 1971).
7. See, for example, N. S. Schwartz, "Beyond John Dewey: Paul Goodman's Theory of Human Nature" (Ed.D dissertation, Rutgers, the State University of New Jersey, 1970).
8. G. Dennison, *The Lives of Children: The Story of the First Street School* (New York: Vintage Books, 1970).
9. S. Kierkegaard, *Fear and Trembling and Sickness Unto Death* (Garden City, N.Y.: Doubleday Anchor Books, 1941), p. 57.
10. As quoted by Hans Meyerhoff in his introduction to M. Scheler's *Man's Place in Nature* (Boston: Beacon Press, 1961), p. xii.
11. P. Tillich, *The Courage to Be* (New Haven: Yale University Press, 1952), p. 138.
12. *Ibid.*, p. 137.
13. H. H. Horne, *The Democratic Philosophy of Education: Companion to Dewey's Democracy and Education, Exposition and Comment* (New York: Macmillan, 1932), p. 421.
14. See, particularly, L. Troutner, "Dewey and the Individual Existent," *The Personalist*, XLVIII (Summer 1967).

15. R. J. Roth, *John Dewey and Self-Realization* (Englewood Cliffs, N.J.: Prentice-Hall, 1962).
16. N. Roseman, "Self Realization and the Experimentalist Theory of Education," *Educational Theory*, XIII (January 1963), 35.
17. H. M. Kallen, "Individuality, Individualism, and John Dewey," *Antioch Review*, XIX (Fall 1969), 314.
18. C. O. Berry, "The Concept of the Self in John Dewey and John Macmurry: A Summary Critique" (Dissertation, Columbia University, 1971).
19. J. Dewey, *Creative Intelligence* (New York: Henry Holt & Co., 1917), p. 30.
20. Berry, *op. cit.*, p. 16.
21. Dewey, *The Problems of Men* (New York: Philosophical Library, 1946), p. 163.
22. Dewey, *Democracy and Education* (New York: Free Press, 1916), p. 2.
23. Dewey, *Human Nature and Conduct* (New York: Modern Library, 1922), p. 12.
24. Dewey, *Experience and Nature* (New York: Dover Publications, 1958), p. 43. Incidentally, according to Berry's analysis many of Dewey's inconsistencies and paradoxes concerning the self stem from these two irreconcilable generic traits of existence. (Berry, *op. cit.*, p. 245.)
25. R. N. Beck, *Perspectives in Philosophy* (New York: Holt, Rinehart and Winston, 1961), p. 151.
26. P. Schilpp, *The Philosophy of John Dewey* (Evanston and Chicago: Northwestern University Press, 1939), p. 543.
27. Dewey, *Philosophy and Civilization* (New York: Minton, Balch, 1931), pp. 251-252.
28. Dewey, *The Influence of Darwin on Philosophy* (New York: Peter Smith, 1951), p. 157.
29. Berry, *op. cit.*, p. 27.
30. Dewey, *Human Nature and Conduct*, p. 58.
31. Dewey and J. H. Tufts, *Ethics* (New York: Henry Holt, 1956), p. 181, as quoted in Berry, *op. cit.*, p. 27.
32. Dewey, *Human Nature and Conduct*, p. 32.
33. *Ibid.*, pp. 24, 25.
34. Berry, *op. cit.*, p. 28.
35. *Ibid.*, p. 44.
36. Dewey and Tufts, *Ethics*, p. 319, as quoted in Berry, *op. cit.*, p. 302.
37. Kierkegaard, *op. cit.*, p. 146.
38. C. O. Schrag, *Existence and Freedom* (Evanston: Northwestern University Press, 1961), p. 51.
39. Dewey, *Creative Intelligence*, p. 30.
40. M. Buber, *I and Thou* (New York: Charles Scribner's Sons, 1958), p. 27.
41. Dewey, *Experience and Nature*, p. 27.
42. Schilpp, *op. cit.*, p. 251. It is somewhat ironic that Dewey is criticized by some for neglecting the centrality of the experiencing self while at the same time he is criticized by others for concentrating too narrowly on human experience.

43. Dewey, *The Influence of Darwin on Philosophy*, p. 227.
44. Dewey, *Experience and Nature*, pp. 8-9.
45. Schilpp, *op. cit.*, p. 532.
46. Dewey, *Experience and Education* (New York: Macmillan, 1938), pp. 41-42. The full quotation reads: "The conceptions of *situation* and *interaction* are inseparable from each other. An experience is always what it is because of a transaction taking place between an individual and what, at the time, constitutes his environment, whether the latter consists of persons with whom he is talking about some topic or event, the subject talked about being also a part of the situation; or the toys with which he is playing; the book he is reading (in which his environing conditions at the time may be England or ancient Greece or an imaginary region); or the materials of an experiment he is performing. The environment, in other words, is whatever conditions interact with personal needs, desires, purposes, and capacities to create the experience which is had. Even when a person builds a castle in the air he is interacting with the objects which he constructs in fancy."
47. Dewey, *Experience and Nature*, p. 232.
48. Dewey, *Human Nature and Conduct*, p. 296.
49. Dewey, *Experience and Nature*, p. 175.
50. "If no Dasein exists, no world is 'there' either." (Heidegger, *Being and Time*, p. 417.)
51. Dewey, *Democracy and Education*, p. 2.
52. M. Natanson, *Literature, Philosophy and the Social Science: Essays in Existentialism and Phenomenology* (The Hague: Martinus Nijhoff, 1962), p. 16.
53. Berry, *op. cit.*, p. 62.
54. Dewey, *Experience and Nature*, p. 166.
55. *Ibid.*, p. 172.
56. *Ibid.*, p. 179.
57. *Ibid.*, p. 184.
58. *Ibid.*, p. 180.
59. *Ibid.*, p. 189.
60. Schilpp, *op. cit.*, p. 530.
61. *Intelligence in the Modern World: John Dewey's Philosophy*, edited and with an introduction by Joseph Ratner (New York: Modern Library, 1939), pp. 462-463.
62. *Ibid.*, p. 825.
63. Berry, *op. cit.*, p. 27.
64. Schrag, *op. cit.*, p. 204.
65. Kierkegaard, *Purity of Heart Is To Will One Thing*, translated from the Danish with an introductory essay by Douglas V. Steere (New York: Harper & Row, 1938), pp. 16, 18-19.
66. The source of this statement was a public address given by Will Herberg in 1965 at University of California, Davis. Arthur Schlesinger, Jr. would agree: "Man generally is entangled in insoluble problems; history is consequently a tragedy in which we are involved, whose keynote is anxiety and frustration, not progress and fulfillment." ("The Causes of

the Civil War: A Note on Historical Sentimentalism," *Partisan Review*, XVI [October 1949], p. 981.)

67. Dewey, *Experience and Nature*, p. 9.
68. *Ibid.*
69. Dewey, *Essays In Experimental Logic* (New York: Dover Publications, 1953), p. 69.
70. Dewey, *Experience and Nature*, Preface, x.
71. *Ibid.*, p. 232.
72. Dewey, *Creative Intelligence*, p. 7.
73. Berry, *op. cit.*, p. 74.
74. S. Strasser, *Phenomenology and the Human Sciences* (Pittsburgh: Duquesne University Press, 1963), p. 7.
75. *Ibid.*, p. 9.
76. As quoted in *Ibid.*, p. 7.
77. C. W. Hendel, ed., *John Dewey and the Experimental Spirit in Philosophy* (New York: Liberal Arts Press, 1959), pp. 113-114.
78. Berry, *op. cit.*, p. 247.
79. *Ibid.*, p. 128.
80. Schrag, *op. cit.*, p. 10.
81. Quoted in W. H. Kilpatrick, *Source Book of Philosophy of Education* (New York: Macmillan, p. 143).
82. Thévenaz, *op. cit.*, p. 26.

ASPECT **B**

Aspect B begins with Eugene Kaelin's essay, "Existential Grounds for Aesthetic Education." Professor Kaelin, like Troutner, indicates where his work stands in relation to Heidegger and Dewey, but moves beyond that to establish systematically the existential grounds not only for aesthetic education, but for all education. In so doing, he also prepares the ground for the three essays which follow his. *

3 | The Existential Ground for Aesthetic Education

E. F. KAELIN

I

As a preamble, my terms will be defined as follows:

(a) "Education" will mean any planned or controlled production of changes in behavioral patterns of human individuals;

(b) "Aesthetic" will be interpreted to describe any phase of those activities involved in the processes of creation and appreciation of works of art, whether the latter be restricted to those variously defined disciplines known as "criticism" and "art history" or the more loosely denominated area of human experience commonly referred to as "enjoyment of the consummatory values to be found in any experience that is *an* experience;"

(c) "Ground" is to be read as a summation term for all those reasons used to justify the program or programs of proposed changes in the patterned behavioral responses of the subjects to be educated, whether individuals or groups;

(d) "Existential" refers to the body of philosophical doctrine, developed primarily in Germany and France as an alternative description of 'human nature and conduct' to that provided by the methods of scientific induction.

My sources are principally the philosophic works of Martin Heidegger in Germany and Jean-Paul Sartre in France, in particular *Sein und Zeit* (1927)[1] of the former and *L'Etre et le Néant* (1943)[2] of the latter.

My program is to interpret the existential literature as affording reasons for adopting one set of educational procedures as opposed to others, which may

*This essay first appeared in *Philosophy of Education,* 1966, and is used by permission and in its original form.

lack sufficient or relevant grounds to constitute an adequate justification either for the inclusion of aesthetic matters in the public school curriculum or for adopting one specific pedagogical technique for the attainment of maximal efficiency within this realm once it is admitted. Although I may not be able to avoid the use of some jargon, an appeal will not be made to the socio-psychological concept of "leisure," the medical concept of "mental health," the anthropological concept of "culture," or, in point of fact, to the vague educational concept of "the whole person."

Too many educators, making appeal to this latter concept, seem to assume that we already know what the whole person is; or, if we do not, that we could arrive at such an understanding merely by adding the parts of the human personality we already have some comprehension of.

The problem may be stated simply as an evaluation of phenomenological existentialism in terms of the claims made for it as constituting a philosophical anthropology sufficiently clear and well enough defined to outline the possibilities of meaningful human activity to be developed by educators. Precedents for this kind of philosophical endeavor may be found in Plato's *Republic*; in the use of Hegel's *Phenomenology of Mind* by the St. Louis Hegelians; and in the more recent applications of Dewey's instrumentalism to the problems of the schools in society.

If I interpret him aright, Dewey's *Human Nature and Conduct* (1922) would afford better materials for a study of this kind than his *Art as Experience* (1934), while his *Experience and Nature* (1925), more confused than either of the others, has correspondingly fewer potentialities for application to the problem at hand. It must be confessed, however, that had I not chosen to interpret "existential" in the sense noted above, I should have been tempted to treat it in much the same manner as Dewey did in this last mentioned of his works. The reason for this substitution should be made clear in the sequel.

II

A close scrutiny of my stipulated meaning of "education," above, may have raised a few eyebrows. That it could be applied, however, to such activities as brain-washing, propagandizing, advertising, preaching, caning or other means of corporeal punishment is nothing to the point. It should be obvious to anyone having been through an educational institution that all these techniques have been used in the name of education—and some of them have succeeded in producing educated persons, in the finer, more difficult sense of the term. After all, ordeal by boredom is still perhaps the most commonly used technique to lead the person to be educated out of the state or condition in which he is found to another, more desirable state. Moreover, until the value notions associated with our concept of a cultured or cultivated individual are made clear, any appeal to this sense as the most proper for the term must appear to beg the very question I should like further to establish.

Reflection upon the success of the cruder forms of education to produce results should merely serve to indicate that some cherished philosophical presuppositions are themselves without ground. For example, in spite of the widespread influence of the functional psychology of Dewey and Mead, idealism in education is not dead; it appears in every proposal to emphasize the liberal arts—at the expense of the fine and practical arts which must be taught in a studio and thus somehow thought to be properly classified with manual training. And God help the teachers of physical education, who in these enlightened years of our Lord are concerned with the improvement of physical efficiency but who, in order to do so, must come into contact with sweating bodies—still the principle of evil in the Christian idealist's world. There is no man lower on the educational totem.

The thing to be educated would on second thought appear to be a consciousness-body, a body-mind, or a minded body whether we happen to be concerned with its physical or its cultural dimensions. In some areas of aesthetic education—those of the dance and in the studio and performing arts, for example, it is perfectly obvious that the only ground for discrimination against their inclusion within the curriculum is the unfounded prejudice of unthinking administrators.

Nor do these men understand the basic materialism of our contemporary technological societies, abetted by our stepped-up programs of scientific education. The only difference between Americans and Russians on this score seems to be the honesty of the Russians: they freely admit to a materialistic account of nature, the world and human conduct. And, for them, brain-washing is perhaps the most effective technique available for their ends.

III

The most viable of contemporary educational dicta is that teachers must start "where the children are." Unfortunately, some have ended there too, but this is not so much an indication of the dictum's falseness as it is inept teaching or lack of a philosophical justification or both. We must start where the children are, because there is no place else to start: the child himself, at any moment of reflection on who or what he is, will always find himself there. *Befindlichkeit,* Heidegger calls it, one of the constitutive moments of a human being's being *there.* Where? In the world, the only place a human being can be and be what he has to be—something other than he is at present.

A first false step from here on in is the assumption that the teacher must determine what his students are by snooping in their backgrounds. The son of a butcher, a preacher's kid, a rivet maker, pitcher or catcher: upper lower, or lower middle class sons and daughters who, by virtue of their classification display one set of values and not another. It has been written that education in aesthetic values has so often failed because middle class teachers have failed to introduce their students into the aesthetic possibilities of lower class experiences: and they could not do anything else, because by definition their own values are "middle class." My own experience would suggest that they often may fail to communicate the importance of high artistic achievement for the same reason. Something is wrong here, of course. If the correlation of aesthetic values and socio-economic strata of society is to be found of any worth in the instruction of art and its appreciation, one should be led to expect the same kind of correlation between "high culture" and the "upper classes." Such does not exist: the upper economic classes have produced nothing but more wealth, having lost even the gentility of the older aristocratic classes. Those who can, do; and those who cannot, make money, whether they teach or not. Because some successful (by the financial criterion) artists have begun to act like bourgeois gentlemen (which designation was an absurd *contradictio un adjecto* for Moliere) we have been seduced into traducing the artistic personality. Social alienation is an unpopular theme in the heyday of the social scientist, so we refer to it, by the force of some unknown logic, as socially determined.

The fact which stands out like a statistician's sore thumb is precisely that of effective creation: it is a blatant and unstandard deviation from the mean—in two senses of the term. Even to be able to set up a correlation between it and anything else we must be able to stipulate the criterion or criteria, and this on aesthetic grounds, of how we recognize it as such. Rosenberg's and Fliegel's book, entitled, *The Vanguard Artist,*[3] is a failure for this reason. It correlates creation with many factors, but fails to stipulate the criterion—other than that the artists polled were "vanguard" and residents in New York City—for determining the aesthetic meaningfulness of their identification. Thus, if my charges are correct, as I believe they are, successful instruction in matters aesthetic would enable even our social scientists to interpret the meaning of their correlations. This would be an unexpected by-product of successful aesthetic education. And until they learn this trick teachers of art or aesthetics have nothing to learn from them. Not even by starting out with an adolescent's love of fast, junky cars could one succeed in the task of teaching aesthetic values. So strong is this love that one is incapable of determining whether the expression "hot rod" refers to the adolescent's automobile or to himself. Society and the individual would be much better off, however, if whatever is named by the term could be cooled down somewhat.

The point of this diatribe, of course, is to indicate that our pedagogical theories have suffered from a disease known as "over-determination." We started out by asking the question, "Who are our students?", and all we have received as an answer is that they are somewhat, a *what* that is inhuman in that it has been essentialized out of its existence.

Since the publication of *Sein und Zeit* in 1927, Heidegger has been saying nothing else. His claim that the categories of ancient and modern philosophy are applicable only to things, not to living human beings, has gone unheeded—either because of the scientism of our age or our failure to comprehend the significance of his pronouncement. If *"Das Wesen des Daseins liegt in seiner Existenz,"* and *Dasein* is what is to be educated, it would behoove us as educators to pay some attention to *Existenz.*

By *Existenz* or existentiality is meant primarily the fact that a human subject is (or is describable in terms of) the ways in which it lives a limited set of possibilities. Both the limitation on the set and the character of the possibilities are determined by what Sartre calls "the human condition," or necessary relationship to some environing situation. The necessity of this relationship is factual, and for this reason the relation itself is called "facticity." The moment one asks the question of the meaning of existence, he becomes the questioner and finds that the significance of his question is tied to the situation in which it arose and that toward which it tends. Ordinarily, however, human beings do not question their own existence: they exist in a "fallen" state in which their mood is one of idle curiosity, their understanding confused by ambiguities, and their discourse surrendered over to empty talk. On the average the everyday character of one human being is to be in the same way every other human being exists: to do, feel, and say whatever "one" is supposed to do, feel, or say. Authentic existence, on the other hand, is a call to true selfhood, felt, understood and expressed in one resolute act of self-determination.

Does such a description have educational implications?

The first impulse is to answer, no. Existentialism is a form of radical individualism, according to which the individual's conduct may be conditioned and motivated, but not determined. School administrators must hold in horror the prospect of a program of education structured to the requirements of each individual to be educated. Thinking in terms of a program with fixed objectives for all students, based upon their socio-economic classification, their supposed future function in society, and the like, is however no meaningful alternative. Such thinking overlooks the fact that the students themselves offer the most meaningful resources for the development of educational aims. Such thinking, if imposed upon the educational process itself, can only be called "idealistic" at best, and "tyrannical" at worst. We must therefore deny our first impulse, and attempt to build a program fitted to the needs of the individual to be educated.

Two suggestions are immediately forthcoming. If the human individual is what he is to be, meaning only by that, that his being is yet to be determined, he is by nature educable; we must only remember that he is to be educated according to whatever hints we may find in the humanness of his nature. Since he is the person who will decide what he is to become, it will appear completely bootless on our parts to insist that the student become one thing rather than another. This is the reason some adolescent behavior may be described as a reaction against the values of parents and teachers. Parents and teachers have not in general succeeded in justifying the value-character of their particular values. Why like Beethoven when the Beatles will do? Any attempt to justify our preferences in this matter by appealing to comparisons and contrasts is to miss the point that any experience may be aesthetic and that only having the experience is a guarantee of its value. Let us start, therefore, where the students are; but let us make sure they come to an understanding of their experiences. Any criterion for judging these must be found in the experiences themselves, and this is what a good course in philosophical aesthetics should provide.

The second, and usually misinterpreted, factor of the educational process is the teacher. He, too, is a human participant who must react with meaning to what we vaguely refer to as "a classroom situation." It is more significant, educationally, to saddle him with a program than it is to insist that children or adolescents adopt the behavioral patterns of cultivated adults. Teaching is an art, not a science; and the responses of the teacher to the classroom situation must be dictated by the necessities of that situation, part of which are precisely the ways in which the students themselves react to the same situation. As an artist he must learn how to "transform the obstacles of the situation into means," to lapse into Deweyan terms. He must work with a medium constituted by those obstacles he finds, and the greatest of these (if we lay aside administrators) is the unpredictable reactions of the students themselves.

Since it becomes clear that the second of my suggestions depends upon a more complete description of the educational possibilities of the first, the remainder of this paper will consist in further treatment of the student's existential condition.

According to Heidegger, the existential constitution of *Dasein's* "being there" is its *Erschlossenheit.* I paraphrase, every human being is characterized by its openness to experience. If the human personality were not open to experience, it would be uneducable—and dead to boot. This openness to experience may itself be experienced: first, as a mood; secondly, as understanding; and thirdly, as expression. My translation of these *existentialia* (the term Heidegger uses for categories applicable to human beings) needs some justification. I cannot play with English in the same way as Heidegger has played with German, moving from *Stimmung* to *Bestimmtheit,* from mood to determination, and hope to be understood. Yet he seems to be making a common-place assertion. Human knowledge—of any kind whatsoever—is determined by a response to the ordering of the qualities perceived within a sensory field. This pervasive quality of a situation (once again, Dewey) is intuitively felt as a modification of a previous "subjective" state.

At this level of experience, moreover, we may be unaware of objects as such, and hence of their abstracted or abstractable significance. Our "understanding" of the mood is our having of the experience, and what we understand in this sense we must come to express (a more general term than Heidegger's *Rede*). These three determinants, affectivity, understanding and expression, are in Heidegger's terms (*gleichursprünglich*) "equi-primordial," by which he means to say that neither has a temporal precedence over the other. We do not first feel, then attempt to understand, and finally succeed in expressing what we have come to understand. We may very well express ourselves first in order to understand what we wanted to express and come to the affective experience with either the understanding or the expression. All he is saying is that the creative idea must be discovered, and will ultimately be revealed only on the condition of being open to the influences of an environment—real or imagined. In pedagogical practice, however, it would appear beneficial to assume that affectivity precedes expression, in order to allow for those vague ideas the student feels he has to express without having the means, the ability, or the determination actually to express them.

We need not commit the intentional fallacy here. We need not assume that the artwork of the student "means" what the student wanted to express. If we are to communicate with him at all, we must start our criticisms with what he has actually expressed, with the quality of his ordering of qualities. In so doing we must be equally as careful to avoid that other dreaded aesthetic pitfall, the so-called "affective fallacy." We commit it when we assume that the significance of an ordering of qualities is our own reaction to a work of art as a purely "subjective" phenomenon, determined by our own private associations. The sentiment or mood of the piece in this way becomes falsely interpreted in the light of our own sentimentality.

If we are to avoid intentionalism on the one hand and sentimentality on the other, one and only one recourse is open to us. The "significance" of a work of art is still to be gauged by its felt expressiveness, but this expressiveness must be controlled by the actual ordering of perceived qualities. Here again the aesthetic category to be applied to the experience is openness. The critic or the teacher in the critic's function must allow his own perception to be guided by what he sees controlled by the student artist's ordered universe. To apply the aesthetic ideals of the Renaissance to a contemporary piece is to denigrate both. And this is the second justification for finding the criterion of aesthetic significance within the experience of the work itself. The first was to allow the student the freedom of *his* expression; the second is to guarantee communication with a truly appreciative audience. To the openness of the student the teacher must be trained to respond with his own. Between the two is the common stimulus of the physical world, screened in the first instance by two bodies (perception), and interpreted in the light of a single prevailing mood.

The critic or teacher's openness, it might be suggested, moves from affectivity, to understanding, and thence to verbal expression. But this scheme too should be interpreted as a single process of equi-primordial determinant moments. The verbal expression, considered as the application of aesthetic categories—such as matter and form or form and content (I prefer surface and depth)—is not, however, to be interpreted as a gloss, commentary, or paraphrase of the artwork's significance; nor should it be attempted as an assessment of the "worth" of the expression measured by the application of an external criterion. Aesthetic categories, when they work, serve to make explicit the implicit ordering of the artwork's context; and any which succeed in this trick are valid for that experience. There is no danger of alienation of the critic from the artist as long as the second-level categories he uses are tested against the context of the experience in question—as long, that is, as openness continues to correspond to openness. The critic merely lays out the experience in terms of the categories applicable to the experience: he gives utterance to this interpretation, and then may be led to an experience (the pervasive quality or the mood) of the piece he has interpreted.

When the critic is a teacher, however, his mode of expression is broader than that of the student artist or of a critic per se. One of the obstacles he must turn into a means is the student's reaction to his own expression; another is the critical process just described. If one set of categories fails to communicate with the student, the teacher must be capable of changing his approach and finding a set which does. To limit himself to a single set of aesthetic categories is as restrictive to his own, and ultimately to the student's original expression, as the demand that the student adopt someone else's style. This likewise is a common failing in the instruction of the arts. Again, the cure is the correspondence of openness to openness guided or controlled by the similar reactions to a common world, or ordering of qualities.

If this description is exact, then there is a sense in which the teacher must be a trained artist. His artistry is not proficiency in one of the creative or performing arts, but in teaching as an art. We refer to the first as "the artist teacher," so I would suggest for the newer concept, "the teacher artist." His is the task of ordering the qualities of the learning experience by controlling the communication between the openness of the student—who must express his own universe—and his own as the first critical appreciator. The teacher artist need not be conceived as an actor, because he is not performing for an audience. That is another way of ordering qualities, but one which may be terribly ineffective since it would tend to reduce the student to the role of a passive audience. There is enough ham in the classroom already; there seems to be no reason to appeal for more.

In summary, the teacher artist is concerned primarily with the universe of the student, of coming to an understanding of the student's expression, of guiding and of offering clear alternatives to the student's means and manner of expressing *himself.* The teacher's own reactions should be limited to having the experience of the student's work, and of suggesting meaningful alternatives. The measure of his success as an artist should be the student's success in expressing himself as an artist. And here as always, the way in which each is an artist is to be viewed as the way in which each overcomes obstacles in such a way as to turn them into means. Toward what? Toward the structuring of a uniquely significant universe of expression.

IV

I have stated above that an existential ground for aesthetic education is possible, given the proper account of the being of human beings; and concluded that the same ground is necessary if the teacher is to be considered as an artist whose universe includes the student's attempts at ordering an individually significant expressive context. The existential categories which enable this interpretation are Heidegger's three determinants of human *Erschlossenheit:* affectivity, understanding, and expression. In what follows I shall merely enumerate the expected results of applying this existential ground in justification of the inclusion of aesthetic materials in the public school curriculum.

First of all, it is fatal for the furthering of human growth, considered in individual or social terms, to interpret the educational process as a means of assimilating the already existing culture (initial appreciation does not mean the assessment of worth—whatever that might mean). The purpose of assimilating a culture is to be able to use it, and to use it in such a way as to surpass it. For this reason, the student must be allowed to make his own contribution. He must be allowed to communicate as he can, and for many students this means to communicate without using verbal symbols. His work is to construct objects which have a significance, in the first instance perhaps only to him, by calling attention to the nature of the world in which he lives. It is for this reason, perhaps, that contemporary pop artists continue to hold our attention—as social critics. Any pre-existent object is for him only a means for thus expressing himself. Cut off this possibility by excluding aesthetic expression from the school curriculum or by limiting it to the assimilation of the culture of the past, and you are wantonly destroying the resources of the human community. Successful criticism applied to contemporary art helps to insure the growth of the community between persons created in the first instance by the artist's aesthetic expression.

Secondly, it does not follow that the individualism of the above account of expression precludes the possibility of education in the field. As educators, we must allow ourselves to be guided by the nature of the beast to be educated, which in the light of the above means the human individual as basically (i.e., so constituted in its being) an openness to experience. We can achieve this state of affairs by allowing our teachers the same sort of freedom in their own art as we have insisted upon for their students. The first and most meaningful act of communication is between human beings allowing openness to correspond to openness, a condition we can fulfill by insuring that each teacher's response be controlled by the ordering of qualities in the students' acts of expression. And the only way I can conceive of this happening is for every teacher artist engaged in teaching an art to be provided with an effective set of aesthetic categories. In a bygone age, we expected this of courses in philosophical aesthetics.

I hope at this point that I have made good on my threat to justify both the inclusion of aesthetic materials in the public school curriculum, and the adoption of a particular manner of developing proficiency therein.

REFERENCES

1. Heidegger, *Sein and Zeit* (Tübingen: Max Neimayer Verlag, 8th ed., 1957).
2. Sartre, *L'Etre et le Néant* (Paris: Librairie Gallimard, 45th printing, 1955).
3. Rosenberg and Fliegel, *The Vanguard Artist* (Chicago: Quadrangle Books, 1965).

Maxine Greene takes us to the heart of existentialism in her opening comment of "Literature, Existentialism, and Education": "Since 1842, when Søren Kierkegaard made indirect communication one of the categories of communication, existential philosophers have been awakening individuals to a sense of their condition through the use of literary devices and forms." But her interest is not only in Kierkegaard. She also considers the works of Nietzsche, Sartre, Camus, Buber, and Simone de Beauvoir, as well as such purely literary figures as Joyce, Melville, Gide, and Rilke. The purpose of these considerations is to open for teachers, through literature, the existential possibilities of choosing, of commitment, of care, and of freedom.

4 | Literature, Existentialism, and Education

MAXINE GREENE

Yes, he thought, between grief and nothing I will take grief.

William Faulkner, *The Wild Palms*

Nathaniel, I shall teach you fervor.

Andre Gide, *Les Nourritures Terres ˋs*

We do not know what we want; however we are responsible for what we are.

J.-P. Sartre, Introduction to *Les Temps Modernes*

Since 1842, when Søren Kierkegaard made "indirect communication" one of the categories of communication, existential philosophers have been awakening individuals to a sense of their condition through the use of literary devices and forms. Kierkegaard's view of his own age had much to do with his decision to beguile people, to stir them up, to make their lives more difficult. "A revolutionary age is an age of action," he wrote, "ours is an age of advertisement and publicity. In the present age a rebellion is, of all things, the most unthinkable. Such an expression of strength would seem ridiculous to the calculating intelligence of our times."[1] Concerned with making "an expression of strength" possible for individuals, he created a literature intended to challenge both calculating intelligence and the calculated

63

enjoyments associated with the "aesthetic" approach to life. His project was to seduce his readers into asking the questions and making the choices that seemed to him to be the "proper and stringent expression of the ethical."[2] But he could function neither as seducer nor as gadfly if he relied upon abstract argument. His readers had to be brought to participate imaginatively in situations where decisive choices were demanded and where there were never enough good reasons for saying that one alternative was absolutely right and the other wrong.

Either/Or involves a dialogue between the intellectually gifted aestheticist "A" and the less gifted but committed ethical thinker, Judge William. Between "A's" essays and the Judge's letters appears the "Diary of a Seducer," based upon Kierkegaard's own experiences with Regina Olsen: the love affair, the wooing, and the broken engagement. Kierkegaard had already decided to give Regina up when he began *Either/Or,* so the account cannot be regarded as diary or confession. Rather, it is a deliberate transmutation of actuality into fiction. The world in which Johannes pursues and then retreats from Cordelia is a concrete world full of ambiguities and open possibilities; moreover, it is suffused by the imaginary. The reader willing to enter into it cannot remain an indifferent spectator. His own consciousness becomes the subject of the Diary, his own awareness of the contradictions between romantic and conjugal love, the problem of fidelity, the discrepancies between the outward appearance of an engaged couple and their inner lives. He is there in person, confronting the necessity to choose either good *and* evil—or not to choose at all. The climax is reached not when Cordelia, repelled by a deliberately unpleasant Johannes, breaks the engagement herself. It is reached when the Judge writes: "If you will understand me aright, I should like to say that in making a choice it is not so much a question of choosing the right as of the energy, the earnestness, the pathos with which one chooses. Thereby the personality announces its inner infinity, and thereby, in turn, the personality is consolidated."[3] Kierkegaard called the work an "incantation," not an argument. He was trying to arouse each reader to "earnestness of spirit," to the consolidation or creation of himself. And this could be done best by means of imaginative literature.

Kierkegaard, of course, was predominantly interested in becoming a Christian; and his primary purpose, as he said, was religious. He thought of himself as a teacher, which "in the right sense was to be a learner"; but he was an exemplary philosopher in the existential sense. He demonstrated this clearly enough when he wrote in *The Point of View for My Work as an Author:*

> I have nothing new to proclaim; I am without authority, being myself hidden in a deceit; I do not go to work straightforwardly but with indirect cunning; I am not a holy man; in short, I am a spy who in his spying, in learning to know all about questionable conduct and

illusions and suspicious characters, all the while he is making inspection is himself under the closest inspection.[4]

As we shall see, this could describe any literary artist. The novelist, for example, has often been presented as a forger,[5] a counterfeiter,[6] a confidence man.[7] In this case, however, the deceit, the cunning, and the indirection—not to speak of the self-inspection—appear to be distinctive characteristics of the existential philosopher; and they help to explain his use of literature.

Kierkegaard was not the only one. There was Nietzsche as well. He used metaphors, epigrams, plays on words, satires, aphorisms. "Whoever writes in blood and aphorisms," he says, "does not want to be read but to be learned by heart. In the mountains the shortest way is from peak to peak; but for that one must have long legs. Aphorisms should be peaks—and those who are addressed, tall and lofty. The air thin and pure, danger near, and the spirit full of gay sarcasm: these go well together."[8] Later, talking about seeking the truth, learning and trying out himself, the character Zarathustra says: "A trying and questioning was my every move; and, verily, one must also learn to answer such questioning. That, however, is my taste—not good, not bad, but *my* taste of which I am no longer ashamed and which I have no wish to hide. 'This is *my* way; where is yours?'—thus I answered those who asked me 'the way.' For *the* way—that does not exist."[9] Once again, the effort is (indirectly, through Zarathustra, the fictional "I") to arouse people to their own subjective awareness—and to awareness of that awareness—so they can seek *their* ways. *Thus Spake Zarathustra* has no more practical utility than a lyric; it cannot be summarized, paraphrased, or used for any end beyond itself. As Sartre puts it about literature in general, "the end to which it offers itself is the reader's freedom."[10]

So it is with Sartre's imaginative works, Albert Camus', Simone de Beauvoir's, Martin Buber's, and those of other existential philosophers. Acting upon his or her existential commitment, each has been concerned with moving persons to reflection upon themselves and to choose what to make of themselves within their own historical situations. Free people write, as it were, their own histories; they are the authors of their own lives. But they must act and choose in terms of the reality given to them by way of consciousness. More often than not, they do not see their own reality. Conventions, presuppositions, proprieties, habitual automatisms, *idées fixés* of all kinds disguise or deform the impinging world; they prevent individuals from returning to "things in themselves." The artist is concerned with such returning, with renewing the reader's own world. "For this is quite the final goal of art:" writes Sartre, "to recover this world by giving it to be seen as it is, but as if it had its source in human freedom."[11]

In *Being and Nothingness,* Sartre discusses "quality as a revelation of being" and the existential symbolism of things. He makes the point that the quality of a thing is nothing other than its being. "The yellow of the lemon, we said, is not a subjective mode of apprehending the lemon: it is the lemon. We have shown also that the whole lemon extends throughout its qualities and that each one of the qualities is spread over the others; that is what we have correctly called 'this.' Every quality of being is all of being; it is the presence of its absolute contingency; it is its indifferent irreducibility."[12] In Sartre's novel, *Nausea,* Antoine Roquentin discovers the absolute contingency of the world. There are only qualities, appearances: there are only labels and abstract categories—nothing more. He is sitting on something named a seat in a tramcar. "I murmur: 'It's a seat,' a little like an exorcism. But the word stays on my lips; it refuses to go and put itself on the thing. . . . Things are divorced from their names. They are there, grotesque, headstrong, gigantic and it seems ridiculous to call them seats or say anything at all about them: I am in the midst of things, nameless things. Alone, without words, defenseless, they surround me, are beneath me, behind me, above me. They demand nothing, they don't impose themselves: they are there." He sees a man half-lying on the opposite seat; he watches his finger scratch his scalp with a nail. Then he jumps off the tram and finds himself in the park. "I drop onto a bench between great black tree-trunks, between the black, knotty hands reaching towards the sky. A tree scrapes at the earth under my feet with a black nail. I would so like to let myself go, forget myself, sleep. But I can't, I'm suffocating: existence penetrates me everywhere, through the eyes, the nose, the mouth. . . . And suddenly, suddenly, the veil is torn away, I have understood, I have seen."[13]

In *Being and Nothingness,* the philosopher has much to say about the relation between things and human reality. He writes much about the psychic meaning of the slimy which is "identical with the symbolic value which the slimy has in relation to being-in-itself."[14] For all his imagery, for all such terms as "sticky thickness," "the sucking of the slimy which I feel on my hands," and "the invisible suction of the past," the nature of the human situation is not revealed as it is in the novel. It is not made available for appropriation by a reader's consciousness in the same fashion, because the reader is not asked to apprehend it imaginatively. It has, therefore, nothing like the impact of Roquentin's metaphysical predicament when he has his vision in the park. "And then all of a sudden, there it was, clear as day: existence had suddenly unveiled itself. It had lost the harmless look of an abstract category: it was the very paste of things, this root was kneaded into existence. Or rather the root, the park gates, the bench, the sparse grass, all that had vanished: the diversity of things, their individuality, were only an appearance, a veneer. This veneer had melted, leaving soft, monstrous masses, all in disorder—naked, in a frightful, obscene nakedness."[15] The terrible nausea experienced by the man who yearns for an orderly, intelligible universe and discovers that existence escapes the boundaries of language and science is the product of the consciousness disclosed in the novel. That nausea can only become significant, however, if the reader gives to it some of his own revulsion at contingency and arbitrariness. He can only give in this way if, for a moment at least, he contemplates existence from an inward and personal vantage point. Contemplating it in this fashion, he may be able to summon up his awareness of the thereness of things and the otherness of human beings, the opaqueness surrounding him, the imperviousness. The illusioned world that is *Nausea* can only be entered by way of his own consciousness at a time when he is capable of bracketing out his common-sense perceptions of benches, gates, trees, and trams. Having bracketed out or set aside what he has learned to see as the reliable particularities of daily life, he can (moving through his consciousness of the patterned events in *Nausea*) see his own reality in a strange nakedness. This means that he can look upon the world as it presents itself to him in its concreteness and immediacy, without the intervention of social recipes and schemata. In doing so, he may also perceive possibilities of human action unthinkable in his everyday world. If nothing else, he may suspect that, if existence is nameless or meaningless, it is up to human beings to restore meanings. Or he may discover what Anny means when she talks about living forward, outliving herself, avoiding fixities and bad faith. At the very least, dimensions of his life will be disclosed for the first time; he will have been helped to recover his world.

This is what happens when the existential philosopher decides to supplement his or her philosophic texts with indirect communication. We need only recall Simone de Beauvoir's *The Second Sex* with its call for the liberation of both men and women, its demand that people dare to be human and to live in good faith, and compare the work with her novel, *The Mandarins.* Here a woman struggles to live her married life in good faith, to confront aging and disillusionment, to choose against her own death because of the remorse her family would suffer. "I am here," Anne thinks at the end of the book. "They are living, they speak to me, I am alive. Once more, I've jumped feet first into life. . . . Either one founders in apathy, or the earth becomes repeopled. I didn't founder. Since my heart continues to beat, it will have to beat for something, for someone. Since I'm not deaf, I'll once more hear people calling to me. Who knows? Perhaps one day I'll be happy again. Who knows?"[16] We need only recall as well the difference between Albert Camus' lucid descriptions of the Absurd in *The Myth of Sisyphus* and such images as that of the "whole beach, pulsating with heat" pressing against Meusault's back in *The Stranger*—or "the benign indifference of the universe" and the "howls of execration" at the novel's end.

We do not suggest that the only effective existential novels are those created by philosophers eager to confront readers with their own reality. We suggest that imaginative literature holds a distinctive significance for the existential philosopher because of his dominating interest in human freedom, authenticity, and the elusiveness of Being. Idealist philosophers may cherish literature and the other arts for their mimetic function or (as Benedetto Croce does[17]) for being themselves spiritual acts through which images and intuitions are clarified and expressed. Pragmatic philosophers may cherish literature and the other arts because they make possible paradigmatic experiences. "An object," wrote John Dewey, "is peculiarly and dominantly esthetic, yielding the enjoyment characteristic of esthetic perception, when the factors that determine anything which can be called an experience are lifted high above the threshold of perception and are made manifest for their own sake."[18] In the one case, literature is expected to communicate a form of spiritual knowledge; in the other, an engagement with literature is expected to provide an experience characterized by wholeness, integration, and the fullest realization of qualitative particulars. Both idealists and pragmatists find in the arts a capacity to promote heightened sensitivity and awareness, perhaps an intensified perception of meaning. But existential philosophers are unique in their view that consciousness, in its intentionality, is as empty and as clear as the wind. This means that consciousness does not contain the ego. "In fact the consciousness which I have of the I never exhausts it, and the consciousness is not what causes it to come into existence; and I is always given as *having been there before* consciousness—and at the same time as possessing depths which have to be revealed gradually. Thus the ego appears to consciousness as a transcendent in-itself, as an existent in the human world, not as *belonging* to consciousness."[19] The individual is therefore constantly in search of himself, encountering nothingness or the dread of nihilation, living among possibles. To find himself, he must become reflective about his situation; he must experience the anguish which is the manifestation of his freedom—which is also "the recognition of a possibility as *my* possibility." Because literature goads a reader to reflexiveness and, at once, to confrontation with his freedom, it becomes a potential means of self-discovery, an aid in the pursuit of being. For the existentialist, then, a literary encounter can be an encounter with the fundamental drama of an individual's life.

In a poem called "Torso of an Archaic Apollo," Rainer Maria Rilke describes a statue in the Louvre which bursts with light and gleams "until there is no place/ that does not see you. You must change your life."[20] Saying this about the impact of art upon the beholder, he is speaking for generations of writers who were not philosophers but whose awareness of the human condition was so similar to that of existential philosophers as to warrant the description "existentialist." In the first of the *Duino Elegies,* Rilke uses angels to represent either imagination or an ideal of undivided consciousness men aspire to and can seldom achieve. He writes:

> Each single angel is terrible. And so I keep down my heart, and
> swallow the call-note of depth-dark sobbing. Alas, who is there we can
> make use of? Not angels, not men; and already the knowing brutes are

aware that we don't feel very securely at home within our interpreted world.[21]

His perception of the void that exists after the death of God led him to the fearful recognition that men themselves, if they were able, would have to create new imaginative orders in empty space, horrified space. Not only did he present an awareness of what Sartre was later to call an indifferent, hostile, and restive world; he knew of homelessness and insecurity, even in the face of what was "interpreted" by the sciences and the old sterile faiths.

Fyodor Dostoyevsky knew as well, and had known long before the *Duino Elegies,* even before *Thus Spake Zarathustra.* In most of his novels—*The Possessed, Crime and Punishment, The Brothers Karamasov*—the recurring existential themes are sounded and explored: freedom, anguish, despair, boredom, guilt, loneliness, dread. We need only think back to *The Brothers Karamasov* in order to summon up that topsy-turvy world inhabited by people who seem to have no everyday reality. Living their lives in extreme situations, they are presented as thrusting consciousnesses; the fiction is composed of what they intend. Ivan Karamasov's "poem" about the Grand Inquisitor suggests some of this and at once reminds us of certain perplexities which have become obsessions in the modern world. In the "poem," the Grand Inquisitor blames Jesus for destroying His own kingdom. He destroyed it by insisting on receiving love that was freely offered "and not the base raptures of the slave." He rejected, therefore, the forces of miracle, mystery, and authority, all of which could have been counted upon "to hold captive forever" the consciences of rebellious men.

> Instead of taking men's freedom away from them, Thou didst make it greater than ever! Didst Thou forget that man prefers peace, and even death, to freedom of choice in the knowledge of good and evil? Nothing is more seductive for man than his freedom of conscience, but nothing is a greater cause of suffering. And behold, instead of giving a firm foundation for setting the conscience of man at rest for ever, Thou didst choose all that is exceptional, vague and enigmatic; Thou didst choose what was utterly beyond the strength of men, acting as though Thou didst not love them at all—Thou who didst come to give Thy life for them![22]

In Dostoyevsky's *Notes from Underground,* the reader discovers one of the most compelling enactments of self-confrontation ever created. Transmuting old conventions having to do with caverns, pits, and being buried alive, Dostoyevsky devised the metaphor of underground to communicate the sense of anguished inwardness or human subjectivity. The cellar inhabited by the Underground Man is located, significantly, in St. Petersburg, a shabby modern city shrouded in dingy, yellowish snow. Without support or attachment, the speaker is struggling to identify himself and at once to understand his being-in-the-world. Not only does he lash out at the Crystal Palace that represents progress and industry; not only does he rebel against abstract formulas, notions of the "normal" and the "reasonable," and the thought of being treated as a "piano-key." Breaking with all aspects of common-sense reality and morality, he has to face the terrible conundrums of anguish and free will; he has to find a way of coping with boredom and with "spite." In his predicament, he exudes the fear and trembling which accompany reflexiveness. To engage with his anguished consciousness is to plunge into the existential dilemma, to suffer free will.

> And yet I think man will never renounce real suffering, that is, destruction and chaos. Why suffering is the sole origin of consciousness. Though I did lay it down at the beginning that consciousness is the greatest misfortune for man, yet I know man prizes it and would not give it up for any satisfaction. Consciousness, for instance, is infinitely superior to twice two makes four. Once you have mathematical certainty there is nothing left to do or to understand. There will be nothing left but to bottle up your five senses and plunge into contemplation. While if you stick to consciousness, even though the same result is attained, you can at least flog yourself at times, and that will, at any rate, liven you up. Reactionary as it is, corporal punishment is better than nothing.[23]

To move from Dostoyevsky to Leo Tolstoy is ostensibly to move from the world of the outsider to the dense concreteness of social reality; but in Tolstoy's works too there are disturbing and incessant evocations of absurdity. In *The Death of Ivan Ilyich* existential preoccupations become increasingly manifest as the civil servant, Ivan Ilyich, is forced by terminal cancer to break with the natural attitude that sustained him throughout his life. An agreeable marriage, promotions in his ministry, a "delightful house," expensive confectioners, the "best people": all the accoutrements of bourgeois living shield him from his own reality. He injures himself slightly. There follows a certain absent-mindedness, a bad taste in the mouth, an ache in his side. Ivan Ilyich visits the doctor, who tells him only what is "necessary and proper." At length a chill comes with despair; he sees that he is going to die. He thinks of the old syllogism, "Caius is a man, men are mortal, therefore Caius is mortal"; and he thinks that what was correct about Caius—"man in the abstract"—cannot be true of him, "a creature quite, quite separate from all others." This is his awakening in the face of death. Suddenly he perceives his own loneliness and forlornness in a place where those he knows best are receding and becoming "other" to him. On the verge of dying (here compared with being thrust into a black sack), he begins to question and to think of choice: " 'What is the right thing?'," he asks. Aware of his family's wretchedness, he feels sorry and thinks that "he must act so as not to hurt them: release them and free himself from these sufferings."[24] In some manner, he has come to be on the very brink of dissolution, of a nothingness where there is only light.

There is Joseph Conrad also, with his continual emphasis upon the inscrutable and the ambiguous and the darkness. In *Heart of Darkness,* there is a remarkable confrontation between the man who has seen reality unmasked and those who persist in living submerged in everyday life. Marlow is sitting on a yawl in the Thames river at a gathering hosted by the Director of Companies; he is moved to tell his companions with their "stay-at-home" minds a yarn about his confrontation with the wilderness. Describing the journey down the silent African river, he tells of how he had to watch for sunken stones and pieces of dead wood. And then: " 'When you have to attend to things of that sort, to the mere incidents of the surface, the reality—the reality I tell you—fades. The inner truth is hidden—luckily, luckily. But I felt it all the same; I felt often its mysterious stillness watching me at my monkey tricks, just as it watches you fellows performing on your respective tight-ropes for—what is it? half a crown a tumble—' "[25] The effect of this is felt by the one man who is awake and who growls, " 'Try to be civil, Marlow,' " as if it were somehow impolite to disclose absurdity. Later, Marlow (having told of the death of the black helmsman, the way his shoes filled up with blood, and his flinging the shoes overboard) becomes more specific.

> "Absurd!" he cried. "This is the worst of trying to tell. . . . Here you all are, each moored with two good addresses, like a hulk with two anchors, a butcher around one corner, a policeman round another, excellent appetites, and temperature normal—you hear—normal from year's end to year's end. And you say, Absurd! Absurd be—exploded! Absurd! My dear boys, what can you expect from a man who out of sheer nervousness had just flung overboard a new pair of shoes!"[26]

To have a normal temperature is to be impervious to the hidden, to the "immense jabber . . . without any kind of sense." It is to be like the manager with his lack of care and concern, the man who never gets sick—and who can never, therefore, see his own reality. To be sick is to experience extremity "in an impalpable grayness, with nothing underfoot, with nothing around, without spectators, without clamor, without glory, without the great desire of victory, without the great fear of defeat." To be sick is to know one's being in the world.

Being in the world, *in* reality; being *there*: this becomes the ground of what is rendered in imaginative literature with increasing frequency as the twentieth century moves on. Franz Kafka evokes the philosophy of Kierkegaard in his presentations of an impenetrable web of institutions, officials, codes, and authorities. In *The Trial,* for example, K. has a job in a bank; he has identity papers; he believes he exists in an ordinary world and in an ordinary network of relationships. Once he is accused and held to be guilty, once he tries without avail to reach the Judge and the High Court, at least to find out of what he has been accused, he falls out of the world. Realizing, on some level, that he in unutterably alone and homeless, he comes in touch with the ground of his own being as he moves closer and closer to the quarry where he is scheduled to die. Yet here, as in *The Castle*, the short stories, and the *Letter to My Father*, there is a sense of something transcendent and unknowable, something expressed in one of Kafka's parables:

> He is a free and secure citizen of the world, for he is fettered to a chain which is long enough to give him the freedom of all earthly space, and yet only so long that nothing can drag him past the frontiers of the world. But simultaneously he is a free and secure citizen of Heaven as well, for he is also fettered by a similarly designed heavenly chain. So that if he heads, say, for the earth, his heavenly collar throttles him, and if he heads for Heaven, his earthly one does the same. And yet all the possibilities are his, and he feels it; more, he actually refuses to account for the deadlock by an error in the original fettering.[27]

This peculiar fettering, too, is part of the existential situation at a particular moment of time. Kafka wrote in the letter to his father that he was absorbing "the negative element of the age in which I live, an age that is, of course, very close to me." And it may be that what we discover in so much of contemporary literature is itself a response to a historical situation, a peculiar "present age."

André Malraux defined himself openly and repeatedly within a particular historical situation as he developed his perception of the absurd. *Man's Fate* (*La Condition Humaine*) is in one sense a specific response to an age of political violence, when the Shanghai Revolution could convincingly serve as an emblem of a boundary situation at its most extreme. In another, more profound sense, however, *Man's Fate* deals with the desperate predicament of men and women adrift in a wholly absurd universe. Each one confronts his or her fate, which may be nothingness or death or simply an inevitable catastrophe. Because the situation is so extreme, each character has no choice but to defy nothingness through action or through a type of mania. Each one (because he is neither "normal," bourgeois, or even prudent) must struggle for self-assertion in the void. Ch'en combats the blankness with terror and self-destruction. Kyo commits himself to human dignity and makes that commitment his personal fate. Katov creates his meaning in a heroism rooted in fraternity; Gisors withdraws into the distancing of opium dreams. Ferral defies nihilation with eroticism and the wielding of power; Clappique gambles, renders his own life a myth and a game. Malraux renders them all as irreducibly private persons and engages the reader with their inwardness. He shows them to be persons fiercely aware of the gulf between their subjectivity and the violent public world in which they must act in order to be. At the end, some of them are transfigured: solitary individuals converge—at the cost of their lives—in an image of Mankind. Katov, having sacrificed his own cyanide to aid a wounded young comrade, walks towards his execution in the boiler of a locomotive with an utterly hopeless dignity. The revolutionary cause has been lost. There remains only death for those who fought.

> He began to walk. Silence fell, like a trapdoor, in spite of the moans. The lantern threw Katov's shadow, now very black, across the great windows framing the night; he walked heavily, with uneven steps, hindered by his wounds; when the swinging of his body brought him closer to the lantern, the silhouette of his head vanished into the ceiling. The whole darkness of the vast hall was alive, and followed him with its eyes, step by step. The silence had become so great that the ground resounded each time his foot fell heavily upon it; all the heads, with a slight movement, followed the rhythm of his walk, with love, with dread, with resignation. All kept their heads raised: the door was being closed. A sound of deep breathing, the same as that of sleep, began to rise from the ground: breathing through their noses, their jaws clenched with anguish, motionless now, all those who were not yet dead were waiting for the whistle.[28]

Existential heroism is heroism on the edge of the precipice, when the abyss yawns inexorably and there is no reason left for hope, no rational justification for bravery. Katov's is the dignity of extremity, and those who follow him with their eyes achieve the only real communion possible in an empty cosmos: a lucid awareness of a predicament they share. Malraux had Blaise Pascal in mind when he named his book *La Condition Humaine.* Pascal said that the human condition could best be represented by picturing a number of men in chains, all condemned to death and being executed one by one before the others' eyes. In their fate the remaining ones could only see a reflection of their own condition. That was what it meant to exist, to be alive.

Indeed, this seems to be the buried assumption in many twentieth century works of literary art. Terrence Des Pres, discussing some of the exemplary ones, writes of an "ethos of survival in extremity" and of a need for a kind of heroism "commensurate with the vastness of desolation in our time."[29] No one who recalls the death camps in Germany, the mental institutions in the Soviet Union, the decimated village societies in Vietnam, the mass expulsions, or the violence of repression around the world, can deny that people in many places live against incredible odds, with death always a condition of their lives. Nor can anyone easily deny that anything is possible in his or her own life.

Des Pres talks about a heroism of survival, of the miracle of mere existence;

and he reminds his readers of the many novels which have recently explored the theme of how to survive as a dignified human being under atrocious, anti-human circumstances. This literary thematic would not have come to be were it not for an initial concern with the human condition in the existential sense—the human condition rather than human psychology, the human condition rather than the social plights of men. So there have been books like Albert Camus' *The Plague,* Alexander Solzhenitsyn's *The First Circle,* Ralph Ellison's *Invisible Man,* and Bernard Malamud's *The Fixer,* all dealing with victims of dehumanizing forces over which no one has complete control. They are not passive victims, however; they are people who struggle to move beyond their victimization, no matter how extreme, in order to keep faith with themselves as men. Dr. Rieux, in *The Plague,* may speak for most of them when he tells Tarrou (the "Saint without God"): " 'I don't believe in heroism; I know it's easy and I've learned it can be murderous. What interests me is living and dying for what one loves.' "[30]

Significantly, Dr. Rieux also asserts that he has seen enough of "people who die for an idea" and that man is not an idea. This scorn of the abstraction is another existential theme which has begun to permeate twentieth century novels. In *A Farewell to Arms,* written after the First World War, Ernest Hemingway's Lieutenant Henry talks about how embarrassed he has already been by the words "sacred, glorious, and sacrifice." And then: "Abstract words such as glory, honor, courage or hallow were obscene beside the concrete names of villages, the numbers of roads, the names of rivers, the numbers of regiments and the dates."[31] This challenge to empty abstractions became a leitmotif in ensuing years; the determination to return to the concreteness and contingency of "things themselves" has found expression in diverse important ways. Writers ranging from Alain Robbe-Grillet in France to John Barth in the United States have tried in idiosyncratic ways to demonstrate how myths, symbols, and metaphors falsify reality by obscuring its contingency. Robbe-Grillet's *Le Voyeur* does without any patterns but those the reader can impose. The story presents what is seen by the murderer, whose fears, gestures, memories, and plans are rendered with neither depth, temporal dimension, nor interpretation of any kind. Implicit questions are raised with regard to literature itself, to novelistic form and language, to character and imagery. In John Barth's *End of the Road,* the questions are made explicit; indeed, the novel itself has to do with roles, masks, abstractions, and a parody of existentialism called "mythotherapy." Jake Horner, the hero of the book, is trying to overcome his "weatherlessness" with role-playing, but has become aware of the way in which myth and language both tend to obscure reality and disguise the "raggedness of things."

Articulation! There, by Joe, was *my* absolute, if I could be said to have one. At any rate, it is the only thing I can think of about which I ever had, with any frequency at all, the feelings one usually has for one's absolutes. To turn experience into speech—that is, to classify, to categorize, to conceptualize, to grammarize, to syntactify it—is always a betrayal of experience, a falsification of it; but only so betrayed can it be dealt with at all, and only in so dealing with it did I ever feel a man, alive and kicking. It is therefore that, when I had cause to think about it at all, I responded to this precise falsification, this adroit, careful myth-making, with all the upsetting exhilaration of any artist at his work. When my mythoplastic razors were sharply honed, it was unparalleled sport to lay about with them, to have at reality. In other senses, of course, I don't believe this at all.[32]

The book concludes with an ambiguous and tearful yearning on Jake's part for the opportunity to take responsibility. He does not know what to do now that Rennie (who was Joe Horner's wife but may have become pregnant through sleeping with Jake) is dead after her abortion. But the book itself is an indication that he did something called "scriptotherapy"; he wrote about what had happened and thereby tried to give it meaning. Like Roquentin in Satre's *Nausea*, he realized somehow that life as it goes on moment to moment has no meaning; it only takes on meaning later, when one tells a story about it, gives it form and point. Also, one falsifies; but so do Malraux's characters when they sacrifice their lives for the "fates" they choose. There remains a tension, as the individual struggles for authenticity, for the kind of heroism that derives from confrontation *in person* of the world as it presents itself to consciousness.

Authenticity and dignity are both unthinkable if the individual agrees to subordinate himself to a system or to define his belonging by locating himself in a hierarchy. Part of the rebellion against abstraction in literature becomes a rebellion against systems, controls, fixities of all kinds. In a tragicomical dimension, the system may resemble Catch-22, which says (as an old woman in Rome tells Yossarian in Joseph Heller's novel) that "they have a right to do anything we can't stop them from doing." "They" may refer to circumstance in general, to the air force, to flying formations, to the syndicate, or to any rigid pattern imposed on the particularities of existence. Yossarian, unable to cope in any reasonable fashion with anti-human forces that confuse identification papers with individual identity, eventually abandons the system by deserting from the army. " 'I'm not running away from my responsibilities. I'm running *to* them. There's nothing negative about running away to save my life.' "[33] In Thomas Pyncheon's mysterious *V*, the enemy is the "Inanimate," automatism or entropy. The danger permeating the novel is "rockhood," or the inability to care. In William Burrough's *Nova Express*, "Reality" itself is a pattern imposed by "a power primarily oriented towards total control," and men's only hope is to retake the universe by restoring the reality that existed before they were manipulated and narcotized.

These novels—and the many others which reiterate the same or similar existential themes—may be thought of as responses to a particular historical situation, now more than a century old. It is characterized by urbanization, industrialization, bureaucracies, technological regularities, manipulations, incipient violence, and the persistence of the "crowd." The only way to become a survivor in such a situation is to rebel against systematic controls and endeavor to see through—or to bracket out—conventional schemata in order to confront one's own naked reality. The novels which present such predicaments are, most often, not the work of existential philosophers or even the work of writers who proclaim an existential orientation. Nevertheless, they give evidence of an increasing prevalence of existential perspectives and phenomenological themes. They make those themes available for inward appropriation by readers capable of grasping them. And it would appear that imaginative literature of this sort can only fulfill its purpose if it is inwardly appropriated, if it enables readers to see more and thus to change their lives. "My task which I am trying to achieve," wrote Joseph Conrad, "is, by the power of the written word to make you hear, to make you feel—it is, before all, to make you see. That—and no more, and it is everything. If I succeed, you shall find there according to your deserts: encouragement, consolation, fear, charm—all you demand—and, perhaps, also that glimpse of truth for which you have forgotten to ask."[34]

If it is indeed the case that many contemporary novels appeal to what Sartre describes as their readers' "freedom," and deal with human situations rather than with character development and specific areas of social life, an existential theory of literature may best explain some of their intentions and account for what they do. There are many points at which existential theory overlaps other theories, many points at which it merges with them. But the peculiar emphasis existentialist aesthetics places upon both consciousness and freedom permits a special clarification—even an unfreezing—of what happens in what appears to be a literature of consciousness.

For the existentialist, a work of literature is the means by which a writer creates himself. When he writes a novel, he builds a self-sufficient structure which embodies in language his consciousness of—or his way of experiencing—the world. Since consciousness is intentional, always consciousness of something, the book presents a "reality," or an aspect of the historical situation in which the writer lives his life. In other words, it reveals the writer's subjectivity under the aspect of the objective; the writer has thus engaged in what Sartre calls "action by disclosure."

The book is an art-object; and, like any other art-object, once it is completed, it exists autonomously in the world. It is a presence, with all its possibilities realized; it no longer exists in any particular relationship with the maker whose universe is revealed in the words that compose the work. Envisaged in total independence and completion, the book resembles for a moment the hermetically sealed object conceived by formalist critics of literature. Examining a Conrad novella, for example, such critics would define it by means of its "significant form." They would study its texture, examine its formal and sensuous values in their relationship, analyze its figures of speech and its images, look at the ways in which attitudes and meanings are finally harmonized. The pleasure anticipated would be predominantly aesthetic, a pleasure aroused and sustained by intricacy of relationship, by the ordering of disparate experiences, by the emergence of a totality.

Like the formalist critic, the existentialist would view the work as something completely made and formed out of words. He would view it as a multivalent structure, with its own internal space and time, disengaged from ordinary life. He would stress, in fact, its unreality and the "unreal world" to be encountered by the reader. For a consciousness to imagine, writes Sartre, "it must have the possibility of positing an hypothesis of unreality."[35] The real must be negated; the ordinary world must be negated; the reader must release himself into his own subjectivity.

It is at this point that the existentialist differs from the formalist and from those like Dorothy Walsh[36] and John Dewey who speak of the "virtual experience" made possible through engagement with a literary work. Sartre speaks of the "generosity" of the reader and of his impatience, of the necessity for the reader to lend the book some of his life. Without the reader, the book would be a dead thing, as "unravished" as Keats' Grecian urn. The reader must work with the author in bringing "the concrete and imaginary object on the scene." The reader must disclose the work of art and bring it into being.

> In a word, the reader is conscious of disclosing in creating, of creating in disclosing. In reality, it is not necessary to believe that reading is a mechanical operation and that signs make an impression upon him as light does on a photographic plate. If he is inattentive, tired, stupid, or thoughtless, most of the relations will escape him. He will never manage to "catch on" to the object (in the sense in which we see that fire "catches" or "doesn't catch"). He will draw some phrases out of the shadow, but they will seem to appear as random strokes. If he is at his best, he will project beyond the words a synthetic form, each phrase of which will be no more than a partial function: the "theme," the "subject," or the "meaning." Thus, from the very beginning, the meaning is no longer contained in the words, since it is he, on the contrary, who allows the signification of each of them to be understood; and the literary object, though realized *through* language, is never given *in* language. On the contrary, it is by nature a silence and an opponent of the word.[37]

Choosing the mode of awareness which is imagination, freeing himself from the everyday, the individual reader finds himself confronting his own consciousness of reality, taking an interior journey in order to see what he may never have seen before. Taking that journey, he helps to create the universe disclosed by the author; he must constitute the aesthetic object towards which the characters and the events of the plot seem to point.

Returning to *Heart of Darkness* for a moment, we recognize that the universe to be constituted there is one that is, on the surface, unfamiliar to most of those who try to bring it into being. Few modern readers have penetrated the jungles of the Belgian Congo in the bitter days of colonization. Few have ever found themselves—in the guise of manager, missionary, or riverboat pilot—standing against the wilderness. But the characters, the villages, even the river here are fictive, utterly "unreal." At the same time, they are almost unendurably concrete. Kurtz, the mysterious ivory-trader, holds actual importance only for the other characters in the tale; he is but an analogue of traders or "humanitarians" or cannibals existing in reality. Nevertheless, the reader becomes desperately concerned about him as Marlow pilots the boat down the river; it becomes absolutely necessary that Kurtz be alive when the boat arrives, that he be there for the "nightmare" of Marlow's final choice. And, fictional though the reader knows Kurtz to be, the discovery of the purported idealist officiating at a primitive ceremony is shattering. This possibility is what is so remarkable about an experience with imaginative literature.

Sartre stresses the fact that a reader comes to a book on his own initiative. A reader agrees to constitute it as an imaginary object; he freely sets aside his everyday reality and freely turns attention to events transpiring in his own inner world. Paying attention in that manner, he discloses a field of pure relations through which he moves under the guidance of the author. Under Conrad's guidance he moves from his own safe place (from his own butcher and his own policeman) to his own "culminating point," perhaps rooted in a childish passion to fill in some "blank space" in experience. The city that resembled "a whited sepulcher"; the Company; the two women knitting black wool; the doctor's warnings; the plague in the jungle; the black shapes withdrawn into the grove to die slowly of disease and starvation; the first mention of "a very remarkable person" named Kurtz: all these are stops on the reader's guided journey down his own inner stream. Sartre speaks of a "silence" which exists anterior to the language of the work and of the way in which the reader objectifies that silence as he approaches the literary object to which the characters and the events point. "At the very interior of this object there are more silences—which the author does not tell. It is a question of silences which are so particular that they could not retain any meaning outside of the object which the reading causes to appear."[38] He means something inexpressible in which the art work originates, something the reader comes upon as he goes beyond what the words say.

Merleau-Ponty speaks of something resembling that silence when he talks of returning to the core of primary meaning in which an individual's knowing begins. He has in mind the perceptual consciousness through which a child first comes in contact with his environment, before he is capable of logical thought. To rediscover that "primordial perception" is to return to things themselves, "to return to that world which precedes knowledge, of which knowledge always speaks, and in relation to which every scientific schematization is an abstract and derivative sign-language."[39] An engagement with literature can make possible such a recovery and return. It can restore what some call the person's spontaneity; it can recall to him his original and authentic vision of things. Most important, it can help him rediscover his actual presence to himself, "which in the last resort is what the word and the concept of consciousness mean."[40]

Conrad's river flowing into the heart of Africa is a symbol and therefore refers beyond itself to all the rivers and roads human beings have travelled in search of salvation or truths or holy grails. Because it is a river taking people towards what is thought to be savagery and chaos, the journey here symbolizes movement backward into history—or downward into the unconscious—or outward into hallucinations and dreams. It may evoke a complex of wildernesses and forbidden frontiers; it may summon up recollections of the River Styx or the River Lethe, as the meanings expand and reverberate within the reader. There comes a moment, however, when the symbol refers beyond the natural world, beyond what can be captured in words.

How does this happen? How can language create an illusioned world—and, at the same time, reflect the reader's feelings back to him? Roman Ingarden (to whom critics Wellek and Warren refer as they try to explain the "mode of existence" of a literary work) speaks of levels or strata within the structure called a novel or a poem. There is first the sound-stratum, on the basis of which "units of meaning" arise. ("A great silence around and above. Perhaps on some quiet night the tremor of far-off drums, sinking, swelling, a tremor vast, faint: a sound weird, appealing, suggestive and wild—and perhaps with as profound a meaning as the sound of bells in a Christian country.") On the stratum of meaning, the words combine into syntactic structures, out of which rises the stratum "of the objects represented, the 'world' of a novelist, the characters, the setting." Ingarden speaks of the point of view made explicit or implied; we might speak of what is intended by the consciousness embodied in the work. Marlow's innerness, for example, is intended in *Heart of Darkness,* an imaginary innerness to which the reader attributes passions and perspectives. The "world" disclosed is what is grasped in the light of Marlow's biography—a world which includes persons who are "other" to him in a variety of ways. Finally, Ingarden speaks of a stratum of " 'metaphysical qualities' (the sublime, the tragic, the terrible, the holy) of which art can give us contemplation."[41] If we see the movement from level to level as a movement within the reader's own subjectivity as he invents or creates the work of art, we can understand the nature of the disclosure Sartre describes.

The recovery or the renewal of the reader's world culminates in what might be called a metaphysical dimension but which might as well be called the interior silence, the original personality.

It is in such silence that the individual begins constituting his original world. It is at such a moment of return that the individual recognizes, as Merleau-Ponty puts it, that "I am the absolute source, my existence does not stem from my antecedents, from my physical and social environment; instead it moves out towards them and sustains them, for I alone bring into being for myself (and therefore into being in the only sense that the word can have for me) the tradition which I elect to carry on, or the horizon whose distance from me would be abolished—since that distance is not one of its properties—if I were not there to scan it with my gaze."[42] Man is metaphysical, he says in another place, "in his very being, in his loves, in his hates, in his individual and collective history. And metaphysics is no longer the occupation of a few hours per month."[43]

Metaphysics, in this sense, signifies a realization of the radical subjectivity of our experience. It signifies a recognition that we have to constitute a novel as meaningful and bring it into being. The author of a novel, Sartre says, sets up landmarks for the reader, but the landmarks are "separated by the void"; it is up to the reader to unite them, to go beyond them and create a whole. An engagement with literature becomes, therefore, paradigmatic; it involves self-transcendence and the creation of orders, even as it enables us to look, by dint of the imagination, upon the great metaphysical constants like birth, death, seeking, relationship—and to return to things themselves.

Camus, writing about "rebellion and the novel," discusses the felt incompleteness of ordinary reality, the desire to possess, and the desire to endure. Human beings strive continually, he says, to find attitudes that will impart a unity to their existence. They reject reality; they long for something better; they yearn to transform. The world of a novel is a "rectification" of the world in which they live, and so the novel satisfies a metaphysical need. It is, on this level, "primarily an exercise of the intelligence in the service of nostalgic or rebellious sensibilities."[44] But if literature is to constitute a significant rebellion, it must make unity possible in an affirmation of some interior reality. And it must, according to Sartre, reveal itself to "the indignation of the reader," an indignation which holds within it a promise to change. To change does not mean simply to alter sensibility or expectation; it means to transcend, to refuse and to realize, to move towards what does not yet exist. If literature can arouse individuals to reflective consciousness, it can arouse them to an awareness of new possibilities, new openings; it may even move them to act upon the freedom that has been addressed.

This brings us back to the question of indirect communication with which we began, since imaginative literature, according to existential theory of literature, has the capacity to awaken human beings to their condition, to make them aware of their awareness, present to themselves. Although existential literature and literature with existential themes may speak more directly to contemporary people, because of the historical situation in which they live, many great imaginative works have precisely the same capacity, if readers are willing to do more than simply read. Sartre places great emphasis on the way the writer is "situationed," and the public for whom he writes. He believes that the literature of any given age is alienated when it is submissive to the state or to an ideology and considers itself a means rather than an end. He considers a literature abstract when it subordinates subject matter to "the principle of its formal autonomy." He thinks of "concrete universality" as all the men living in a given society and the need on the part of the author, who wished to embrace such a totality, to define "a concrete and finite duration" by his choice of subjects, which would "define his situation in social time." No work of art is timeless; no work of art is an ideal object. Wellek and Warren write that it has the capacity always to become an object of experience but is not identical with any experience. It differs from numbers, say, because it has something which can be called "life."

> It arises at a certain point of time, changes in the course of history, and may perish. A work of art is 'timeless' only in the sense that, if preserved, it has some fundamental structure of identity since its creation, but it is 'historical' too. It has a development which can be described. This development is nothing but the series of concretizations of a given work of art in the course of history which we may, to a certain extent, reconstruct from the reports of critics and readers about their experiences and judgments and the effect of a given work of art on other works. Our consciousness of earlier concretizations (readings, criticisms, misinterpretations) will affect our own experience: earlier readings may educate us to a deeper understanding and may cause a violent reaction against the prevalent interpretations of the past.[45]

There appears to be no reason why this approach to concretization cannot be reconciled with an existentialist approach to literary art. Wellek and Warren are, by implication, talking about choosing particular concretizations with an awareness of the present moment and an awareness of the past. They do not speak of disclosures, but concretization may be conceived as a form of disclosure for particular people at particular times. *Antigone* may have opened up one set of possibilities in the Classical period, another in the seventeenth century; it may still, in another concretization, arouse people to an awareness of themselves today. Their responses may be intensified by knowledge of the "pity and terror" once presumably evoked, although few spectators and fewer readers will expect to experience the same catharsis at the present time. An understanding of the nature of an ancient connection between the law of the state and the moral law may add a dimension to what is created out of *Antigone* by contemporary audiences and readers, although they are clearly not the public to whom the tragedy was addressed. The same may be said of *Hamlet* or *Phèdre* or *Tom Jones* or *The Divine Comdey*. Each such work, in particular historical settings, can be chosen anew.

Sartre writes: "One cannot write without a public and without a myth—without a *certain* public which historical circumstances have made, without a *certain* myth of literature which depends to a very great extent upon the demand of this public. In a word, the author is in a situation, like all other men. But his writings, like every human project, simultaneously enclose, specify, and surpass this situation, even explain it and set it up, just as the idea of a circle explains and sets up that of the rotation of a segment." And then: "To understand what [*Phèdre*] is, it is necessary only to read or listen, that is, to make oneself a pure freedom and to give one's confidence generously to a generosity."[46] It is important to know how the meanings of particular works, like the idea of literature itself, fluctuate with social movements, but it is equally important to understand that every work of art is in some manner unconditioned and that it holds its own world in suspense.

The implications for education are manifold, as they are for the teaching of literature. The historical situation in which education now takes place is marked far more than Kierkegaard's by the spread of "advertisement and publicity." Depersonalization has increased with technology and corporate structures; it becomes ever more difficult to resist the blandishments of the crowd, to survive as an authentic individual. A malaise, therefore, permeates the schools and universities. Apathy and *ressentiment* are expressed on all sides. Educators tend frequently to respond with proposals for more "personalized" or "humanized" teaching and learning; these take the form of affective programs, ideas for encounter groups, noncognitive experiences, heightened trust.

To attend to existentialist views on indirect communication and a literature that appeals to human freedom is to become aware that "rebellion" is only likely if persons are enabled to confront their own reality. Martin Heidegger, writing about truth as "unconcealment," says that the work of art can be a locus of truth and throw an extraordinary light on things.

> Man cannot master much of what *is*. Only little gets known. What is known remains inexact, what is mastered insecure. What *is* is never, as may all too easily appear, our handiwork or even merely our representation. If we contemplate this whole as one, then we apprehend, so it appears, everything that *is* in general, even if we apprehend it crudely enough. And yet: beyond what *is*, not away from it but before it, something else happens. In the midst of what *is* as a whole an open place is present. A clearing, a lighting *is*. Thought from the direction of what *is*, this clearing *is* in a greater degree than what *is*. This open center is therefore not enclosed by what *is;* rather the illuminating center itself circumscribes everything that *is*, like the Nothing that we scarcely know.[47]

If educators were to concern themselves with the "unconcealment" of such clearings, if they were to help students stop dissembling, teachers and students both might become aware of nameless possibilities within themselves.

Works of literature offer visions of possibility to the existing person. Encounters with them can be significant if those visions are understood to be of a reality imaginatively apprehended. The imaginative mode of apprehension, as we have seen, breaks with the stereotyped, the conventional, the mundane. It can enable an individual to explore his inner horizons, to reflect upon his own consciousness and his own knowing. Such reflexive consideration of the activity of his own consciousness, like the synthesizing of materials in inner time, may have the effect of freeing the person to understand that he—living in a historical situation and acting on it—has constituted the meanings of his own experience. It may have the further effect of freeing him to understand that he is the one who must go on constituting the meanings by which he lives.

Just as primordial perception becomes the ground of later rationality, so may reflective consciousness become the ground of learning in many fields. Conscious of himself, present to himself in the world, the individual can reach out in many directions to develop cognitive perspectives for the sake of ordering his own life-world. If he continues, by means of aesthetic experiences of diverse kinds, to take interior journeys, he is not likely to become alienated from himself when he becomes involved with the academic disciplines. Literature and the other arts ought not to be used as a corrective for depersonalization or empty formalism. They surely ought not to be used as purely sensual or noncognitive experiences. If they do appeal to the "pure freedom" of the individual, if they do enable him to confront his own reality, they ought to be offered as always present possibilities—beginnings, not culminations, origins, not means or ends.

Imaginative literature can only take on this kind of significance, however, if students are given opportunities for disclosing what they read to themselves. The teacher, aware that works of art do not automatically become occasions for self-confrontation, must do what he can to make the works available, without enforcing his own, or current critics', interpretations. He must make it possible for his students to learn to take particular stances with respect to novels, poems, and short stories, to engage in particular modes of perception, to exclude conventional modes of coping with the world. They must in some manner learn the central importance of the imaginary and the ways in which works of art differ from documents, articles, case histories. The difference, obviously, is that documents report on or interpret phenomena in the public, intersubjective world—the "real" world. Imaginative literature creates illusioned worlds, equivalents or analogues, perhaps fundamentally "unreal." In contrast to the transparencies of discursive literature, the language of imaginative literature is like a mirror. The reader does not look through it to referents in the external world. He finds in it reflections of his own feelings and perceptions. He finds pointers to the interior silence, the original self.

Attentiveness and wide-awakeness are important; so is the ability to generate, out of the reader's accumulated experience, the structure of the literary work. Only then can he be released into his own subjectivity, his own inner time; only then can his imagination move beyond the artist's traces "to project beyond the words a new synthetic form," an order of meanings distinctively his. · The experience with literature—*any* experience with a literary work of art—must end in private possession, just as it begins. The teacher's object can only be to launch the student on his own journey, to goad him to his own action and his own choice, to confront him with possibles.

A consideration of imaginative literature, then, may remind us that the teacher can only be present to his students if he appeals (as writers do) to their freedom. He can only be present if he himself is engaged in searching and choosing, if he is committed, and if he cares. The teacher of literature certainly wants his students to realize how criticism can open works of literature to them; he wants to communicate some awareness of the norms that govern attentive reading. Most of all, he wants to help his students feel that outside his talk and their talk, something exists on its own—beckoning each person, soliciting each one to stop dissembling and refusing, to uncover what is real for him. The teacher, having identified himself as a lover of art and freedom, can only offer possibility. He can only try to free his students to love in their own way. If he succeeds, if they dare to chance the jungle river and the underground and the void, there will be interior journeys taking place in the classroom. There will be movements towards meaning, assertions of freedom. People will be learning to rebel.

REFERENCES

1. S. Kierkegaard, *The Present Age,* A. Dru, tr. (New York: Harper and Row, 1962), p. 35.
2. Kierkegaard, "Either/Or," in *A Kierkegaard Anthology,* R. Bretall, ed. (Princeton: Princeton University Press, 1947), p. 105.
3. Kierkegaard, "Either/Or," *op. cit.,* p. 106.
4. Kierkegaard, *The Point of View for My Work as An Author: A Report to History,* W. Lowrie, tr. (New York: Harper and Row, 1962), p. 87.
5. Cf. J. Joyce, *Finnegan's Wake* (New York: Viking Press, 1930): Shem the Penman, who stands for Stephen Daedalus, is a sham, forger, fraud, and fake. He is modelled after Jim the Penman, a notorious forger. But to be a penman, in the context, is to be a writer and an artist.
6. Cf. A. Gide, *The Counterfeiters* (New York: Modern Library, 1955).
7. Cf. T. Mann, *Confessions of Felix Krull Confidence Man* (New York: New American Library, 1951) and H. Melville, *The Confidence Man* (New York: New American Library, 1964).

8. F. Nietzsche, "On Reading and Writing," *Thus Spake Zarathustra: First Part*, in *The Portable Nietzsche*, W. Kaufman, ed. (New York: The Viking Press, 1958), p. 152.

9. Nietzsche, "On the Spirit of Gravity," *Thus Spake Zarathustra: Third Part*, in *The Portable Nietzsche*, p. 307.

10. J.-P. Sartre, *Literature and Existentialism (What is Literature?)* B. Frechtman, tr. (New York: Citadel Press, 1965), p. 48.

11. Sartre, *Literature and Existentialism*, p. 57.

12. Sartre, *Being and Nothingness*, H. E. Barnes, tr. (New York: Philosophical Library, 1956), p. 603.

13. Sartre, *Nausea*, L. Alexander, tr. (Norfolk, Conn.: New Directions, 1959), pp. 169-170.

14. Sartre, *Being and Nothingness*, p. 611.

15. Sartre, *Nausea*, pp. 171-172.

16. S. de Beauvoir, *The Mandarins* (New York: World, 1956), p. 610.

17. See B. Croce, "Aesthetics," in *Philosophies of Art and Beauty*, A. Hofstadter and R. Kuhns, eds. (New York: Modern Library, 1964), pp. 556-576.

18. J. Dewey, *Art as Experience* (New York: Minton, Balch, 1934), p. 57.

19. Sartre, *Being and Nothingness*, p. iv.

20. R.M. Rilke, "Torso of an Archaic Apollo," C.F. MacIntyre, tr., in *Rilke: Selected Poems* (Berkeley: University of California Press, 1958), p. 93.

21. Rilke, "The First Elegy," *Duino Elegies*, J.B. Leishman and S. Spender, trs. (New York: W.W. Norton, 1963), p. 21.

22. F. Dostoevsky, *The Brothers Karamasov*, C. Garnett, tr. (New York: Random House, 1945), p. 302.

23. Dostoevsky, "Notes from Underground," *The Short Novels of Dostoevsky*, C. Garnett, tr. (New York: Dial Press, 1945), p. 152.

24. L. Tolstoy, "The Death of Ivan Ilyich," L. and A. Maude, trs., in *World Masterpieces Since the Renaissance*, M. Mack et al. eds. (New York: W.W. Norton, 1956), p. 1982.

25. J. Conrad, *Heart of Darkness* (New York: New American Library, 1950), p. 103.

26. Conrad, *Heart of Darkness*, p. 120.

27. F. Kafka, "Reflections on Sin, Pain, Hope, and The True Way," *The Great Wall of China: Stories and Reflections*, W. and E. Muir, trs., (New York: Schocken Books, 1960), pp. 293-294.

28. A. Malraux, *Man's Fate*, H. Chevalier, tr. (New York: The Modern Library, 1936), p. 329.

29. T. Des Pres, "The Survivor: On the Ethos of Survival in Extremity," *Encounter*, September 1971, p. 4.

30. A. Camus, *The Plague*, S. Gilbert, tr. (New York: Alfred A. Knopf, 1948), p. 149.

31. E. Hemingway, *A Farewell to Arms* (London: Jonathan Cape, 1952), p. 186.

32. J. Barth, *End of the Road* (New York: Avon, 1964), p. 96.

33. J. Heller, *Catch-22* (New York: Simon and Schuster, 1961), p. 440.

34. Conrad, "Preface to *The Nigger of the 'Narcissus'*," in *Myth and Method: Modern Theories of Fiction*, J.E. Miller, Jr., ed. (Lincoln: University of Nebraska Press, 1960), pp. 30-31.
35. Sartre, *The Psychology of Imagination* (New York: Citadel Press, 1948), p. 265.
36. See D. Walsh, *Literature and Knowledge* (Middletown, Conn.: Wesleyan University Press, 1969), pp. 80-92.
37. Sartre, *Literature and Existentialism*, pp. 43-44.
38. Sartre, *Ibid.*, p. 44.
39. M. Merleau-Ponty, *Phenomenology of Perception* (London: Routledge and Kegan Paul, 1962), p. ix.
40. Merleau-Ponty, *Phenomenology of Perception*, p. xvii.
41. R. Wellek and A. Warren, *Theory of Literature* (New York: Harcourt, Brace and World, 1956), p. 152.
42. Merleau-Ponty, *Phenomenology of Perception*, p. ix.
43. Merleau-Ponty, "Metaphysics and the Novel," *Sense and Non-Sense*, H. L. and P.A. Dreyfus, trs. (Evanston and Chicago: Northwestern University Press, 1964).
44. Camus, *The Rebel* (New York: Alfred A. Knopf, 1954), p. 233.
45. Wellek and Warren, *op. cit.*, p. 155.
46. Sartre, *Literature and Existentialism*, p. 44.
47. M. Heidegger, "The Origin of the Work of Art," in Hofstadter and Kuhns, *op. cit.*, p. 6-8.

Philip Phenix, in "Unamuno on Love and Pedagogy," introduces Miguel de Unamuno as a philosopher of education; only one other piece on Unamuno has appeared in the literature of philosophy of education. Phenix makes this introduction through an explication based on his own translation of Unamuno's* Amor y pedagogía, *a work not yet published in English. In his explication of this short novel on education, Phenix provides us with further discussion of the themes treated by Kaelin and Greene.*

5 | Unamuno on Love and Pedagogy

PHILIP N. PHENIX

During the past year I have had the rewarding experience of discovering Spanish civilization. One of my discoveries was the Spanish philosopher Unamuno, whom I had known about vaguely for the past twenty years but had never encountered face to face in his writings. And the special delight of this discovery was that he turned out to be a philosopher of education! I met him in *Amor y pedagogía*,[1] a novel that calls to mind Rousseau's *Emile*, and that in my opinion merits as much as does *Emile* a place among the classics of educational philosophy. Like Rousseau's work, Unamuno's *Love and Pedagogy* is one of the relatively few books of major philosophers explicitly devoted to education.

Unfortunately, *Amor y pedagogía*, first published in Spain in 1902, has never appeared in English translation and so has not been available to the majority of English-speaking students of the philosophy of education. Since plans are under way for an English translation of the work, I am hopeful that the book will before long become generally known to American readers and will contribute to the enrichment of the curriculum in the philosophy of education. [As of mid-1973, the translation had not reached publication. —Editor.]

The purpose of the present paper is to introduce *Love and Pedagogy* to those among you who do not know this work, and through it, to acquaint

---

*J. Willers, "Unamuno Centennial," *Educational Theory*, XV (October 1965), 317-320.

This essay first appeared in *Philosophy of Education*, 1968, and is used by permission and in its original form.

you with the educational thought of a man who is generally acknowledged as the most original and impressive Spanish philosopher of the present century, and indeed, as one of the world's leading modern philosophers.

Miguel de Unamuno was born in 1864, in Bilbao, in Basque country. He took his doctorate in philosophy and ancient languages in the University of Madrid. The greater part of his professional life he spent at the University of Salamanca, where he was first professor and later rector. Dismissed from his post as rector because of his political opposition to the Spanish monarchy and to the military dictatorship of General Primo de Rivera, he went into exile in France, but with the advent of the Republic in 1930 he resumed his post at Salamanca, only to lose it again in 1936 when the Nationalists came to power. He died the same year.

Unamuno was a prolific author, in a variety of literary forms: novel, poetry, essay, drama, biography, memoirs. While his best-known explicitly philosophic work is *The Tragic Sense of Life,* all of his writings are expressions of his philosophic outlook. Since it is characteristic of him to deny the possibility of philosophic system as an ordered body of doctrine, the more informal modes of literary expression, such as the novel or the play, become his more important means of philosophical exposition. Furthermore, Unamuno's philosophical standpoint is deeply personal, and thus requires as a vehicle for its best articulation literary forms that communicate the drama of subjective personal existence. These characteristics obviously link Unamuno with the Existentialists, among whom he is commonly classified. He had studied Kierkegaard and had resonated to his spirit. He shared with Kierkegaard and with our contemporary Sartre the communication of philosophy through the vehicle of imaginative fiction.

But we must take care not too readily to label and classify Unamuno, even as an Existentialist. For it was characteristic of him that he belonged to no party and founded no school. He had no faithful following as did his contemporary, Ortega y Gasset, the other major Spanish philosopher of the twentieth century. Unamuno was the perennial disturber of easy assumptions and comforting illusions. His was a life of constant combat, without and within. His "tragic sense of life," the central thread running through everything he wrote and lived, meant the use of the irresolvable contradictions that are intrinsic to all authentic human experience, to sustain and confirm life rather than to deny it.

Yet far from regarding himself as a solitary individualist, Unamuno conceived of his mission as the re-discovery and the re-articulation of the distinctive Spanish spirit, which he considered to be symbolized in the figure of Don Quixote—that fantastic embodiment of divine madness, boundless aspiration, romantic chivalry, and transcendence of common sense and the commonplace. This spirit, by the way, found concrete historic incarnation in the discovery of the New World, in the unbelievable exploits of the Spanish conquistadores, and in the inexhaustibly interesting developments and paradoxes of the emerging Latin American civilization up to the present day.

Unamuno speaks to the universal human predicament, in all times and situations, with the special accent of one who had been profoundly formed by the uniquely rich resources of Spanish culture, intricately compounded of Latin, Gothic, Christian, Hebraic, and Arabic elements mysteriously fused within the austere crucible of the Iberian peninsula, and subsequently modified by interaction with the most advanced forms of modern European civilization. He thus speaks as a representative man, representative of all mankind and of his own people, but always as a rebel and a disturber, in order to drive himself and his readers to the deeper levels of their own being, never leaving them content with the conventionalities, whether ordinary or sophisticated, that obscure the meaning within the agonizing mystery of the human condition.

Love and Pedagogy is Unamuno's only book explicitly on the subject of education. It was his second novel, written after he had been teaching for ten years at the University and just after his appointment as rector. Arturo Barea says of Unamuno in those early years in Salamanca, "He brimmed over with plans for works of poetry, imaginative prose and scholarship. He turned his philological lectures into exciting experiences for his students, by infusing them with his love and respect for the creative word."[2] In those days Herbert Spencer's philosophy of panscientism was in vogue, and many saw in the new scientific rationalism the cure for all human ills and a sure foundation for the educational practice of the future. Unamuno saw nothing but disaster in what seemed to him a surrender of authentic human values in favor of blind faith in popular pseudoscientific panaceas. His response was a sustained satire on what he termed "sociological pedagogy," by which he meant a program of education designed to produce perfect human beings by the application of supposedly scientific pedagogical techniques. *Love and Pedagogy* is in effect a "thought experiment" in which Unamuno aims to demonstrate dramatically the human consequences of such an educational program. By his more ample empiricism, expressed in terms of a fictional narrative, he seeks to take account of human factors denied by narrow dogmatic scientific rationalism.

Critics have generally agreed that as a work of literary art *Love and Pedagogy* is not really successful. Unamuno's opening words in the Prologue to the novel reflect this opinion: "There are those who believe—perhaps with justification—that this work is an unfortunate, a most unfortunate blunder on the part of its author." (p. 9) And then, with tongue half in cheek, as he speaks so often throughout the book, he says, "The present novel is an absurd mixture of wisecracks, clowning, and nonsense, with a bit of sensitivity here and there submerged by a flood of intellectual contrivance." (p. 9) He admits that he has apparently made no effort in the novel to justify those who criticize him for ridiculing science and pedagogy and not (as befits a man of science and an educator) merely pseudoscience and pedagogical fanaticism. He grants, too, that his characters are really caricatures, that he uses them as puppets to say what he, the author, wants to express.

It seems to me that the key to Unamuno's intention in his playful self-depreciation as an author is provided in this passage in the Prologue: "We may surmise that underlying all the jests and buffoonery, not always in the best taste, is a denunciation of the veneration of science and pedagogy that the author renders in spite of himself. If he turns against intellectualism in such a manner, it is because he suffers from it to a degree few Spaniards can match. So we suspect that in trying to set himself straight he ridicules himself." (pp. 12-13) Such self-objectification is characteristic of Unamuno. He does not sit smugly in judgment on the follies of others from the safe vantage point of an assured philosophic position. In his characters—even the most grotesque of them—he sees himself mirrored. The conflicts that propel his plot forward reflect the contradictions that are the source of his own tragic sense of life and of the despair that is the deepest ground of his hope.

Unamuno, no mean critic even of himself, thought well enough of his novel more than thirty years later to say in a Prologue-Epilogue to the second edition: "In this novel for which I again write a preface there is in germ—and more in germ—the best and most of what I developed later in my other novels: *Abel Sanchez, Aunt Tula, Nothing But a Man, Fog,* and finally, *St. Emmanuel the Good, Martyr, and Three Other Stories.*" (p. 16) Thus by the author's own appraisal, his *Love and Pedagogy* is not, as its somewhat curious melodramatic content might suggest, a minor literary aberration within the corpus of an otherwise reputable philosopher, but a seminal and representative work. It is interesting from the vantage point of educational philosophy that, as in the case of John Dewey, for Unamuno the educational theme was not a side issue to which he applied philosophical perspectives gained in other contexts, but that he demonstrated clearly how education evokes the most fundamental and general philosophical reflections.

But what does Unamuno mean by "philosophy"? Clearly, he does not mean an activity that can be confined within the limits of objective discursive expression. He advises his readers that all of his works, whether in the form of novels or otherwise, and especially his philosophical writings, are, strictly speaking, fiction or legend. His stories, he says, are "intense dramatic tales about the deepest personal realities, without that staged realism which usually lacks the truth, the eternal truth, the reality of personality." (p. 16) According to Unamuno, his literary activity has been a continual unfolding of the "deep caverns of feeling," of which the Spanish mystic St. John of the Cross spoke. Unamuno's life and his literature are not two, but one. So he says: "As I have gone on living—and dying—my novels have gone on living—and dying." What a contrast here with Unamuno's great hispanic contemporary, Rubén Darío, for whom literature was the sovereign way of escape from the sordid realities and oppressive failures of personal life! To Unamuno, great works of philosophy are imaginative expressions of the deepest truth—the truth of personality.

For Unamuno, to write a novel on the theme of education is itself an educative act, which to be authentic must be performed in the spirit of the novel itself. Hence he addresses the book "to the reader," and not to the reading public as an anonymous mass. Being concerned about touching the individual in the inner recesses of his personality, Unamuno talks "as though there were just the two of us, each hearing the breathing and occasionally the heartbeat of the other, as in the confessional." (p. 18)

It is not that Unamuno is unmindful of the social bearings of education. Quite the contrary. Because he is so deeply concerned for the well-being of his own people and of mankind, he is all the more dedicated to education for the authentic humanness of the individual person. Thus, in his Prologue-Epilogue to the second edition, written amidst the gathering clouds of civil war in the early 1930's, Unamuno declared sorrowfully: "If for more than thirty years I have meditated painfully on love and pedagogy, how much I now have to meditate on love and demagogy. Poor Avito Carrascal [one of the characters in the novel] wanted to make a genius out of his son, but by means of demagogy we want to make citizens out of our children, and what is worse, out of the children of our neighbors, who are their natural and spiritual parents. Citizens that are republicans or monarchists, communists, or fascists, believers or unbelievers." (p. 18) Faced with the dismal reality that "the child belongs to the State and must be handed over to the pedagogues—demagogues—officers of the State in the public school system" (p. 18), Unamuno could only echo the cry of the unfortunate victim of scientific pedagogy in his book, as he watched the animals in an experimenter's laboratory: "The poor guinea pigs! The poor guinea pigs!" For Unamuno, the only education worth having is the kind in which one ceases to be a guinea pig and enters upon the path of knowing himself as a unique and irreplaceable person. This is the theme that is developed in *The Tragic Sense of Life,* which work, says Unamuno, is a novel, as is *Love and Pedagogy.*

Love and Pedagogy, as I indicated earlier, is a tale of a man who tries to make his son a genius by means of scientific pedagogy. Don Avito Carrascal was avid for science, confident that by means of science (especially the social sciences) every human problem could be solved. He had made a heroic effort to manage his own life in all its aspects by scientific principles. A favorite saying of his was that: "Only science is the guide of life," but ever and again the unbidden counter-thought would insinuate itself: "Is not life the guide of science?" Still, consciously, he insisted that man, who has made the gods in his likeness, can do anything, and in particular that by means of scientific education all men can be made geniuses.

Avito, of course, mirrors Everyman—Unamuno, you, and me. He is avid for science because he thinks that science, the discipline of prediction and control, holds the promise of the future. He clings to science passionately ("Is not life the guide of science?") because he is so desparately hungry for life. He turns from the past because the past is dead, and death is the one great and perennial enemy of man, who is defined by his longing for immorality. This is the central theme in all of Unamuno's writings—the insatiable hunger for everlastingness as the distinctive mark of man. But man is also a being with reason, which tells him that he made the gods, not vice versa, and that the traditional myths of the immortal soul are illusions. Thus modern intelligent man is faced with the agonizing necessity of responding affirmatively to the hunger for life without denying the conclusions of reason.

Carrascal attempts to resolve the dual demand by a passionate devotion to science as the seal to the promise of the future: not science as abstract truth, but as the basis for the concrete embodiment of truth in persons by means of scientific pedagogy. In the character of Avito, Unamuno is suggesting, somewhat as Plato did in speaking of the eros of the teacher, that the great motive for teaching is the teacher's hunger for immortality, and the promise of eternalization that in one sense is realized in the learning of his pupils.

In order to insure perfect laboratory conditions for the great experiment in scientific genius-making, Avito could not be content with being an ordinary teacher. The only way to be absolutely sure of success was to become a father, so as to have complete control of the teaching-learning process from the very beginning. Unfortunately, however, for pure scientific pedagogy, since science had not yet advanced to the point of test-tube generation of persons, Avito had to enlist the cooperation of a female.

As in the traditional Christian ethos, woman—and sex—proved to be the occasion for the fall of man. For Unamuno, the female represents the nonrational element in human life. She lives more by intuition and feeling than by intellect. With her comes to the fore a wholly different means of achieving immortality, through the bearing of children. Like the passion for knowledge, the sexual passion has its origin in the hunger for everlastingness. Both passions are expressions of the same all-pervading human awareness of approaching death and of the all-controlling determination to render meaningful and hopeful an existence lived under that threat. *Love and Pedagogy* revolves around the conflicting claims of love—sexual love—and the inculcation of knowledge as responses to the hunger for immortality.

Early in the account of his son Apolodoro's education Unamuno introduces a new character who thenceforth plays a central role in the drama, and whose participation lends special interest to the story for philosophers of education. For this person is a veteran scientific philosopher, much respected by Avito, to whom he turns for guidance in carrying through his pedagogical plan. In Fulgencio Entreambosmares Unamuno portrays a philosopher actually making pedagogical prescriptions, supposedly on the basis of his philosopher's insight. It appears to me that Unamuno at many points uses don Fulgencio as the mouthpiece for his own ideas, but also as a vehicle to ridicule philosophic rationalism. Thus, whenever Fulgencio is depicted in his role as an abstract theorizer, he is a comic figure, but whenever he is shown faced with the necessity of making a concrete recommendation that will affect Apolodoro, he shows a profound personal concern and humane wisdom that belies all his facile theorizing.

When Avito asks for his aid as an educational advisor to Apolodoro, Fulgencio responds with what may well reflect the central ideas of Unamuno's own philosophy of education. "You attribute an important role to your son in the human tragicomedy. Is it the one that the Supreme Stage Director designed for him? This is a tragicomedy, Avito my friend. Each of us plays his part; we are being drawn by wires when we think we are doing something—this doing is nothing more than acting; we recite the part we learned in the beyond, in the darkness of the unconscious, in our shadowy pre-existence. . . . And in this theater the great one is the hero, . . . he who takes his role seriously and is absorbed by it and pays no attention to the audience nor cares a straw for the public, but who achieves a truly life-like representation. . . . And there are—listen to this carefully, Avito—there are those who on some occasion put their own line into the play . . . that line, oh, that line! Those who survive will survive because of that line. In the whole life of each man there is no more than a moment, only one moment of liberty, only one time in life when one is truly free, and on that moment, on that moment, yes, which once gone will not return, like all the other moments that pass away, on that metadramatic moment of ours, on that mysterious time, all our destiny depends. . . . That line, my friend Carrascal, is what the actors put into the dialogue on their own account, it is what they add to the work of the playwright. The line! One has to watch for its time, prepare it, guard it carefully, and when the time comes put it in, put our line, whether it be long or short, into the dialogue, and then the play goes on. By virtue of that line we survive—that line, indeed, that the Great Prompter whispers to us. . . . Your pedagogical task is to prepare him for his line." (pp. 51-53)

Everything in education, then, according to the philosopher don Fulgencio, is to be judged by reference to the authenticity and creative freedom of the person. It is authenticity and true liberty that alone qualify us for immortality. Insofar as we live in response to external compulsions, merely fulfilling what is expected of us in our social roles, we shall be swept on into oblivion like all else in the natural order, but insofar as we succeed in being creators and not merely creatures, we manifest a quality of being that is in principle immune to temporal dissolution.

When Apolodoro reached adolescence, another teacher entered his orbit, Hildebrando F. Menaguti, a sacrilegious poet, "a priest of Our Lady of Beauty," apostle of love and of the works of artistic genius that love inspires.

Just as Avito typified the scientific positivism of a Herbert Spencer, so popular when Unamuno was writing, so Menaguti symbolized the escapist aestheticism of the Parnassians or of the iberoamerican modernists, of whom Rubén Darío was high priest. Here was a teacher whose lessons made sense to Apolodoro. "What a kaleidescope the world is," he thought, "but a kaleidescope that smells of perfumes that inflame the blood, especially in springtime and in youth." (p. 82)

When Apolodoro fell in love with Clarita everything became clear. The confusions and obscurities of the insane world of logic and science disappeared, and a whole new world of zest and delight opened before him. For the first time he understood, because for the first time he loved.

But before long Clarita decided that her prospects were better with a more conventional type of boyfriend, and so she left Apolodoro with his shattered dreams. He sought consolation in writing a short novel about his love affair, thus realizing Menaguti's teaching that "ordinary loves end up producing children, but heroic loves produce poems or paintings or symphonies" (p. 99), but this work met with complete indifference on the part of the reading public.

Crushed by his catastrophic failure, both in love and in art, Apolodoro went to see don Fulgencio in hopes of getting some light on his desperate problem. In the resulting scene, in which the old philosopher breaks down and pours out his heart to the young Apolodoro, it seems to me that Unamuno expresses the pivotal concepts and concerns of his entire philosophy. Amid sobs, he confesses that the disease from which our age suffers, which he himself and Avito also had, and with which they had spent years infecting Apolodoro, was erostratism, named after Erostratus, who burnt down the temple of Ephesus in order to make his name imperishable. Today, he said, we don't any longer believe in immortality, and we are terrified of death. Anybody who denies this is a liar or a fool. To live is to long for eternal life. Because we cannot believe that we will survive death, we settle for the substitute of immortalizing our names. The thirst for immortality is the source of all art: through art we try to leave the impress of our being on something permanent. It is said that play is the source of art. And what is play? It is an effort to transcend logic, because logic leads to death. So play too is a manifestation of the hunger for immortality.

When Unamuno talked of immortality, he did not have in mind the traditional idea of disembodied souls or of saints singing around the throne of grace in a transcendent heavenly realm. What he put on the lips of don Fulgencio belonged also on his own: "They call me a materialist. Yes, a materialist, because I want a material immortality, with bulk and substance." (p. 111) This same longing for enduring existence is the only real ground he has for believing in God. The rational arguments for the existence of God lead only to doubt and disbelief. I believe in God, not because my reason convinces me, but because I need him so much. "I need God," says Unamuno through Fulgencio, "in order to make me immortal." (p. 111)

The nearest thing to a real, substantial, material immortality is to have children. Menaguti wrote poems, but he had no children. Don Fulgencio, though married, had only his book of aphorisms and his *Ars Magna* to immortalize him. How poor and lifeless these relics of a life are in comparison with the concrete continuation of personal life in the life of a child! And so Fulgencio concluded his impassioned session with Apolodoro with the counsel: "Have children, have children, Apolodoro!"

Regarding himself as a failure both in love and in art, Apolodoro saw no reason to continue living. His little sister Rosa, who had not prospered under her father's pedagogical tutelage—girls, he argued, being the material element in the matter-form combination, need essentially a curriculum of physical education—had finally withered away and died. Clarita had married. One night in a delirium of loneliness and longing for Clarita, driven by the half-conscious urge to fulfill Fulgencio's precept for immortalization, Apolodoro had taken advantage of the sympathetic servant-girl, Petra, who as a consequence became pregnant. Overcome with remorse, he decided the time had come to end the misery of it all. Now, he thought, he would find out what lay beyond death. Shutting himself in his room, he prepared a noose in a cord fastened to the ceiling. He thought for a moment that he might look silly hanging there like a sausage—another failure—but he concluded that his act was really sublime. Thus concluded the education of the genius—or was it only the beginning?

In the final scene of the novel, Avito tries to apply to Apolodoro the latest techniques of scientific resuscitation—his last desperate teaching move—but to no avail, while Marina, Avito's wife, cries uncontrollably, "My son! my son!" At the end, Avito, taking up the mother's cry, now from the heart, falls fainting into the arms of Marina, who, comforting him, whispers, "My son," to which the poor pedagogue replies from the unsounded depths of his soul, "Mother." And so, concludes our author: "Love had triumphed."

Unamuno's book does not end with the conclusion of the novel. Like his contemporary George Bernard Shaw, don Miguel was addicted to prefaces and epilogues, in which he reflected on what he had written. In some respects these are the most interesting parts of his books. In *Love and Pedagogy* the Prologue, the Prologue-Epilogue, and the Epilogue all contain fairly sizable passages in which the author discusses his business dealings with the publisher, who has certain minimum size specifications for the book, requiring "filler" material, which the various prologues and epilogues are meant to supply. Nothing would appear less fitting than such discussions, until one sees what Unamuno does with the existential moment presented to him. In the Epilogue, for example, starting from the criticism that a novelist should not degrade his work of art by intruding commercial considerations, he quickly moves to sketch out an analysis of the relation between art and the common life, not dissimilar to Dewey's, and thus enriches the central thesis of the novel about the existential unity of life and about the need to concretize spirit in the man of flesh and blood. In this way Unamuno not only pokes fun incidentally at the superficiality and mechanical mentality of the world of commerce, but also employs the occasion to demonstrate how the conflict between the poet and the publisher may be creatively used, in a minor episode in the tragic drama, to affirm life rather than to negate it.

In the Epilogue, Unamuno also tells his readers what happened to the various characters in his drama after the death of Apolodoro. Menaguti, the poet, who had first suggested the idea of suicide to Apolodoro, tortured by a sense of guilt, at first furtively sought forgiveness from the God in whom he could not believe, and then, while wasting away with tuberculosis, wrote a book called *The Death of God.* Don Fulgencio meditated on the question as to whether death is not the true metadramatic moment; and set himself the project of studying suicide in the light of such combinations as the death of life, the right of the death of life, and the duty of death. Petra, rendered both widow and mother by Apolodoro, was adopted by Avito and Marina as their own daughter, and Avito, who, as might be expected of one with a fixed deductive set of mind, had learned absolutely nothing from his experiences with Apolodoro, eagerly awaited the arrival of the grandchild, who would surely be a genius, because this time he, don Avito, would take complete charge, and would see that there would be none of the poisonous influences that had led Apolodoro astray, including don Fulgencio, "to which Marina could only respond: 'For God's sake, Avito, for God's sake! Still more of that?' "

Following the Epilogue, Unamuno has included a curious supplement, purportedly from the pen of don Fulgencio, entitled: *Notes for a Treatise on Cocotology,* which consists of an introduction to the science of making folded paper birds. Again, it would seem at first glance that such material would have no place in the novel and that it had no bearing on the main thesis of the book. Closer scrutiny shows how very relevant it is. The Treatise demonstrates how, simply by successive folds in a square of paper, one can evolve a series of basic forms which mirror the structure of the actual cosmos, and even lead to the postulation of God. The imperfection of the forms is due solely to the fact that the paper has a finite thickness. If the paper were vanishingly thin, then the perfect ideal world, only approximated by the ordinary paper figures, would be realized. Imperfection, then, is due to individual material embodiment, and perfection consists in pure abstraction.

For Unamuno, of course, the Treatise is a satire on rationalistic speculation. He wants to expose the rationalistic hoax that pretends to construct the whole of this world and the other world as well out of nothing at all, and thereby to underline his own conviction that the primary source of knowledge is the concrete individual—the man of flesh and blood. This is not to say that Unamuno had no interest in and feeling for rationalistic speculation. He was quite at home with it, and directed his satire at such extravagances within himself as well as at those in others. It is a fact, too, that Unamuno had a personal interest in paper-bird making, and was wont to present his creations to his friends—an idiosyncrasy for which he was well known.

The Treatise belongs naturally in the one book Unamuno wrote on education, in view of the traditional interest children have in making paper birds and because of the idea of learning through imaginative construction that such activity symbolizes. One may surmise that had don Fulgencio taught Apolodoro as a young child, he would certainly have used cocotology, to the delight and edification of his pupil. In this connection, I was surprised and delighted last summer, shortly after reading *Amor y pedagogía*, to find one Sunday morning in Chapultepec Park, in Mexico City, a man attired in cap and gown addressing in the open air a sizable group of fascinated listeners of all ages on the subject of cocotology, telling its meaning, history, and importance, demonstrating the production of an amazing variety of interesting creatures and leading his audience step by step in making their own little birds.

Reflecting on the book as a whole, we find that the message of Unamuno is surely clear. In the end love—concrete, personal affection—triumphs over cold abstraction, though not without tragedy. The meaning of life does not consist in the denial of reason in favor of irrational emotion. We must live, says Unamuno, with both reason and feeling, but, recognizing, with Pascal, that the heart has reasons of which reason knows not, and that the highest reason is to acknowledge, accept, and live by the hope that our hunger for immortality inspires.

I suspect that heterodox though he be from a theological standpoint, Unamuno has consciously or unconsciously drawn heavily in his story from the Christian epic. In a sense Apolodoro was a Christ figure—he was the only son, sent from God (as his name implies). He was a messianic figure, in that he was expected to be the perfect one who would become the exemplar for all mankind. But his perfection turned out to be of a different order. He did not conform to the traditional pattern, but insisted on contradicting the pedantic logic of the scribes. And so he died (was not in effect Jesus a suicide, too, though other hands were the instrument?); but before he died, he laid the foundation of his continuing life on earth. Was not Petra the rock on whom this Christ-figure founded his hope for the future? And did not the only moment of humanity in Avito, when from the depths of his heart he cried "Mother," this single metadramatic moment that qualified him for everlastingness, spring from the death of Apolodoro? And did not the glimmerings of real love between Avito and Marina also stem from

Apolodoro's death, and from their reconciliation did there not emerge their concern for accepting the servent-girl Petra as their own and thus unfold the possibility of future generations begotten and nurtured in love?

Judgments about the aesthetic, philosophical, and educational value of Unamuno's *Love and Pedagogy* will surely not be unanimous. Many will find the characters too exaggerated to seem real, the plot too obvious and too contrived, and the sentimentality too blatant. For me personally, as for Unamuno, the characters were genuine people. As he wrote in the Epilogue: "I am not the one who gave life to don Avito, to Marina, to Apolodoro, rather they are the ones who have grasped life in me after having wandered through the limbos of existence." (p. 130) I found the action economically related and convincingly ordered. As for sentimentality, I will only confess that one of the qualities in Spanish culture that most delights my Puritan being is just such unashamed expression of emotion as Unamuno reveals.

Philosophically, one may find Unamuno too fond of paradox, too critical of logic, too exclusively preoccupied with the solitary individual, and too willing to trust the reasons of the heart—to which I would respond that it seems to me the most fundamental problems of existence may best be formulated in terms that transcend the ordinary categories of rationality, that Unamuno gives ample evidence of his respect and understanding for logic within its proper limits, that his passion for the unique person is developed within the context of his profound concern for his people and for the well-being of mankind, and that he makes an important contribution in insistently raising the issue of the epistemic import of our vital persuasions. It should be insisted that Unamuno does not settle that issue; he examines it and bears witness to his own experience of the energizing effect of the tragic sense that the enduring inner conflict between abstract reason and the hunger for immortality creates.

Finally, one may find the educational issues in Unamuno's book far afield from those that exercise contemporary Americans. For my part, the chief value of Unamuno's work is to drive the educational discussion back to the fundamental human issues. It seems to me that in the last analysis most of our educational conflicts and confusions are symptoms of a deep-seated insecurity about the meaning of life, and that Unamuno not only points to the cause of the insecurity and to the source of meaning, but also by means of an extraordinarily picturesque and winsome story suggests some concrete ways in which education can contribute to the healing of men and nations.

REFERENCES

1. Unamuno, *Amor y pedagogía* (Madrid: Colección Austral, Espansa-Calpe, S.A., 1964).
2. A. Barea, *Unamuno* (New Haven: Yale University Press, 1952), p. 14.

David Denton, whose efforts in recent years have been directed toward the explication of teaching itself, rejects, in "That Mode of Being Called Teaching," both substantialist and functionalist definitions of teaching, and argues that teaching is a special mode of being-in-the-world, a mode which cannot be reduced to anything other than itself. The question of understanding teaching becomes paramount, and, in response to that question, he moves beyond a purely existential position, as well as that of his earlier works, to an incorporation of certain insights of Heidegger, Straus, and Habermas. The style of his essay is that of the dialogue which permits discourse at three different yet interacting levels: professor, teacher, and author.

6 | That Mode of Being Called Teaching

DAVID E. DENTON

"Method by itself cannot abolish the recalcitrancies of existence."
—Buchler, *The Concept of Method*

We plunge into contingency, ambiguity, and tensionality. We bodyforth into a sphere of intentionality and nihilation. We step into the surge of reverberations of a particular lived-reality. Into this abyss of madness, of apparent nonsense, we throw concepts and words and terms in an attempt to provide meaningful structure. We attempt order with schedules and outlines. We try to explain it all. We set forth role descriptions. We operationalize our terms in an effort to quantify that which is going on. Out of these attempts come formulas, or, to use Goodman's term, formats[1] for teaching, methods for researching teaching, and numerous conceptual analyses of the talk about teaching. That person who wishes to be called teacher soon develops a facility for differentiating among the arguments for and against the competing formulas. According to the formats, teaching is communication, modifying behavior, classroom management, serving as a resource person, guiding youth, influencing society's tomorrow, functioning as a change agent, processing information, establishing I Thou relationships, et cetera, et cetera, et cetera.

With one or more of the formats in hand, our new teacher walks into the classroom and quickly discovers that coercion is necessary to make the situation conform to the method, that police-action is becoming his actual function, that chronic fatigue is his reward at the end of the day. One day, early or late in his life, he looks on himself as though he were standing outside that classroom, looking at himself through a closed window. From that new and sudden perspective, his own movements seem absurd, his gestures meaningless, and his prior commitments sheer folly.

> The shock of awareness—
> the experience of nothingness,
> of no-thing-ness,
> the moment of degree zero—
> explodes from the emptiness of his depths,
> reverberating against the walls of the class-
> room, creating dissonance among the students.

At and in that moment, our teacher confronts the necessity of choice. Many possibilities are open to him. To illustrate certain ones, he may leave the profession, acquire from older teachers and behavioristic psychologists necessary coping mechanisms, or he may define himself as a being who, in teaching, transcends the limits of the formats of functionality. That choice, however, does not provide a definition; it merely opens possibilities for a new understanding of what it is to be a teacher.[2]

THE TEACHER AND THE PROFESSOR

In searching out just what these possibilities may be, our teacher seeks out a friend who, for the purposes of this work, happens to be a professor of existential philosophy. He enters the conversation by expressing where he must start: the study of teaching must begin in wonder, in amazement, *that* it is. To begin otherwise is to deny that it is. To ask, "What is teaching?" is to presuppose a metaphysic from which substantive answers regarding the nature of teaching can be drawn. To ask the "why" of teaching is to reduce it to terms appropriate to one's theory of explanation. To ask for a taxonomy of uses of the word is to ask for the typical rather than the unique, for the standard rather than for the protean; at best, such a taxonomy will tell one only uses of the term, not of teaching itself. These questions are possibilities for later inquiry, but are not the origin; further, they remain possibilities only so long as they are not used to deny teaching. By looking unflinchingly at that which is called teaching—that is, without averting one's gaze from substantive answers, explanatory theories, or analyses of uses—one can see a hole of nothingness bounded by the arc of intentionality, a hole both mysterious and bright.

Our teacher and our professor are now joined in a common undertaking: to explicate and understand that mode of being called teaching in a way that will not negate the existential reality of the lived world of the classroom. This undertaking will return their attention to the critical comments contained in the professor's opening remarks; if they accept his criticisms, they will then have to ask, "How can we even talk about teaching?" After that, the question of the mode of understanding sought will face them. At that point, certain additional aspects and problems in the existential analysis of teaching can be set forth.

The Professor's Critique

Our existential analysis must begin within the situation itself; any protocol for interpretation and explication is to be generated from within the situation being described. Terms such as "phenomenological description," "hermeneutical understanding," and even "existential psychoanalysis," have been used to refer to aspects of this analysis, but their explication at this point is not necessary, and would take our focus away from that which the two of us are trying to see. If we need them, we can come back to them.

Grounding our description and interpretation in an existential situation itself has as one consequence the setting aside of a priori answers to questions which may emerge from the situation. It eliminates substantialist answers to the question of "what," for such answers have, historically, presupposed that the nature, or essence, or reality, of that which we live is not that which we live, but is prior to, more enduring than, and ultimately more real than that which we live. A substantialist definition, then, does not provide an opening of possibilities, but, rather, carefully points to the nature or essence or reality which transcends that lived-reality. For example, Socrates, in replying to Meno, differentiated between definition and what he called illustration with the former pointing through the particulars of illustrations to the nature of that in question. Other examples can be selected from Aristotle, St. Thomas Aquinas, and on to Kant and the modern period. Grounding our description and interpretation in the lived situation leads to a rejection of substantialist answers for another reason, namely, that an a priori definition of teaching constitutes an imposition on that situation, an imposition with normative force: the situation must be made to conform to the definition.

In our time, few writers in the literature of educational thought have pursued the question of "what"; the problems of substantialist definition are generally recognized. Substituted for the question of "what," however, has been the question of "why." Thinkers have always concerned themselves with the question of "why," but only in modern times has the substitution of "why" for "what" been so systematic. The substitution in education has led to patterning after the forms of explanation used in the social and behavioral sciences which, in turn, have been patterned after the natural sciences. Although these forms of explanation vary in details, they have certain common elements: covering laws, either general or probabilistic, are required; particulars—instances, cases, behaviors—must be subsumed under the covering laws; and meaning of the particular is obtained by demonstrating its relation to the covering law. Nagel's work[3] is perhaps the best summary, explication, and defense of this approach to explanation. Hempel[4] has extended the approach to the discipline of history, and Hull[5] has made one of the most explicit attempts in psychology to include psychological explanation under the forms of the natural sciences. Teaching, learning, and counseling theories abound with such attempts, for a notion of theory, borrowed from the natural sciences, brings with it a notion of explanation. (What is called for, but not in this discussion, is a fundamental critique of the nature of educational theory.)

You see, my teacher, that if we ground our description and interpretation of teaching in the existential situation, we shall have to reject the approach of scientific explanation as well as that of substantialist definition. If we seek understanding of a being-who-teaches from within the situation, the meaning of the particular will be obtained from the teacher in her world with others, not from some a priori law, even a probabilistic one. The term "particular" itself presents a difficulty. Existentially, human-beingness is not reducible to the terms of particularity, for human-beingness is not an instance of a general case. Or, to put the matter in different words, intentional action is not reducible to behaviors or to any other fractionalized, fragmented terms required by the principle of subsumption. Further, the search for explanation takes our focus from the situation itself to the theory. The question, "What is happening?" is quite different from the question, "What caused it?" and the choice between the two establishes the direction and nature of one's inquiry.

Our teacher interrupts: Let me see if I can put into my own words your criticisms to this point. If we begin with definitions, we distort that which is actually lived by determining, even before we get in to the situation, the criteria for what we will see and not see, what we will accept and not accept. If we begin with explanation, we give primary attention to causes rather than to the situation itself; we screen out phenomena not accounted for by the theory; and we actually explain only fractions, parts of persons and intentional actions, never persons and intentional actions themselves. Whether I agree or not, I think I understand you, but, as yet, you haven't clarified an earlier charge you made against analyses of uses of teaching terms.

Professor: True, I have not. My general charge is that analyses of the uses of terms have been conducted in such a way that the mode of being called teaching eludes the grasp of the analysts. The criteria of exactness and standardization[6] preclude the personal, the intentional, the protean. Green,[7] for example, admits that teaching is an open-textured, vague concept, yet he cannot analyze concepts at that level. To meet the requirements of his method of analysis he must reduce teaching to such terms as training, indoctrinating, conditioning, showing, and instructing. These terms he calls molecular and, thereby, provides his own demonstration of his reductionism. (Some people are still striving to find that atom. If one should ever find that atom and look at it closely, one would see what it is in what it is not: holes bounded by no-thing.) For Scheffler,[8] teaching is an achievement term inferred from learning. If learning has taken place, we may infer that teaching has been done; if no learning occurs, as he defines it, no teaching has been done. Pullias and Young, in *A Teacher is Many Things,*[9] back away from such narrowly prescribed analyses with the deliberate use of open-textured terms of description, in their case, metaphors, but then they use their metaphors as descriptions of sets of expected behavior, that is, of roles. Further, they admit in the title that the teacher is many things. The language of roles and the language of things is one language. Teaching is a mode of being in the world and, as such, is neither describable nor analyzable with the language of things. Analyses of the types illustrated here err in attempting to sever teaching from teacher, doing from being.

The teacher again: I don't understand you now. Isn't it obvious that teachers "do things," conduct activities, initiate processes?

Yes, teachers do. Perhaps greater clarity can be had if we play with the line, "I am walking." If we were to conduct what I shall call here a functional analysis of the sentence, "I am walking," one conclusion would be that the "I" and the "am" are only space-fillers necessitated by the rules of grammar. They are meaningful only in the context of grammar, not that of function. An ontological analysis would reverse that order, making "walking" second-ary, but not denying it. "I am walking" would translate into "being-who-walks," and the walking would become part of the definition of being, but being would not be reduced to walking. Now, if we substitute teaching for walking in the sentence, it reads "I am teaching," and we prepare to do a functional analysis analogous to that done to the original sentence. "I" and "am" have already been denied, and, when we find that the functional entailments of "teaching" are difficult if not impossible to determine, teaching too will be. Other terms, the functional entailments of which are relatively clear, will have to be substituted, terms such as "telling," or "speaking," or "showing," terms which are logically analogous to "walking." If, however, we substitute "being-who-teaches" for "being-who-walks," teaching becomes a part of the definition of being, but being is not reduced to teaching. But more, teaching is not reduced to something other than itself. Two alternatives follow from this "playing with the line." One can conclude, with the analysts, that "being" sentences are indeed meaningless, or we can contend that our language evidences a domain for which the methods and criteria of the analysts are not at all appropriate. Those who wish to stop this sort of discussion and get back to their functional analyses have a precedent for doing so: by generalizing the functional description to include the teacher under the categories of that description, the being-who-teaches becomes defined merely as a functionary.

Teacher: When I think back on my teacher education courses and my own experience in the classroom, your criticisms certainly make sense, but they force me to ask more questions. For example, just what is there to see and talk about in teaching if teaching is not reducible to doing? And if theoretical language and the language of things won't fit, what language will?

The Teacher Talks of Teaching

In my imagination I am back in the classroom, yet I'm not there; I'm here. In a sense I am in it at the same time I am at a distance from it, and, though that puts me in a bind, if I attempt to get out of the bind, I'll be dealing merely in abstractions about the classroom, on one hand, or lost in the minutiae of the classroom, on the other. In neither case will I be able to see the lived-reality of that classroom. I must have gotten that term "lived-reality" from you, Professor. It isn't mine, not yet. Yes, I know that teaching is; I know that I have projected myself into the world as a teacher; I know that basically I love students; but all too often these "knows" get lost when I step into that confusing caldron.

If I accept your position, Professor, that to see teaching one must begin in wonder and amazement that it is and, further, that teaching is a moment of human interconnectedness which can't be reduced to anything other than itself, I am in yet another bind: I am a teacher, yet I don't know how to talk about it. Following you, I must lay aside most, if not all, of the concepts and terms I've learned in my teacher education courses, for most of those came from the social and behavioral sciences with their theories of explanations of roles and behavior. They appealed to me at the time; I wanted to know the why of everything. I guess I was getting ahead of myself, wanting to know the "why" before I knew the "is" of which I was asking why: The more I talk to you the more I seem to be digging myself into a deeper hole. But I can't go back to where I was. That moment of seeing myself through the window, that moment of awareness, though it has yielded up to this point only a sense of emptiness and confusion, has established a direction, and I shall pursue it.

This is a difficult task, Professor. My training has conditioned me to look at my teaching world through the glasses of each discipline. When I look through my sociology glasses, I see roles and role relationships, formal and informal authority structures, and communication networks. When I look through the glasses of psychology, I see achievement and underachievement, responses and reinforcements. With the architect's glasses, I see something else again. And, I suppose this could go on and on until one had exhausted the number of glasses, right? Arthur Eddington wrote *The Nature of the Physical World,* he said,[10] while sitting at two tables. One table had extension, substance, and scars, and pressed against him when he touched it and leaned on it. The other table was made of electrical charges which moved so rapidly that his sheet of paper was also held in a stable position. For Eddington, the physicist, the second table was the real one and the one from which his thought took its departure. I suppose, Professor, there could be an even larger number of tables: table as art object, table to eat from. It's interesting that there could also be two or more Eddingtons: social, political, religious, biological. But none of these was the Eddington with whom his wife and colleagues lived and worked. They lived and worked with the flesh and bone, sometimes irascible, always intentional, experiencing body called Eddington. Perhaps there is a clue in all this to help me try to talk about my teaching world. In describing teaching, many descriptions are possible, but what description, Professor, actually speaks of that world which the students and I live?

The professor reminds her of her commitment to pursue the problem unflinchingly, of the fact that it is his world he is trying to talk about, and the professor cannot do it for him. The professor does tell the teacher that, to see the lived-world, we have to put aside two common notions of seeing. One of the notions is that seeing is a projection either of some subjective selfhood or of learned stereotypes; such seeing is possible and common, but it prevents our "getting into" the actual situation. The other notion is that seeing is analogous to a camera's receptivity, that it is passive and non-intentional; even the possibility of this is questionable, but, if such seeing could be had, the one who sees would be excluded from the situation. Existentially, seeing is constituted of seeing what is, in its experiential givenness, and what might be. Seeing is thus the perception of that experienced as opposed to that observed. Noting the questioning look on the teacher's face, the professor illustrates: One never observes the possibilities of one's life, yet, to the extent that those possibilities play a part in the direction of life, one sees them. One does not observe his body or time; rather, he experiences them and can say he sees them. One does not observe another's meanings, yet he can say, "Yes, I see what you're saying." Further, one does not observe an action, for coexisting with overt movements are intentionalities, commitments, projects, enthusiasms, and subsidiary awarenesses, all of which are characteristics of experience, not observable entities or processes.

Teacher: I think I understand what you are saying. I put aside—or bracket out, as you philosophers say it—the language of abstraction and fragmentation, the "glasses" of specific disciplines, and, as a being-who-teaches, see the lived-situation. That throws me right back into the center of things, doesn't it? All right, I'm back in my teaching world; earlier, I called being in that location a bind. Perhaps it still is, but now I think I know where to look. Now, I shall look, not at the probable confirmation of a theory, but at the expressions of those beings, including myself, who make up that world. On your advice I read Kwant's *Phenomenology of Expression*[11] and, as a result of that reading, am prepared to see, not only expressions in words, but also silences, gestures, movements, and productions as well. On my own, Professor, I also read of Doris Humphrey's notion of rhythmic differentials,[12] and that really speaks to my world of teaching.

But in introducing the names of Kwant and Humphrey, I'm getting out of my classroom again. May I share with you some of my students' recent comments? During a group activity the other day, Johnny blurted out that he didn't have enough room, that everyone was crowding him. Kathryn, at the end of a class yesterday, exclaimed, "The period's over already?" This morning, I walked in on a most heated, passionate discussion of the responsibility for last week's snafu: Ralph, Kent, or the group? At the end of the day, "Big John" frequently tells me that I like someone else better than him. Little Lynne, voicing nothing, touches me in the hall. Elaine is obviously infatuated with me, hovering about, telling me of her family, dressing like me, and talking of becoming a teacher too. And, "Devilish Dave" is always countering me with, "I thought you were saying something else." And Fred, my most cooperative student, suddenly, for no apparent reason, said no to the whole task. I am aware that these are examples of student language, not scientific or theoretical language, yet these examples do illustrate where we daily live.

We exist, in intentional action which cannot be reduced to molecular terms. Johnny's concern was with what might be called lived-space or the space-for-him. Kathryn was expressing her experience of time, which had little to do with the schedule in the principal's office. Ralph, Kent, and the group were engaged in determining responsibility, in reference not to rules, but to creation and initiation of activity. "Big John," Little Lynne, Elaine, and "Devilish Dave" were all expressing the erotic, the sexuality of our world. And Fred, that most cooperative student who said no, was expressing the very existential grounds of freedom, his ability to stop the flow of the determined to open new possibilities for himself, and, thereby, our world. Professor, I can already anticipate your summary. You're going to say that the existential questions expressed by my students are those of spatiality, temporality, authenticity, sexuality, and tensionality, with all of these being aspects of the larger question of intentionality.

Professor: Who can say more?

Teacher: I can ask more.

I am still attempting to talk about my own teaching. It seems to me that there is a danger, in using your terms, of locking in another set of a priori categories. I may have to come back to your terms; we may have to live on the fine edge of such dangers; but the language which emerges from my classroom on an exciting day categorizes little and points not at all to specific referents. The students' talk, and mine, too, would be labelled by some as being only expressive noises or emotive language. It is emotive, Professor, but it is talk which moves out to fit the fullness of the teaching and classroom experience. When I search the literature on teaching, I find few who actually talk about teaching at all; rather the discussions are about learning, management, programming, evaluation, and other facets of teaching, but not about teaching itself. Perhaps the language of teaching is similar to the language of love in that it is about an experience so holistic, so immediate, and so close to us that we can't say what it is. Confronted with the difficulty of talking about such experiences, we either reduce the experience to the fractions of its wholeness or we talk about what it is like. For me, teaching cannot be reduced to classroom management or evaluation any more than love can be reduced to sex, marriage, romance, or what have you. That leaves me the other alternative, doesn't it?

Professor: Yes. The language of primordial experiences, such as teaching and loving, is always an "is like" language.

Teacher: I'm beginning to see that you never intended your terms to function in a direct, referential way. Maybe your terms, such as spatiality and temporality, to the extent that they refer to anything, refer to possibilities of being, rather than to what you called observables. If that is so, then my talk of teaching must consist of symbols, metaphors, which signify in a plurality of ways not only what we are doing in the moment but the possibilities of the moment, the negations and affirmations in the moment which open us to projections beyond the moment.

Professor: Wheelwright called those symbols 'plurisigns.'[13]

The professor points out that Wheelwright's plurisigns are made up of intermingled metaphors and that the teacher's talk of teaching can be done with metaphors. He warns, however, that "metaphor" must not be interpreted as analogy, but as a set of terms that permit one to speak of experience and possibilities, and the mystery and hiddenness of their fundamental reality. He reminds the teacher that there is no "It" for 'It' and, yet, there is that mysterious ground which makes possible 'It'.

Our teacher now begins an exploration of metaphorical language as a way of talking about his world of teaching. He soon finds that the bibliography on metaphor is almost overwhelming; he is most impressed with the work of Bachelard,[14] who, after establishing himself as a foremost philosopher of science, turned to metaphor as the only way of describing the lived-world of human beings. In the study of teaching, he finds the work of Linda Scott,[15] whose work was inspired by Bachelard's, most helpful. Scott was attempting to find a language that would describe teaching in a non-reductionistic way, primarily to overcome the fragmentation of teaching into so-called cognitive and affective domains. But Scott was also reaching beyond that to a mode of description which would take into account spatiality, temporality, authenticity, sexuality, and tensionality; she found that mode of description in the sexual metaphor. After an analysis of the many metaphors used for describing teaching, Scott concludes that six sexual metaphors—rapist, seducer, sexual partner, prostitute, voyeur, and exhibitionist[16] —describe the various ways in which teachers and students interact. Coming at the question from entirely different reasons and grounds, Margaret Grote, in her article, "Teaching and the Sex-Act,"[17] arrives at a similar conclusion. Our teacher exclaims, "Well, when I agreed to give up the linguistic glasses of scientific and theoretical language, I didn't know I was going this far!" But our professor suggests that he not merely accept the work of Scott and Grote, but consider them as one "is like Y" possibility for his world.

I have spent days going through the literature, Professor, and I need time to absorb, sort out, and make my own choices with respect to what I read and reflect on. While I do that, can we talk about something else?

They Come to Understand

Professor: Yes and no, dear Teacher. Yes, we can shift our focus away from the talk of talking about teaching, and, no, we cannot stop asking about that mode of being which we are. The explication of being, a task never fulfilled, remains our task, however. We dwell in a world which can never be fully worded, though it awaits our wording for its disclosure. Paradoxical? Confusing? Conflicting? Of course, but no more paradoxical, confusing, or conflicting than our world of teaching, that world of intentional action, individuated and shared meanings, affectional ties, tensive relationships, in which there is always the possibility of one's saying no. And you, as a being-who-teaches, are a cocreator and coexistor of that world, a world you are now attempting to understand through wording it in an authentic way.

I would contend that on your first day in that classroom you already understood and that what you are attempting now is an explication of that initial understanding.

Teacher: I must interrupt at this point. I thought understanding my behavior and that of my students resulted from a comparison of those behaviors with normative data obtained from studies of human development and learning. Only after seeing that relation could I say that I understood myself or my students.

Professor: You have sketched one type of understanding, but, to see if this is the type of understanding you want, let's go back to your reference to Eddington. If we were to approach Eddington from the direction you suggest, we would look for behaviors and behavior patterns, the descriptive statements of which could be subsumed under some covering statement, statistical law, or explanatory hypothesis; then we would demonstrate the relationship between the descriptive statement and the explanatory one, obtaining thereby, a statement of understanding. Perhaps we wish to understand why he became a physicist, but regardless of the specific content of the question, by demonstrating just how the particular behaviors of Eddington (the instantial statements) relate to the covering statement (the explanatory law), we arrive at an understanding of Eddington. But what have we come to understand? Not the existential Eddington, not the Eddington with whom his wife lived and with whom his colleagues worked; rather we have come to see those parts of him specified by our theory and for which the theory provides covering statements. In doing all this, though we have arrived at an objective, logically valid conclusion regarding Eddington, we have moved to a considerable distance from the flesh-and-bone, holistic person. Because of this movement away from the actual person, the objective mood of understanding is really a deficient mode of seeing human beings.

Teacher: We discussed this same point, in other terms, earlier, didn't we? You keep forcing me back into that classroom. You persist in your contention that the locus for understanding a world is from within that world, don't you?

Professor: You make it sound as though I were imposing a theory, or method, or model. I'm not. But, if one is to understand in terms other than the language of fragmentation and the principle of subsumption, one must vigorously commit himself to the systematic laying aside of those terms to regain the richness and surety of his primordial, original understanding of the lived-world.

Teacher: You just now mentioned another term, Professor, that of original understanding. Does that refer back to your claim that on my first day I already understood? If so, are you preparing to set forth a taxonomy of levels and types of understanding?

Professor: No. Let's approach the matter in the manner of Erwin Straus, who calls this original understanding "symbiotic understanding."[18] Symbiotic understanding takes place in an alingual world, a world of sensing, sympathetic experiencing, and feeling. It is premature to call that a world; it is, rather, an environment or setting, and we have a feel-for, an intuitive grasp of the expressions of, a sense of the whole. This sense of the whole is prelinguistic and precognitive; tonality and tempo are its media, and its time is Now, its space, Here. And, though precognitive body-feels, tonality, and tempo, Now and Here are not to be lost, for their loss leads to a deficient understanding of lived-reality, the direction of educating is toward the cognitive and the future. This direction establishes the direction of our understanding of your world of teaching.

When you walk into the classroom, you walk not into a world, but into a setting. You have an immediate grasp of the whole. Then begins the task of making explicit and interpreting that which is there, with the referent for "that which is there" being the complete range of expressions, as you defined that term earlier, to be found there. You and the students together do the explications and interpretations, and, though the direction is toward the cognitive and the future, there is a sense in which each day is a new beginning, for we never leave our bodies, which are always Here, and we are not without feelings, which are always Now. To recast in other words, the movement, brought about through explication and interpretation, from symbiotic to reflective understanding is not to be conceived of in linear terms, but as a transcending of the moment while not negating the moment, thereby creating new meaning in the moment. Yes, another tension, requiring a tensive language for its description, but that is where you live as a being-who-teaches.

Teacher: If I understand you, you are saying that my interpretations of what is happening will make explicit what is already understood. Is that correct?

Professor: Yes, and the way you state it is very similar to Heidegger's statement: "Any interpretation which is to contribute understanding, must already have understood what is to be interpreted."[19]

Teacher: I'll leave the footnotes to you; I'm searching for something in my own experience that will help me understand all this. If I may use a textual example rather than one of action, I think I can clarify for myself what you're saying. When I read a poem for the first time, I usually read it very rapidly to get a feel for the whole poem. And I get it. Yet if someone were to insist that I talk at that moment about the poem, I would be at a loss for words.

Professor: Explication and interpretation take place most effectively through dialogue.

Teacher: That's true. But let me continue. I agree that there is an immediate grasp of the whole; then, on rereading, some parts, allusions, and images are quite obvious in their intent. After the initial interpretation, the task becomes more difficult, and I have to resist the temptation to bring in psychoanalytic, sociological, and other protocols of interpretation. So, I go go back to the patient explication of what is given. I attempt to unpack meanings by seeing the relationships between specific words and phrases and the whole poem. I try to look at the poem from a variety of perspectives. And I ask two questions of the author and of myself: What was the mythic dwelling place of the poet, and what were his transcending projects? What is my mythic dwelling place, and what are my transcending projects? The text of the poem now goes beyond the words to encompass the depths of being of the poet and of me, the futurings of the poet and of me. The poem becomes a lived-reality, a dialogue. And the explication and interpretation take place within the fullness of being.

Professor: You're beginning to open yourself to your own being. You not only went beyond the words of the poem, you went beyond my words. You now have the keys for understanding the lived-world of your classroom.

THE AUTHOR INTERVENES

Before you go your separate ways certain points deserve further elaboration and elucidation. In focusing on teaching, not as a set of functions or even actions, but as a mode of being, you have brought to attention the entire range of problems in an existential "analysis." There are three of these implicit in your discussion, which need to be made more explicit. "Problems" is a troublesome term in itself; these three actually illustrate points of difference, and some strain, within existential phenomenology. We may identify them in this way: the categorical analysis of existence versus pointing to the concrete; the directness of truth versus the hidden-ness of truth; and, the question of the final description. The questions of generalization, of probability, and of language will have to be addressed, at least briefly, in grappling with the above points.

You have both used certain categorical terms, such as "temporality," "spatiality," etc. But Buber's 'Thou' and Camus' 'rebellion' could also be used in this way. If one attempts substantialist definition and systematization of these, one has not an existentialism, but another essentialism, an inherent problem in any philosophy about existence. One way out of the difficulty is to not attempt a philosophy about existence; rather, through use of anecdotes, novels, plays, and poems, point to existence, at the same time embodying existence in the literary work. Few, Kafka being a primary example, have been willing to remain at that level. Others, such as Sartre, Marcel, Unamuno, and Camus, have attempted both, yet even in the best examples of their works, there is a gap and a tension between their philosophical essays and their literary pieces. One cannot read Camus' *The Myth of Sisyphus,* for example, expecting to find therein some philosophical principle for the explanation of his novel *The Stranger,* or find in *The Rebel* the principle for interpreting *The Plague.* Each is a different form for explicating the various modalities of the lived-world. That critic who mandates rational coherence, or at least consistent method, will always be frustrated by existential description.

But existential description is not just first-person account. Generalized terms are appropriate to such description as are generalizations. How to obtain those without developing another essentialism is the problem. We may avoid the difficulty by looking at certain possibilities regarding the terms, forms, and functions of the generalizations. Certain generalized terms have been used throughout this discussion, but it should be added that the terms of existential description are not necessarily single words or even sentences; an entire work may serve as a single term. Allemann's analysis of Kafka[20] and the study by Ross and Freed of Alberto Moravia[21] serve to illustrate this point well. Fundamental to all such terms is the descriptive metaphor, which points in an *epiphoric*[22] way to the surface and depths of experience while, at the same time, in a *diaphoric*[23] way transcends the particular experience, creating new meaning in the process. Existential description, then, does not rest with the depiction of some "out there" reality, but participates in the creation of reality. It functions to open new possibilities for seeing, but, to the extent that the description is *epiphoric,* the seeing is always a situated seeing; thus the trap of subjective idealism is avoided. As the description functions to open new possibilities of seeing, another trap, that of substantialist definition, is also avoided, for the terms are not categories of a priori meaning, but linguistic "categories" which open us to create new meaning in our worlds. New descriptive terms, in opening new possibilities of meaning, provide the opportunity to raise additional questions regarding the objects of consciousness, aspects of the lived-world. They free us from frozen categories of perception and conception, making possible a return to the richness and variety and anguish of our lives, a richness, variety, and anguish negated whenever the describer attempts to bracket himself out of the description.

The question still remains regarding the form of the generalization. Put simply, the form is that of the narrative. History, both individual and social, is a type of narrative, and in every history, no matter how particular, there is something general, for, as Habermas puts it, "someone else can find something exemplary in it."[24] On the other hand, no matter how general the narrative, if the themes or actions can be taken out of the context of that history and appropriated by persons to their lived worlds, the general is translatable to an individuated situation. In this movement from general to particular and back again, it must be clearly understood that no fractionalizing of moments of intentional action takes place. Holistic, intentional actions may be found to be congruent even across context boundaries; in those cases, we may speak of generalizing. But any reduction of those moments of intentional action to behaviors, personality variables, or quotients of any kind lead only to abstractions, not to generalization. Narratives, personal and social, may in certain moments cohere, and we may therefore speak of generalization. Abstraction, on the other hand, results from fractionalizing and subsumption. Existential description will lead to generalization but not to abstraction.

We may summarize to this point by saying that categories of description do not necessarily lead to an essentialism if it is understood that the terms of description are openings of possibility, not substantialist definition, and that one may generalize from his particular situation if he understands that the form is that of the narrative, and the trap to be avoided that of abstraction.

In our endeavor to talk of that mode of being called teaching, we quite obviously wish for our account to be a true one. We therefore ask, "Where do we begin our inquiry?" And the answer, "From the perspective of existential phenomenology," is with the problem of the lived-body, meaning the embodied-being-in-situation. Earlier, I stated the problem as a conflict between claims for the directness of truth versus the hidden-ness of truth. By focusing on the lived-body, the outlines of the difficulty can be quickly sketched. Can the being-in-situation know with the clarity sought by Husserl and the lucidity claimed by Camus? Or, can the being-in-situation never know without the aid of an objective interpreter as Freud would have it? Or, is the being-in-situation capable of hermeneutical understanding, an interpretation in which some matters are clearly open to seeing, others remain as interpretations, and yet others forever mysterious? Existential phenomenologists, since Heidegger, have accepted hermeneutical understanding, although differing in their understandings of it. Julian Marías' position is not atypical and will illustrate the general position. He argues that all we have are interpretations but that interpretation is not all, for "reality is something that makes me make interpretations."[25] Kisiel's exposition[26] of the current debate in German philosophy indicates to what extent the early claim of phenomenology to a direct knowledge of the phenomena of consciousness has been brought into question. Even Paul Ricoeur, who was considered to be among the most Husserlian of the French phenomenologists, has now extensively modified his position at this point, working dialectically with the materials of what he calls psychoanalytical hermeneutics.[27]

What all of this has to say regarding our explication of that mode of being called teaching is that certain phenomena of that teaching-world can be immediately grasped and will be understood immediately, for the context is also immediately given along with the phenomena. In the language of gestalt theory, we could call this a moment of insight, a moment in which the figure and ground are presented simultaneously, and the relationship is immediately grasped. But what the above also says is that understanding, in most instances, will require hermeneutical interpretation, for most phenomena of the classroom do not present themselves in a manner which yields immediate insight. Beyond all this, however, is the ground for a claim I shall make, namely, that there is a definite limit to what we can know and understand about our classrooms and our teaching. That ground is the lived-body which is always prior to, and yet present with, the wordings of our worlds. Our interpretations are based on that ground and can never encompass it. The locus of the mystery of being is there. In your classroom, there will be some things immediately graspable, some things which can be interpreted, but you and your students will remain fundamentally mysterious. Mystery, however, is not an object of fear: we fear the unknown, the not-yet known. Mystery surprises us, delights us, astonishes us, and leads us to exclaim that it is.

When is the description of that mode of being called teaching ever complete? The answer is never, not because the number of "variables" is too great, the time too short, or the "instruments" inadequate, but because mystery can never be fully disclosed. If mystery could ever be fully disclosed in words, the worder would then be annihilated. There are phenomena to be grasped and to be interpreted, but there is always the limit. Neither mystery nor the known contingencies of your world can be captured within the boundaries of a probability table. Even though you live in contingency, probability has nothing to do with your teaching. Even though you are grounded in mystery and living in contingency, relativism is not implied, for each intentional action is absolute. Either you speak or you don't; either you give a command or you don't; either you put it on the board or you don't; the student responds or he doesn't. Each moment is absolute. If the description is never complete, when is it ended? Whenever you choose.

Professor: Is the intervention finished?

Author: Your question says it is.

Teacher: I'm going back to my classroom.

THE TEACHER RETURNS TO THE CLASSROOM

I return to the classroom, for I have projected myself into the world as a being who is called teacher. Yes, I am a called teacher. In that projection I called, from the mysterious depths of my being, on the world, and the world called on me to be. I have responded to the call in choosing that mode of being called teaching. That is quite literally a calling, a vocation. That call, however, imposes neither substantialist nor functionalistic definition on me; rather, that call, and my response to it in choice, constitute a hole of possibility, a hole bounded by the arc of my intentionality, a hole both bright and mysterious.

REFERENCES

1. P. Goodman, *Speaking and Language* (New York: Random House, 1971), pp. 200-223.

2. D. Denton, *The Language of Ordinary Experience* (New York: Philosophical Library, 1970), Chs. II, V, VI.

3. E. Nagel, *The Structure of Science* (New York: Harcourt, Brace and World, 1961).

4. C. Hempel, "The Function of General Laws in History," in *Theories of History*, P. Gardiner, ed. (Glencoe: Free Press, 1959), pp. 1-5.

5. C. Hull, *Mathematico-Deductive Theory of Rote Learning* (New Haven: Yale University Press, 1940).

6. D. Denton, "Education's Egocentric Predicament," in *Philosophy of Education*, D. Arnstine, ed. (Edwardsville, Ill.: Studies in Philosophy and Education, 1969), pp. 143-148.

7. T. Green, "A Typology of the Teaching Concept," *Studies in Philosophy and Education*, III (Winter 1964-65), 284-319.

8. I. Scheffler, *The Language of Education* (Springfield, Ill.: Charles C Thomas, 1962).

9. E. Pullias and J. Young, *A Teacher Is Many Things* (Bloomington: Indiana University Press, 1968).

10. Cited in E. Straus, "The Sense of the Senses," in *Persons, Privacy, and Feeling*, D. Van de Vate, ed. (Memphis: Memphis State University Press, 1970), pp. 71-91.

11. R. Kwant, *Phenomenology of Expression* (Pittsburgh: Duquesne University Press, 1969).

12. D. Humphrey, *The Art of Making Dances* (New York: Holt, Rinehart and Winston, 1960), p. 104.

13. P. Wheelwright, *Metaphor and Reality* (Bloomington: Indiana University Press, 1962), p. 57.

14. G. Bachelard, *The Poetics of Space* (Boston: Beacon Press, 1969).

15. L. Scott, *Teaching, Action and Metaphor* (Ph. D. dissertation, University of Kentucky, 1972).

16. *Ibid.*, p. 97.

17. M. Grote, "Teaching and the Sex-Act," *Educational Theory* (Spring 1971), pp. 187-192.

18. E. Straus, *The Primary World of Senses* (Glencoe: Free Press, 1963), pp. 194-202.

19. M. Heidegger, *Being and Time* (London: SCM Press, 1962), p. 194.

20. B. Allemann, "Metaphor and Antimetaphor," in *Interpretation: The Poetry of Meaning*, S. Hopper and D. Miller, eds. (New York: Harcourt, Brace and World, 1967), pp. 103-123.

21. J. Ross and D. Freed, *The Existentialism of Alberto Moravia* (Carbondale: Southern Illinois University Press, 1972).

22. Wheelwright, *op. cit.*, pp. 72-73.

23. *Ibid.*, p. 78.

24. J. Habermas, *Knowledge and Human Interests* (Boston: Beacon Press, 1971), p. 263.

25. J. Marías, "Philosophic Truth and the Metaphoric System," in Hopper and Miller, *op. cit.*, p. 48.

26. T. Kisiel, "Ideology Critique and Phenomenology: The Current Debate in German Philosophy," *Philosophy Today*, XIV (Fall 1970).

27. As explicated by D. Ihde, "From Phenomenology to Hermeneutic," *Journal of Existentialism*, VIII (Winter 1967-68), 111-132.

ASPECT **C**

Aspect C is first disclosed to us in J. Gordon Chamberlin's "Phenomenological Methodology and Understanding Education." Professor Chamberlin, who is perhaps the most Husserlian of philosophers of education, argues that phenomenological method is the most appropriate approach to seeing the is-ness of education. In arriving at that claim, he carefully explicates Husserl's method, demonstrates the use of that method in the analysis of the structures of education, and contrasts it with other methods, especially the method of linguistic analysis.

7 | Phenomenological Methodology and Understanding Education

J. GORDON CHAMBERLIN

I

> ... the thinker never thinks from any starting-point but the one constituted by what he is.[1]

Phenomenology offers educators a fresh way to view their field. Employing a new perspective involves searching for a map to guide one's explorations of a new territory, learning appropriate terminology and identifying fresh clues about the way philosophy may be related to education. Traditionally educators have assumed that one first works out or adopts a philosophical position and then proceeds to discern its implications for education. A phenomenological approach challenges that deductive procedure. Its method draws educators to look first at the thing itself in careful reflection on the meaning of education, for until it is clear what education is it will be unclear how philosophy and education are, or may be, related.

In attempting to understand a new philosophical approach an educator always stands in the middle. He has already been exposed to many educational ideas and institutional structures. He has had many teachers and has interpreted and reinterpreted both what has happened to him and his responses to those events. He has formed distinctive patterns in the way he thinks about his work. He cannot recapture the naiveté of his pre-schooling experience nor the innocence of his first encounter with formal educational programs.

This wealth of experience, including the deposit of a centuries-long stream of historical developments in the field, has become a world of meaning enclosed in, and intimately related to, his total life-world. Along with all of his other experiences, what education means is a significant element in the way he thinks of his total past and anticipates his future. His life-world is shaped as he encounters and interprets the vast social process, education, of which he is a part; he lives the meaning education has for him.

Whether a child is being shown how to play marbles, or an adult is being introduced to the study of anthropology, the process of education moves within a typical general structure. While this structure is obvious in schools it is important to recognize that the same structure characterizes many activities which precede schooling or are carried on beyond the reach of schools.

STRUCTURE

Each society embodies a legacy of patterns for what children should learn and how they should be helped in that learning. Someone is held responsible for providing educational activities (sponsor); these activities always involve consciously selected patterns (procedures); someone is responsible for conducting the activities (operative); of course those who are to be helped in learning are always involved (learners); and there is always a constituency concerned with the outcome of the educational activity (constituents). These, then, are the integral structural elements through which the educational process is carried on. By looking carefully at informal educational activities we are able to see clearly the simple essential anatomy of education unencumbered by the vast accretions which formal schooling systems have added.

The sponsors of informal education may be the clan, religious institutions, or the state, who hold parents responsible for initiating and conducting educational activities by accepted procedures. In some things parents share responsibility with each other, while in others there is a clear distinction between the responsibility of the father and of the mother. In some instances, when a family develops unique standards or goals for their children, the parents may be the sponsors of particular learning. And if there are several children, parents may sponsor arrangements whereby older siblings engage in helping their younger brothers and sisters in their learning. Tradition may sponsor informal education in the sense of a diffuse social expectancy accepted by all members of the society about who is to provide help in learning. More explicit sponsoring may come from grandparents or the enlarged family. In some things religious institutions sponsor educational activities for the very young; and in other instances it is the state or the tribal council which provides for the earliest informal educational activities.

Procedure of informal education may be highly stylized or left to individual choice. In many societies, play is expected to help children learn adult skills and social behavior. In some societies, as in some families, children's play is regulated and timed, whereas in others no attempt is made to arrange the kind of play, its frequency, or the dynamics of groups at play. Informal education may follow stylized play at all ages in celebration and festivals, just as it may follow stylized forms of apprenticeship training for occupations.

Informal patterns of education revolve around the operatives who help learning take place. They may be parents, siblings, or relatives. They may be friends or chance acquaintances. Help may be provided directly, as when a father shows his son how to assemble a toy, or indirectly, as the son reads the printed instructions in the toy box. The operatives are those held responsible by society for helping others learn.

Every person is a learner. Much of what he learns he does by himself. He observes, he experiments, he responds to stimuli that crowd in upon him second by second, he explores his changing body and his changing surroundings, he interprets the events happening around him and reinterprets them repeatedly as he remembers them in the light of new events, he tries and fails and tries and succeeds and then tries to discern the differences—all of this is "natural" and "human." In addition, all people are expected, or required, by their social existence to learn many things which they cannot learn by themselves, for which they need the help of others. All people at one time or another are the recipients of informal help in learning, and this process is not limited to childhood. It is important to distinguish between general learning, which a person can do by himself, and helped-learning, which requires the assistance of others, and it is equally important to recognize that each may be carried on in either formal or informal educational activities.

Education is encircled by a constituency which depends upon the helped-learning taking place. Housebuilders depend upon the apprenticed carpenter just as a family depends upon the mother's having learned how to cook from her mother before her.

In formal schooling this five-part structure becomes more elaborate and explicit: boards of education sponsor activities and specify procedures; administrators and teachers are employed to carry out planned activities in standardized ways; learners are required by law or by the hope of employment to attend these activities for set periods of time; and the constituents include the community which wants children kept off the streets for most of the day, employers who need trained workers, and the school system itself which requires replacement of its operatives.

PROBLEMS

When an educator seeks to reexamine what education means for him, he does so in the context of his own particular experiences of this structure and the educational process flowing through it. But every educator is aware of long-standing basic problems of the field which prompt repeated efforts to gain a more adequate insight into what he is doing. How is the distinctiveness of education to be understood? Why is there such confusion of philosophies? Why have educational programs accumulated such accretions of social functions? Among the conflicting objectives how are appropriate goals to be determined? What are the implications of the symbolic role education has acquired in many societies?

That education is a social process is obvious, for it engages individuals and groups in interaction and cooperation. That its structure is similar in some ways to the structures of other basic social processes is also obvious; the parallels between school structures and business structures have often been noted. The distinctive differences, however, are to be seen in the processes served by the structures. Commerce deals with distinctive material, objectives, controls, measures of accomplishment, and relation to society at large. Other major social processes such as government, the arts, and religion, have equally distinctive characteristics. Educators are handicapped because although philosophers often refer to education as a process none has attempted a careful, systematic exploration of the essential nature of that process.

Educators are concerned, also, by the multiplicity of philosophies of education. The problem is created by the expectation that an educational system or program can be built around a particular philosophical position. In fact, however, educational programs draw together people with diverse philosophical commitments and incorporate traditional procedures which have their roots in still other philosophical stances. It is difficult to imagine a situation in which there would be a genuine consensus of philosophical standpoint among all the participants in an educational program.

And to propose that what is really needed is another, more adequate philosophical position from which we can deduce a resolution of prior philosophical conflicts in the field is only to repeat what each new philosophical movement of the past has attempted unsuccessfully to do. Only when the prior basic work of identifying the nature of the educational process is carried out will educators be able to direct educational questions at philosophical positions, and maintain a true dialogue between the two fields.

Historically, education has been marked by constant accretion and complexity. Education is such a basic social process that it is found in every human community, expressing man's aggressive tendencies to control or influence others as well as his yearning to understand the meaning of his existence. Every society has developed educational patterns which reflect its cultural characteristics, and a vast array of educational forms now jostle each other in intercultural contacts. The result is continual elaboration of additional functions, institutional structures, and organizational systems. As an increasing proportion of the social energy and resources of a society are devoted to educational activities, problems of policy become insistent. Thus, whenever education is discussed, concern tends to focus first on immediate issues of taxes, busing, curricular materials, tenure, and buildings. It becomes increasingly difficult to discern the essentials upon which one might base valid judgments or appropriate actions about such matters.

An additional indication of the accretion is the expanding list of what many societies expect education to produce. The most common temptation in thinking about education is to start by designating goals. As we have already indicated, the failure to clarify what the educational process is raises serious questions about the validity of such an approach. The appropriateness of a goal depends upon the nature of the process which is asked to produce it. To be sure, every educational activity has an outcome, but the problem for educators is how to appraise the relationship between educational activities and their intended outcomes. In some instances the results of an educational activity can be identified and measured at once, while in others the objective depends upon future development and is so intertwined with other influences that it is impossible to develop valid measurements for guiding subsequent educational activities. Thus, most educational programs are submerged in a welter of conflicting expectations of outcome which the process may or may not be able to carry out.

"To be educated" usually implies formal education, and the phrase has a variety of meanings for different people. To some it is a value in itself, to others a means of upward social mobility, and to still others it is the mark of progress for a country. For some it means to be wise, for others to be privileged, and for a few to be idealistic. The vast sums of money expended upon educational systems can seldom be justified by an empirical measurement of social utility. Schools have become symbols with meanings basic to a nation's self-image. This elevation of education to symbolic status in a society poses particular problems for philosophers of education, which cannot be resolved by the deductive mode, yet the question is directly relevant to the meaning education has for the huge constituency of contemporary educational activities.

As we have already noted, an educator who attempts to understand his field finds himself in the middle of the developments just reviewed. Simplistic notions of education as the teaching-learning transaction, of education as schooling, or of education as a measure of national prestige, are helpful neither in planning nor in evaluating what is done in activities called education. Whether he is aware of it or not, each educator interprets his experience and these problems from the perspective of some philosophical point of view—his convictions about human nature, social responsibility, the way the mind functions, ethical standards. A serious reexamination of what education means for him requires a philosophical methodology appropriate for a critical re-viewing of both his experience and his present philosophical commitments. But since educators have not yet been provided with a view that will clarify the nature of the process and offer a starting point for deciding what education can and should do, they are justified in looking for a fresh perspective.

II

> Education must shift its attention from things and minds, to the relation between the experiencing subject and the experienced object.[2]

Ernest Moore, reflecting the influence of William James and Charles S. Peirce on the meaning of "experience," recognized that the contributions of those men could have significant implications for education, although he was unable to employ their insights for a convincing answer to his own question, "What is education?" He had, nevertheless, asked a question that educational philosophers have seldom attempted to answer, and he had indicated a promising direction in which to search for an adequate answer.

Moore's question can be answered empirically by a sociologist who examines educational institutions and explains how they operate, but when he does so he tends to assume that "education" can be equated with "schooling." An anthropologist can answer the question by tracing the function of educational activities in various cultures, but by doing so he assumes that the definitional question has already been answered. If Moore's is to be considered a philosophical rather than an empirical question, the answer will depend upon the kind of philosophical methodology employed.

During the past decade educational philosophers have turned increasingly to linguistic analysis as a highly refined methodology for carrying out a program of critical rethinking of educational concepts. Analysts have been aware that:

> Part of the problem involved in talking and thinking about education is the variety of definitions and views of education which is offered to us on all sides. We are, in fact, literally bombarded with a multitude of competing definitions which tempt us to choose among them.[3]

In this situation the task of analysis in education, according to Israel Scheffler, is "the disentangling of different contexts in which education is discussed and argued, and the consideration of basic ideas and appropriate logical criteria relevant to each."[4]

Helpful as it has been to have analysts disentangle the multitude of educational concepts and definitions, examining the language about education has not yet answered Moore's question. The issue of whether education is a distinctive kind of process, a discrete object to which language about education refers, is sidestepped.

In his study of *Ordinary Language Philosophy: Historical Perspective*, E. K. TeHennepe identifies the concern of Wittgenstein with going beyond language use to aspects of things which are "hidden because of their simplicity and familiarity."[5] TeHennepe quotes John Austin:

> In view of the prevalence of the slogan "ordinary language," and of such names as "linguistic" or "analytic" philosophy or "the analysis of language," one thing needs special emphasizing to counter misunderstandings. When we examine what we should say when, what words we should use in what situations, we are looking again not *merely* at words (or "meanings," whatever they may be) but also at the realities we use the words to talk about: we are using a sharpened awareness of the words to sharpen our perception of, though not as the final arbiter of, the phenomena. For this reason I think it might be better to use, for this way of doing philosophy, some less misleading name than those given above—for instance "linguistic phenomenology," only that is rather a mouthful.[6]

TeHennepe finally asserts:

> I believe it is more accurate to say that ordinary language philosophy seeks its solutions, not from psychology or any other of the sciences (as Natanson suggests), but in "grammar"—in an admittedly peculiar sense of "grammar." If we try to track down this sense in which the solutions offered are "grammatical," we come finally to a concern for "what it makes sense to say." And I suggest that we are then much closer to the phenomenologist's concern for "eidetic structures" or "structures of meaning" than to anything psychological or scientific.[7]

In countering "the charge that ordinary language philosophy is purely and trivially linguistic,"[8] TeHennepe has identified affinities of concern between "ordinary language philosophies" and "continental philosophies," but does not thereby claim that their methodologies are the same. The methods of ordinary language analysis are inadequate to the task of examining the "eidetic structures," the essential characteristics of the process of education. Phenomenology may offer a more appropriate methodology.

HUSSERL'S METHODS

Understanding the central element in the phenomenological method properly begins with the initiator of the contemporary phenomenological movement, the German Edmund Husserl.

During the early twentieth century, Husserl addressed the problems of "experience" from a somewhat different perspective than William James, but he had read James and claimed to have been deeply impressed by his thinking. From a background in mathematics Husserl had come to question current theories of knowledge, realizing that how one perceives objects—

whether persons, trees, principles, angels, or social processes—is understood by examining the consciousness which a subject has of them. He wrote that "all basic forms of being an object are predetermined by the nature of cognition."[9] But this was no simple idealist assertion for, as Alfred Schütz points out:

> Phenomenological philosophy claims to be a philosophy of man in his life-world and to be able to explain the meaning of this life-world in a rigorously scientific manner. Its theme is concerned with the demonstration and explanation of the activities of consciousness of the transcendental subjectivity within which this life-world is constituted.[10]

Although Husserl's work was original and led to significant new methodological tools, it was built upon prior developments in philosophy. Paul Ricoeur writes:

> Phenomenology has a past which situates it within the history of occidental philosophy and connects it with the Leibnizian and Kantian sense of "phenomenon"...phenomenology continues the transcendental of Kant, the originary of Hume, and the doubt and cogito of Descartes. In no way does it represent a sharp mutation in philosophy.[11]

While Husserl gave particular and extended effort to developing the phenomenological method, he exploited only a few of its possibilities. Others who followed—Max Scheler, Martin Heidegger, Jean-Paul Sartre, Maurice Merleau-Ponty, Paul Ricoeur—employed the method in a variety of ways, so there is no one orthodox procedure which can be held up as the authoritative phenomenological method. The method varies according to the particular phenomena being studied and the thematic attention given them. Heidegger employed the method in his early work in examining "the existence of human being," while Merleau-Ponty gave particular attention to the "body-world" and Sartre focused on "freedom." But variety of methodology is also found in Husserl's own work. Ricoeur notes that even in the parts of his work where Husserl applied his method:

> They do not constitute one homogeneous body of work with a single direction of orientation. Husserl abandoned along the way as many routes as he took. This is the case to such a degree that in a broad sense phenomenology is both the sum of Husserl's work and the heresies issuing from it.[12]

Husserl contended that he was always starting over, that in a sense the method requires one to commence repeatedly.

The lack of a single clearly articulated set of methodological steps has generated even greater differences among Husserl's interpreters, many of whom disagree strongly with each other in their appraisal of his contribution. But Richard M. Zaner believes that whatever the differences among Husserl's critics the phenomenological method can be seen in terms of a general analogy:

> Learning to think phenomenologically is very much like learning to read and actively use these records, the maps, guideposts, markings, and other paraphernalia of the explorer's and mapmaker's trade. The sense of phenomenological statements is very much like that of an explorer's statements, for the meaning of both is similarly twofold: in so far as they claim to be descriptions of the "land," *they are at once epistemic* (knowledge-claims concerning the land itself) and *communicative* (that is, invitations and guides intended to enable others to know what to look for.)[13]

The method, according to Zaner, is a kind of "disengagement and reflective apprehension of what you have until now been unaware of,"[14] but it is necessary to carry on that disengagement and reflection "systematically and then methodically to explore in depth what then is disclosed to us."[15]

Phenomenology has become a broad stream with many currents. The term "phenomenology" is in vogue and often used loosely. Though significant phenomenological analysis has contributed to work in such fields as sociology, psychiatry, esthetics, and philosophy of religion, its use in education has been very limited, primarily in connection with existentialist commitments.

A few educators have been deeply influenced by Heidegger and the French existentialist phenomenologists, and seem to hold that existentialism provides the stance and phenomenology the methodology for philosophy of education. However, this view does violence to both philosophical traditions. Existentialism has its own method, which is literary and dramatic, so it can hardly depend upon another. Existentialists come in all shades and shapes. Walter Kaufmann contends:

> Most of the living "existentialists" have repudiated this label, and a bewildered outsider might well conclude that the only thing they have in common is a marked aversion for each other. . . .The three writers who appear invariably on every list of "existentialists"—Jaspers, Heidegger and Sartre—are not in agreement on essentials.[16]

Assuming that Kaufmann represents the situation fairly, phenomenology and existentialism have at least this in common: both defy simplistic summary, so that their relationship depends upon what is meant by each. Under these circumstances it is difficult to hold that phenomenology can serve as a method either for existentialist analysis or to implement existentialism in education. And conversely, valuable as the existentialist stance is for the orientation of educators, the methods of existential analysis cannot provide the help educators need with the very basic problem: "What is education?" Until educators can answer the question they are condemned to the futility of trying to relate philosophical positions, whether existentialist or any other, to an unknown quantity—"X"—and therefore are unable to fulfill their crucially important role of helping both participants and constituents reexamine the meaning of education.

Because phenomenology provides a rich set of methodological procedures for analyzing the essence of objects, we will explore the major elements of Husserl's method, giving attention to those aspects which seem to relate most directly to the particular problems faced by educators. At each step the distinctive character of education should shape the claim which educators may make upon phenomenology.

Selected Methodological Elements

Husserl set a demanding task for himself. His objective, as he wrote in *Ideas*, was "to establish phenomenology itself as an eidetic science, as the theory of the essential nature of the transcendentally purified consciousness."[17] Only by care in the exercise of the different movements of the method can one come to a clear understanding of the structure of consciouness and therefore of the way meaning is constituted. The method which Husserl developed and elaborated over the years included a number of elements which interrelate so that each depends on the others. A general statement of the steps in the method of essential analysis is provided in *Ideas* where Husserl wrote:

> It [phenomenology] has to place before its own eyes as instances certain pure conscious events, to bring these to complete clearness, and within this zone of clearness to subject them to analysis and the apprehension of their essence, to follow up the essential connections that can be clearly understood, to grasp what is momentarily perceived in faithful conceptual expressions, of which the meaning is prescribed purely by the object perceived or in some way transparently understood.[18]

Following these steps engages an educator in recognizing that the phenomena, the "pure conscious events," are the "appearances" which education has for him, and that to analyse and apprehend their essence is to clarify their meaning.

Kockelmans holds that to understand phenomenology as a method it is necessary to dwell upon the fundamental themes of "intentional" and "constitutive" analysis:

> The essence of things, therefore, can be determined only by returning in an intentional analysis to the acts of our consciousness in which any being constitutes itself *originally* as "this" or "that." This assertion appears a necessary consequence flowing from the application of the idea of intentionality to human knowledge.[19]

Husserl had indicated his central insight into the nature of consciousness, namely that all thinking is thinking about something. He used the term "intentionality" to refer to the correlation between the object and the appearance of the object to consciousness. He wrote:

> It belongs as a general feature to the essence of every actual *cogito* to be a consciousness *of* something. . . . That an experience is the consciousness of something. . .does not relate to the experimental fact as lived within the world. . .but to the pure essence grasped ideationally as pure idea.[20]

And Herbert Spiegelberg adds:

> It is only in Husserl's thought that the term "intentional" acquired the meaning of directedness toward an object rather than that of the object's immanence in consciouness. Also, it was only with Husserl that the acts thus directed were called "intentions" and referred to "intentional objects," i.e., objects that were the targets of intentions.[21]

To discern the meaning of an object (idea, process, person, house) one does not respond to one's perceptions of that object from one perspective only. Such a view may be profile, but the consciousness is aware that a house can be viewed from many other perspectives, and that all the different perceptions are still of the same object. Intentionality refers to the total meaning of the object which is always more than what is given in the perception of a single profile or perspective. Husserl used two Latin terms, *noesis* and *noema,* to indicate the intimate relationship between intentionality as total meaning (*noema*) and particular acts of perception (*noesis*) of the object. In this way he discerns how consciousness, in dealing with what is given in perception, does so in the light of data that are not perceived.

In attempting to determine the essence of an object, one may employ a methodological device which Husserl termed free fancy in the framing of particular illustrations. No matter how many perceptions of an object one has perceived, it is still possible to imagine others. So a person may use "imaginative variation" to extend the range of aspects to be considered in discerning the meaning of an object. If what is "necessary" to its being and to its meaning is confirmed by each additional imagined variation, or "free fancy," its essence is established.

> Hence, if anyone loves a paradox, he can really say, and with strict truth if he will allow for the ambiguity, that the element which makes up the life of phenomenology as of all eidetical science is "fiction," that fiction is the source whence the knowledge of "eternal trust" draws its sustenance.[22]

Whatever appears to a person is always perceived within some context, termed by Husserl its horizon. Though there may be many objects within that horizon, a person may give attention to this or that object, or to this or that aspect of an object, and thus "thematize" the field of perceptions.

In the educational domain, while attention may focus on one profile of an object, the object cannot be understood except in terms of its total relation to its context. For instance, the idea of education as a teacher-student relationship is but one element in a vast complex of meanings of the educational process and cannot be understood except in the context of that total range of experience and meanings. For an educator that horizon would include a person's interpretation of each aspect of his direct participation in educational activities, both informal and formal, what he has read about the subject of education, ideas and attitudes he has heard expressed by others directly or indirectly, the problems educators face, and his own reflections upon all of his exposures. Intentional analysis strives to clarify the appropriate inclusiveness of that horizon, what is necessary to the meaning of education and what may be excluded.

These concepts—intentionality, *noema/noesis,* horizon, theme—are employed by Husserl as devices to aid in bringing out meanings, in unveiling implicit aspects contained in actual states of consciousness. They help make meanings explicit as well as disengage constituent elements in given meanings. Kockelmans notes:

> Noematically considered, the intentional analysis endeavors to make explicit in consciousness all meanings which were only implicitly indicated in the effectively given datum. In fulfilling this function, it takes into account all the essential influences exercised by the internal horizon and the thematic field.[23]

In order to focus attention upon the way meaning is constituted in consciousness, it is necessary to adopt a phenomenological attitude and "bracket" the natural attitude. By "natural attitude" he means the common sense, ordinary assumptions a person makes that things he sees are what they seem to be in everyday experience, that meanings are obvious. The natural attitude, he contends, applies general knowledge to particular cases and then reduces new generalizations, employing logical powers to relate isolated cognitions to one another.

> It progressively takes possession of a reality at first existing for us as a matter of course and as something to be investigated further as regards its extent and content, its elements, its relations and laws.[24]

In Husserl's method, to bracket the natural attitude involves consciously setting it aside in order to give attention to its assumptions and presuppositions. Though there is among critics of his position a difference of opinion regarding the implications of this reduction, which he calls the epoche, Husserl asserts that setting aside the natural attitude need not lead to a denial of the world; it is a step of transcendence taken for methodological purposes in order, finally, to vindicate common sense knowledge by scientific establishment of its transcendental foundation.

Alfred Schütz amplifies on the relation of bracketing to meaning:

> It is only after I "bracket" the natural world and attend only to my conscious experiences within the phenomenological reduction. . .that I become aware of this process of constitution (of a world). . .the problem of objective and subjective meaning. . .only comes to light after the carrying out of the phenomenological reduction.[25]

> . . . meaning is a certain way of directing one's gaze at an item of one's own experience. This item is thus "selected out" and rendered discrete by a reflective Act.[26]

> Meaning does not lie *in* experience. Rather, those experiences are meaningful which are grasped reflectively. The meaning is the way in which the Ego regards its experience. The meaning lies in the attitude of the Ego toward that part of its stream of consciouness which has already flowed by.[27]

Perhaps the most difficult phenomenological step for any educator or philosopher of education is to set aside the common assumption that education is a natural, exact science, to be understood and conducted by the empirical laws of the human sciences. This scientific assumption cannot be examined and evaluated by the procedures of the empirical sciences. But it is just this assumption that needs to be examined and evaluated if one is to clarify the essence of what education is. And, asserts Husserl, this can be done by setting aside these assumptions and reflecting upon one's own intuitive experiences of education in all its modifications. Such a step should lead one then "to grasp what is momentarily perceived in faithful conceptual expression," that is, in description, for "phenomenology is a descriptive discipline" as it studies consciousness in the light of intuition.

Gerd Brand, commenting on this aspect of Husserl's method, writes:

> Intentional analysis is so unlike construction that Husserl called it descriptive. But just as constitution is not construction, neither is description depiction. . . .Description is not something in itself but gets its determination from that which is to be described; and as description it is determined in such a way that it keeps at a distance everything that is not a determination showing what the thing is. . . .Thus, in the description with which it uncovers functioning intentionality, intentional analysis is in its own way active and passive, receptive, descriptive, and constitutive at the same time.[28]

One need not be a disciple of Husserl to recognize the illumination that the basic elements of his method may bring to the study and practice of education. This is, of course, not to suggest that an educator can list his problems and then turn to phenomenology for answers. The open-endedness of the method does mean, however, that as an educator begins to develop the phenomenological attitude he will be open to the possibility of seeing surprising things; new problems may emerge for him.

The perspective which the method offers to educators and to philosophers of education aids in the primary step of discerning the essential character of the educational process, but this is only the beginning of their responsibility. Philosophy of education involves the practice of education as well as an understanding of the field. When one attempts to help learning take place, whether in an informal or a formal setting, one meets a learner who already occupies a life-world of meaning, who is in the middle of his own experience. The steps which Husserl developed for careful reflection of one's own experience also give a helper insight into the way that learner constituted his life-world and ways he might be helped in learning a particular matter.

At the end of the fifth of his *Cartesian Meditations* Husserl acknowledged the criticism that had been leveled at the subjectivism of his position, namely the charge that phenomenology, as a transcendental philosophy, cannot solve the problem of objective knowledge, and lapses into solipsism. Husserl denied the charge on the basis of his extended examination of intersubjectivity in that fifth "meditation." Having given elaborate explication of his view of the way the ego is constituted, he held that part of our primordial intuitive knowledge is that every ego shares an intersubjective community with other egos who are subjects at the same time that they are also "objectivated transcendencies." Husserl did not minimize the problems involved when one holds that "the only conceivable manner in which others can have for me the sense and status of existent others. . .consists in their being constituted *in me* as other."[29]

He noted that while each person by reflection can grasp his own subjectivity first and then as an object secondarily (I can feel one of my hands with the other, etc.), with another subject the sequence is reversed; one is first aware of the other as object and secondarily as alter ego. This awareness comes in part through what Husserl called "pairing" by which "two data are given intuitionally. . .as data appearing with mutual distinctness, they *found phenomenologically* a unity of similarity and thus are always constituted precisely as a pair."[30]

In the "harmonious behavior" one recognizes an "animate organism" belonging to another "world," analogous to one's primordial world. In fact, wrote Husserl:

> It is implicit in the successful apperception of others that their world, the world belonging to their appearance-systems, must be experienced forthwith as the same as the world belonging to my appearance-systems; and this involves an identity of our appearance systems.[31]

Since education, whether informal or formal, is a social, that is, an intersubjective, activity the problems with which Husserl was dealing in this work are of crucial importance to the practice of education. In commenting on the fifth "meditation" Quentin Lauer has made the significance of the issue for education quite explicit.

> It may be that two subjects experience things (or *some* things) in exactly the same way, but there is no way of *knowing* that this agreement is anything but general. Thus, the world is commonly constituted, but the result is a common world with different modalities, so that the one world is for different subjects both the same and different.[32]

Husserl's basic concern in developing phenomenology becomes clear in his work on the difficult problem of intersubjectivity. As Lauer points out:

> The problem of the other, known as a subject, is not confined to phenomenology. Every philosophy must recognize among its field of objects one object which is like none of the others; it is presented not only as known by the knower but also as knowing the knower.[33]

Whenever one person is engaged in helping another person learn something, both helper and learner are involved in all the problems of two subjectivities—a common world but different life-worlds, and attempting to discern the meaning which the other is trying to communicate. Husserl does not deny the reality of objects of the everyday world, but he does sharpen the question which educators must face in every attempt to help learning take place. His method of viewing subject-object problems suggests directions for both educators and philosophers of education.

One of the consequences of such a view should be a deepened awareness of the futility of designing educational programs and methods as though the meaning which a person has constituted in his experience is easily accessible. The realization of the complexity of establishing "commonness" of meaning, even with a common language and the "social construction of reality," between two subjects should challenge the confidence of most contemporary teacher educators that teachers can be trained, that learning can be programmed, that the banking model of education is valid. And the problem is no less for philosophers of education in their attempt to understand one another.

Educators are less in need of a universal, empirically verifiable definition of education than they are of help in reflecting on their experiences of education and their intuition of the meaning which education already has for them and for companion participants. It would be well for educators, in attempting to understand education, to respect what Dorion Cairns offers as the fundamental methodological principle of phenomenology:

> No opinion is to be accepted as philosophical knowledge unless it is

seen to be adequately established by observation of what is seen as itself given "in person." Any belief seen to be incompatible with what is seen to be itself given is to be rejected. Toward opinions that fall in neither class—whether they be one's own or another's—one is to adopt an "official" philosophical attitude of neutrality.[34]

The phenomenological emphasis upon neutrality is particularly important for educators who are under pressure to think in terms of what education should be or do rather than of what it is. This pressure calls for a conscious effort to bracket all presuppositions, standards, norms, and prior commitments of education, not in order to deny their existence or importance, but simply as a methodological move to facilitate genuine intuiting, and to see clearly the presuppositions in their natural attitude. Thus the essence of the process of education can be discerned and can enable analysis and description in its full phenomenological richness.

<h1 style="text-align:center">III</h1>

These communities (such as Church, State, Law) although essentially grounded in psychical realities. . .reveal themselves as a new type of *objectivities of a higher order*. . .which defy all psychologistic and naturalistic misinterpretations. Such are. . .all concrete cultural organizations which as hard realities determine our actual life. . . .All these objective entities must be described in the way in which they come to be presented according to their fundamental types and in their proper order of formation, and *the problem of phenomenological* shaping set and solved in their case.[35]

Husserl did not list education among the "higher orders," yet education is a cultural entity which as a "hard reality" determines many things within its own process and may in some ways "determine our actual life." The phenomenological task of describing education "in the way in which [it] comes to be presented" involves educators in relating to philosophy in a way which differs sharply from their traditional pattern of relationship. As we have already observed, a philosophy of education is usually thought of as a position from which implications or applications may be deduced for educational practice. The assumption of deductive application in education fails to recognize the absurdity of trying to apply an articulated, carefully developed system of thought to an object that has not been identified, described, or characterized. Such an approach only confuses the issue in education because the way a philosophical stance may be related to education depends upon what the essence of education is. The confusion can be allayed only if phenomenological analysis of education precedes any attempt to determine the implications of a philosophic standpoint—existentialist or any other—for the educational domain. Habitual educational thinking, thus, is challenged basically by the methodological priorities of the phenomenological attitude, which questions all educational and philosophical assumptions, not only for the field in general but also for every individual who thinks about or participates in education.

When an educator comes to understand the phenomenological method he does not thereby have a new view of education; he merely has the facility for a new way of viewing education. The phenomenological method is valuable to educators not because it will produce a new consensus, but because it can be employed by each educator in reflecting upon the educational stream in which he stands. Educational activities are marked by a common structure and process, but what education means to each person depends upon the interpreting subject. Education always involves social relations, but differences of interpretation and meaning provide the basis for the continual dialogic interaction which stimulates all levels of educational activity.

Phenomenology provides direction for an activity of reflection rather than a product, a stance. By self-consciously exploring the way the meanings he holds have been constituted in his consciouness, and by reflection upon the direct and indirect deposit of his own experience, an educator has a facility for clarifying what the educational process is for him, as well for reexamining the meaning of his own philosophical commitments. This is not to imply that once such a reexamination is done the basic questions are answered. Since education as a social activity is a dynamic process reflecting historical conditioning, and since each educator is a historical being whose situation and thinking are in continual flux, phenomenology offers a method for repeated reexaminations of the meaning of new developments. And with a clearer understanding of both the subjective roots of his own philosophical position and the nature of the educational process, an educator may be able to interpret more adequately the meaning education has for others and thus be able to help them discern that meaning for themselves.

Once an educator sees the significance of the descriptive-intuitive approach to understanding his philosophy and his views of education, he can use the phenomenological method to expose his own presuppositions and assumptions. When he has developed both the phenomenological attitude and some familiarity with using its methods to reflect upon the meaning of education for himself and others, he may be ready to engage in more extensive analysis of particular aspects of education. The distinctiveness of education can be examined in terms of the meaning it holds for each component of the structure. The perspectives of sponsors, learners, operatives, and constituents overlap and intertwine in a complex of expectations and interventions. Education cannot be encompassed in factual explanations of its organizational structure and movements of the process; these weave a web of meaning for all participants, and intentional analysis offers ways of probing the fascinating variations of meaning. These meanings express implicit philosophical assumptions and commitments to education's symbolic roles. And only as the distinctiveness of the educational process begins to emerge from the fog of confusion can the problems of appropriate objectives and procedures be examined productively.

We have been using the term "educator" to refer to persons involved in the educational process. It is important to see that the term is not limited only to operatives of educational activities. All of the participants who share integrally in the process—sponsors, operatives, learners, constituents—share in shaping that process. The common assumption that education is a "teaching-learning encounter" fails to take into account the fact that while the immediate participants (teacher and learner) come together with many kinds of expectations which express their own interpretations of education, that activity is encompassed and shaped by the myriad diverse expectations of sponsors and constitutents as well. A father's views on education are a formative factor in his daughter's interpretation of what her teacher says in the classroom. The architectural decisions of sponsors are formative factors in the interpretation by a community, or a teacher, or a learner, of the meaning of schooling. Each participant in an educational program acts in terms of what education means to him and what he assumes education means to all other participants.

Thus "educator" can properly refer to any participant, and the intentional analysis of education can explore at each step the complex interaction of diverse perspectives on meaning which are involved in every educational program. The meaning which education has for any individual subject, therefore, necessarily involves an interpretation of the meaning education has for other subjects who share the process because their views are inevitably part of each person's own experience of education. This interconnection of meanings is a major aspect for attention in any analysis of education.

Phenomenology is of direct practicality in its emphasis on discerning what is in one's experience of an object or a state of affairs. This focus and the methodological suggestions for analysing what *is* have value in any social activity where the perspective which a subject brings to a situation is a crucial factor in the appraisal leading to decisions. The emphasis upon what *is* can assume particular importance in education, which is under the pressure of so many normative expectations. Before spelling out all the "worthwhile" things education should be doing, it is necessary to examine how various concepts of "worth" have already been incorporated into educational activities and procedures.

The phenomenological approach, by focusing attention on the persistent problems of meaning, offers practical assistance in this examination, for beyond the facts, skills, and behavior which are in the foreground of educational preoccupation, lie the basic issues of what meaning these have for participants and how meanings develop in the continuing reconstruction process of the consciousness.

The project of phenomenological description remains always unfinished. On the one hand this may be discouraging to those who still secretly long for absolutes and permanence in their worlds, but, on the other hand, it is encouraging to realize that to the extent that one does grasp the meaning and significance of the phenomenological approach, one can begin to employ it at once in educational activities.

REFERENCES

1. M. Merleau-Ponty, *Phenomenology of Perception* (New York: Humanities Press, 1970), p. xix.
2. E. C. Moore, *What is Education?* (New York: Ginn, 1915), p. 251.
3. J. Soltis, *An Introduction to the Analysis of Educational Concepts* (Reading, Massachusetts: Addison-Wesley, 1968), p. 2.
4. I. Scheffler, *The Language of Education* (Springfield, Ill.: Charles C Thomas, 1968), p. 9.
5. E.K. TeHennepe, *Philosophical Investigations* (New York: Macmillan, 1953), par. 129.
6. E.K. TeHennepe, "A Plea for Excuses," in *Philosophical Papers,* J.O. Urmson and G.J. Warnock, eds. (New York: Oxford University Press, 1961), p. 130.
7. E.K. TeHennepe, *Ordinary Language Philosophy: Historical Perspective* (Ann Arbor: University Microfilms, 1969), p. 46.
8. *Ibid.*, p. 41.
9. E. Husserl, *The Idea of Phenomenology,* W. P. Alston and G. Nakhnikian, trs. (The Hague: Martinus Nijhoff, 1964), p. 18.
10. A. Schütz, *Collected Papers, I, The Problem of Social Reality,* M. Natanson, ed. (The Hague: Martinus Nijhoff, 1962), p. 120.
11. P. Ricoeur, *Husserl; An Analysis of His Phenomenology* (Evanston and Chicago: Northwestern University Press, 1967), pp. 3ff.
12. *Ibid.*, p. 4.
13. R. M. Zaner, *The Way of Phenomenology* (New York: Pegasus, 1970), p. 36.
14. *Ibid.*, p. 47.
15. *Ibid.*, p. 50.
16. W. Kaufmann, *Existentialism from Dostoevsky to Sartre* (Cleveland: World, 1970), p. 11.
17. Husserl, *Ideas; General Introduction to Pure Phenomenology,* W.R. Boyce Gibson, tr. (London: Collier-Macmillan, 1969), p. 161.
18. *Ibid.*, p. 174.
19. J.J. Kockelmans, ed., *Phenomenology: The Philosophy of Edmund Husserl and Its Interpretation* (Garden City, N.Y.: Doubleday, 1967), p. 139.
20. Husserl, *Ideas,* p. 108.
21. H. Spiegelberg, *The Phenomenological Movement,* I (The Hague: Martinus Nijhoff, 1969), 107.

22. Husserl, *Ideas*, p. 184.
23. Kockelmans, *op. cit.*, p. 145.
24. Husserl, *The Idea of Phenomenology*, p. 14.
25. Schütz, *The Phenomenology of the Social World*, G. Walsh and F. Lehnert, trs. (Evanston and Chicago: Northwestern University Press, 1967), p. 37.
26. *Ibid.*, p. 42.
27. *Ibid.*, p. 69.
28. Kockelmans, *op. cit.*, pp. 214f.
29. Husserl, *Cartesian Meditations*, D. Cairns, tr. (The Hague: Martinus Nijhoff, 1964), p. 128.
30. *Ibid.*, p. 112.
31. *Ibid.*, p. 125.
32. Q. Lauer, *The Triumph of Subjectivity* (New York: Fordham University Press, 1958), p. 156.
33. *Ibid.*, p. 152.
34. D. Cairns, "An Approach to Phenomenology," in *Philosophical Essays in Memory of Edmund Husserl*, M. Farber, ed. (Cambridge: Harvard University Press, 1940), p. 4.
35. Husserl, *Ideas*, p. 389.

In "The Multiple Realities of Schooling," Clinton Collins draws on his study of the works of Alfred Schütz as well as his studies with Schütz. The essay explores those limits of an objective sociology which are revealed when the social world is viewed from the perspective of an experiencing individual. Collins describes phenomenologically the various levels of reality corresponding to first-, second-, and third-person experiences. From there, he proceeds to analyze how social reality in the schools is constructed from experiences at each of these levels. On the basis of this analysis, he indicates how teachers can facilitate students' awareness that their life-world consists of the interpenetration of multiple realities tied together by the symbols of their own lives, that movement from one level of reality to another enables them to avoid coercion by institutions at any single level of reality, and that schooling can contribute to the exercise of freedom by challenging students to alter their perspective by moving from one level to another.

8 | The Multiple Realities of Schooling

CLINTON COLLINS

PHENOMENOLOGY AND SOCIOLOGY

The Social Construction of Reality,[1] by Peter Berger and Thomas Luckman, has recently called attention to the possibility of a synthesis between the continental tradition in sociology, which includes the thought of Marx, Durkheim, Simmel, and Weber and the phenomenological method for analyzing individual experience which owes its chief formulation to the philosopher, Edmund Husserl. Foremost among the thinkers who have worked toward such a synthesis is the late Alfred Schütz, much of whose writing has become generally known only since his death in 1960, with the publication of three volumes of his *Collected Papers.*[2]

For those accustomed to the positivistic sociology now dominant in American universities it is no doubt difficult to imagine the basis for a synthesis between sociology and phenomenology, since the methodologies associated with those two disciplines appear so disparate. Sociologists typically examine the products of human actions for an underlying structure which will reveal the functions those actions perform within the society.* Phenomenologists begin their inquiry with the same life-experiences, but reflect instead upon the process by which individuals know those experiences. Separating the two disciplines is the classic conflict between macro- and micro-perspectives which sets in opposition those who assign primacy to society with those who assign primacy to the individual.

The need for a synthesis of these two perspectives is most keenly felt in those areas of institutional practice beset by practical difficulties, difficulties emerging at this time of rapid cultural change. It has become an article of faith in recent years that teachers need greater familiarity with the social and behavioral sciences in order to become efficient managers of classroom learning. The world as experienced by the teacher, however, is not the same as the world experienced by the social scientist. The social scientist deliberately adopts the stance of a detached observer of an objective world. In the case of the positivistic social scientist, the objects experienced are apprehended as related by complex bonds of cause and effect, which can be known correlationally in the form of ratios of probability. The teacher, on the other hand, acts as a practitioner in an intersubjective world in which he is attempting to establish mutually beneficial relationships with others.

The world of everyday life in which teacher and students interact is intersubjective in the sense that each person takes the existence of others as persons for granted. That is, each assumes that others are, like himself, endowed with consciousness and motivated by desires which are the basis for their free choices. This assumption is continually reinforced to the extent that the conduct of others is what one would expect a person such as oneself to do in a similar situation. To that extent one person understands the actions of another.

According to Schütz's phenomenological sociology, if the social scientist is to deal meaningfully with the experience of practitioners in everyday life, he must develop an objective frame of reference which honors the subjective point of view. For the phenomenological sociologist, the subjective meanings inherent in the conduct of actors engaged in everyday life are important factors in gaining a comprehensive understanding of interactional relationships, such as that between teachers and students. The phenomenological sociologist, therefore, develops sets of objective concepts (e.g., "types," "roles," etc.) which refer to the intersubjective nature of everyday life. He gathers information from the intersubjective world both by analyzing the subjective reports of others and by engaging in subjective interpretation of social phenomena from the detached perspective of the scientist rather than as an actor in the situation under study.

*Intended here is a description of what has been called the structural-functionalist position.

Philosophy of education, following John Dewey, has urged upon the teacher the need to achieve consistency between the goals he seeks and the means he chooses in their pursuit. Choice of goals and means, however, is limited by the practioner's understanding of the situation in which he chooses. The phenomenological perspective applied to the social reality of the school holds the promise of contributing to the liberation of the practitioner by providing a more comprehensive perspective from which to view his world. The philosopher of education is, therefore, well advised to explore the possibilities of this new perspective.

This essay is an attempt to describe phenomenologically various levels of reality experienced by teachers and students, and thereby to provide a means of seeing continuity between the macro-level of institution and the micro-level of individual experience. Schütz's sociological category of "the stranger"[3] is employed to illuminate the position of the student facing the social reality of the school. In conclusion I argue prescriptively for recognition by teachers of the multiple realities in which individuals live; of how movement from one level of reality to another enables the individual to avoid the coercion by institutions experienced at any single level of reality; and of how education contributes to the individual's awareness of his freedom in this respect.

ON MULTIPLE REALITIES

Schütz credits William James with having shown that a person's sense of what is real varies according to what he is attending to. That is to say, it is not only the aspect of the world which changes as the individual's involvement alters, but, to the extent that by his attention he constitutes his world, individuals may be described as moving from one world to another, or from one order of reality to another. According to James, "Each world *whilst it is attended to* is real after its own fashion; only the reality lapses with the attention."[4]

Both James and Schütz assert that, among the multiple realities in which a person lives, one is paramount. For James the paramount reality is that of the senses and of physical things; for Schütz it is "everyday life," the world of physical objects and events as they become part of the commonsense knowledge shared by members of a cultural community.[5]

Schütz's description of the paramount reality, however, does not take into account important divisions within the individual's experience of everyday life, divisions based on the different perspectives from which he experiences it. The individual experiences everyday life alternately from the first-person perspective, the second-person perspective, and the third-person perspective. The first-person perspective yields the inner reality of the stream of consciousness, explored by William James and made the principal voice of many twentieth-century novels. The second-person perspective is that of partners in dialogue. In dialogue, two people continuously reconstruct a reality that is both shared and private, and which expands geometrically, each partner contributing a dimension in contrast to the straight-line increments occuring in a stream of consciousness. Martin Buber is the foremost analyst of this level of reality.[6] The third-person perspective is that of people when they are engaged preeminently in institutional life, in which they relate to each other on the basis of certain shared expectations regarding roles. The mode of the first-person voice can be characterized as "phenomenological," in a nontechnical sense; the mode of the second is "dialectical," again not in a technical sense; and the mode of the third can be called "political," in the broadest sense.

The above is the kind of classification one gets by looking at reality from the perspective of the lived-world of the person prior to conditions under which objectivity becomes an issue. Objectivity becomes an issue at the political level. In the stream of consciousness one's grasp of reality is not liable to disconfirmation. Things are experienced in the process of becoming, but what they become is not taken as evidence against what they have been. Neither is there a need for a criterion of objectivity in dialogue: reality becomes whatever the partners can confirm each other in. Socrates, for example, describes the dialectic method as two people helping each other to see, to think, and to act. The wise man who "sees a thing when he is alone," therefore, "goes about straightway seeking until he finds someone to whom he can show his discoveries, and who may confirm him in them."[7]

Emerging from a dialogue, however, the partners take different perspectives to their relationships with others outside the dialogue, that is, to the third parties of the dialogue. It is when former partners give discrepant reports of their relationship to a third party that their objectivity comes into question. In Edward Albee's play, *Who's Afraid of Virginia Woolf?*,[8] for example, the evenly matched protagonists, George and Martha, interrupt the dialogue of their marriage in order to win the allegiance of a new couple on campus to their respective personal points of view. To George and Martha the reality of their son's existence is not in question until each parades himself as a parent before the other couple. At that point objective truth becomes the concern of Nick, their guest. The audience is compelled to see the situation almost simultaneously from within the dialogic relationship of George and Martha, and from the third person perspective of Nick, the biologist, trying to grasp the objective reality. Nick's wife has found what is perhaps as good a defense as her husband, the objective scientist, since she remembers nothing that has been said or done. Blissful ignorance, when one is belatedly made privy to the dialogue of a contentious husband and wife who have been together for twenty-three years. Nevertheless, the play has something positive to say concerning Buber's life of dialogue: the reality which George and Martha experience together is more palpable than that pursued by scientists.

Typically, introduction of objective reality results in a shift of perspective from the experiencing individual to that of an hypothesized neutral observer of that objective reality. If the active individual's perspective is retained, however, the quest for scientific objectivity can be seen as pursued for political purposes. By means of the appeal to objectivity the person both protects himself from the dialogical constructions of partnerships to which he is not privy, and gains some measure of control in that domain in which each of us exists as a third part to relationships which are potentially threatening to us. The person with expert knowledge of a zone of reality to which others will accede, in spite of what is experienced in their stream of consciousness or in their dialogic relationships, thereby gains considerable power over the everyday affairs of men. His power is further enhanced in a society in which people feel alienated because of the impersonality of most of their social relationships, so that objectivity becomes their chief source of a sense of security.*

Although it is a defense against powerlessness, scientific objectivity can cause alienation to the person who pursues it. There is a tendency to orient oneself to an objective world by constructing a depersonalized version of oneself; that is, to play down the importance of one's stream of consciousness and of one's dialogic relationships, and present oneself to others as a predictable object in a predictably objective world.

Consider, for example, the teacher who bears the burden of knowledge from the social sciences regarding socioeconomic class differences among his students, and how this affects the probability of their success as students. The teacher has gained from his knowledge some measure of political power by which to control the potentially explosive situation created when children from different socioeconomic class backgrounds are placed in competition with each other. At strategic points he can forestall the competition or mitigate its effects.† If the teacher becomes caught up in his role as classroom manager, however, he may lose sight of his relationship to individual students. There is, as Buber argues,[9] at least the possibility of educational dialogue between student and teacher. This may be forfeited if the teacher identifies too closely with the political role which his objective knowledge is designed to facilitate.

By its size and form of organization the typical public school classroom is a political arena in which the teacher's primary task is to maintain leadership and control. The increasing emphasis on the teacher's utilization of expert

---

*It is circular to argue that one pursues objectivity because that is where the truth lies. The truth is what a person trusts (I owe this definition to the noted philosopher, Horace Kallen); it is therefore implicit in his actions.

†A primary reason many teachers favor homogeneous grouping of students according to scholastic ability is probably in order to reduce the degree of social-class difference among members of a class, and thereby make their political task as classroom managers less difficult.

knowledge from the social and behavioral sciences is in part a recognition of the political facts of life in the schools. However, it is difficult to move from the political relationship to one of dialogue. To be sure, the teacher retains other areas of life in which dialogue is possible; alienation is never total. But its presence in the world of work lessens the individual's commitment to his career, and provides an example of alienated labor to the young, who are to that degree discouraged from career commitments of their own.

DIALOGUE AND TYPIFICATION

Our inquiry into the social reality of teachers and students begins with the assumption that there are multiple realities which interpenetrate in everyday life. One reality should not be regarded, however, as a progression from the previous reality. Individuals live alternately in these different realities throughout their lives. Nevertheless there is a sense in which the dialogic reality is temporally primary in an individual's biography. The individual comes to conscious awareness in dialogue with significant others.[10] It is the primary socialization of the child in face-to-face relationships with the significant others of his home and family that forms the prototype for all subsequent social relationships, in the sense that all other social relationships can be interpreted as derived from it.[11] Dialogue is also a primary stage in the development of the "social self," that is, the self which is available to the individual's stream of consciousness. George H. Mead offers what has become a classic account of how the individual's self-awareness emerges in reflection upon his communicative interactions with significant others.[12]

The life of the child in the face-to-face relationships of the home takes on the character of routine, that is, the child learns to make typical responses in typical situations in which others are acting in typical fashion. Even in the face-to-face relationship, the child apperceives the significant others in his social environment by means of these typifications.[13] The typifications of other persons serve to hold in experience those whom one has lived with in dialogue when they are no longer present in face-to-face situations.

Alfred Schütz gives the example of the young soldier separated from home and family for the first prolonged period.[14] At home the soldier is part of a primary group* in which the partners experience one another as unique personalities sharing in a "vivid" present, each other's plans, hopes, and anxieties, so that each becomes a part of the personal history of the other. When the soldier leaves home, the vivid present is replaced by memories. By means of typifications, he keeps the other as part of his experience, but he loses the sense of the other's uniqueness which was part of the face-to-face relationship. The personality of the other is no longer experienced as a whole, but is remembered in the form of typical responses in typical situations.

*Schütz took the term "primary group" from the social theory of Charles Cooley.

When the absent soldier writes a letter home, he addresses himself to his typification of the family member.

The former child who has left the home often longs for the reestablishment of these primary relationships, but they cannot be reinstated as they were, because the time in between has altered what is relevant to each of the partners. The shared plans and hopes which were the result of dialogue have been replaced in each individual's experience with a new set of expectations which have not been shared. Dialogue must begin anew; the events in the lives of the partners which took place outside it are accessible to the dialogue only in the form of typifications.

Typifications provide the individual with recipe knowledge* by which he can negotiate in the common-sense reality of everyday life. Outside the primary group most of his relationships are truncated, that is, the sense of a shared present of two unique persons does not emerge. Instead the individual relates routinely to the other as typified in a situation experienced as typical. This is the substance of relationships experienced from the third-person perspective.

UNDERSTANDING THE SUBJECTIVITY OF THE OTHER

The initial experience of relationship is one of dialogue. Therefore, the individual, in his typification of the other, is aware that the actions of the other which he apprehends as typical are expressions of a conscious subject like himself. The individual apprehends the other as a subject, rather than merely as an object, that is, as an independent consciousness which is an autonomous source of motivation. He therefore understands the actions of the other as having been chosen. Max Weber's concept of *Verstehen*[15] refers to this understanding of the subjective purposes of the other as expressed in his actions in everyday life. Even when one's knowledge of the other is in the form of typifications, the typifications refer to a human subject.

One's awareness of the subjectivity of the other is based on the imaginative projection of oneself into the situation of the other (his "here" and "now"). This is done on the assumption that his motives are similar to what one's own would be given the same situation. A more reflective, imaginative leap is required in order also to take into account the historical-biographical situation of the other, yet full understanding of his subjective motives would require understanding of his biography in as full detail as it is accessible to him. As a consequence, any determinate understanding of the subjective motives of the other is not possible. Awareness of this limitation is itself built into one's understanding of the other.

Typification of the other's actions and motives is a means of minimizing

---

*"Recipe knowledge" is Schütz's term for habitual knowledge which governs practical affairs in the commonsense world of everyday life.

this indeterminacy in order to permit routinized interactions to go forward unreflectively. But the other is not only one whose actions may be understood as typical and, therefore, familiar; he is also that which is fundamentally different from oneself: he is *radically* other. It is this which makes the *Verstehen* of the social world distinct from scientific explanations of the natural world. Animistic belief, by bestowing subjectivity on objects of the natural, as distinct from the social world, credits those objects with the same kind of radical otherness that persons have as originating points of volition.* In like manner, the individual does not understand his own actions as if they were completely determined. The active self is a partial stranger to the self known in reflection, possessing the radical otherness of an independent source of volition.†

In institutional life the radical otherness of the other becomes a threat to one's sense of the institution's cohesiveness. The individual cannot, therefore, participate as a whole in the common world of the institution. There is a part of the individual that remains aloof from identification with any group. By holding the self aloof from total involvement in the institution, the individual establishes a basis of opposition between himself and the institution. The institution is known in experience as a form of social organization to be used and at the same time held at bay, so that it is not allowed to usurp one's individuality. As a result the institution becomes reified, that is, it becomes seen as an object having an existence apart from the lives of the people who participate in it.

Reification of institutions is an extreme form of objectivation.[16] The individual comes to think of the social world from the macro-perspective, in which the workings of institutions take on a reality that is seen to dwarf the lives of individuals, including oneself. The fact that institutions are sustained by the actions of individuals is not forgotten, but from the extreme, objective perspective, the actions by which individuals sustain their institutions are seen merely as typical performances by typical actors. Subjectivity is thereby lost sight of, the individual becomes understood as subsumed under the institutional roles he alternately occupies.

The macro-perspective, in which institutions are reified and individuals subsumed under them as performing typical roles, must eventually give way to dialogue and a return of awareness of the subjectivity of the other. Unless a social science is available which can establish a continuity between these two perspectives, however, the institution and the other must exist for us in

---

*In this sense, human volition, though it is sometimes interpreted as one among other kinds of causes of action, differs from other kinds of causes in that it exists apart from prior determination. Individual volition is not liable to prior determination because up to the point of action the individual retains the power to say, "no." See J.-P. Sartre, *Being and Nothingness* (New York: Washington Square, 1966), H. Barnes, tr.

†Mead's concept of "I," the human actor, is never fully accessible to the concept of the self given to awareness, i.e., the "me."

separate realms of meaning. As a consequence, when prescriptions for the education of the young are based on social science inquiry into the institution of schooling, they are likely to overlook much of the meaning which the experience of education has for the individual teacher or student.

Alfred Schütz has endeavored to establish continuity between our understanding of the other and our knowledge of institutions, by a dialectical mode of inquiry in which the same situation is considered alternately from the perspective of the subjective experience of an actor in the life-world, and from the objective perspective of the phenomenological sociologist.* In order to illustrate the application of Schütz's method to the understanding of the schools as institutions, we shall interpret how one type of social situation which Schütz has analyzed finds its analogue in schooling.

THE STUDENT AS STRANGER

In sociological literature, schooling is traditionally treated as an institution which provides secondary socialization for the young, in contrast to the primary socialization provided in the home.[17] The family provides the young person with his initial orientation to social reality. Unless the school comes to supplant the orientation acquired in the home—which happens only in rare instances to individuals with compelling reasons for abandoning their world of primary socialization—the effect of the school on the orientation of the young is necessarily superficial in comparison with that of the home. Generally, schooling is not accompanied by the strong emotional identification with significant others which characterizes learning in the home.

Berger and Luckman see a need for teachers to make their teaching relevant by linking the subject matter to what the child has learned in the home, since "an internalized reality is already there persistently 'in the way' of new internalizations."[18] In actuality, however, teachers make relatively little effort to make their subject matter relevant, despite their awareness of the strong influence of the home. Instead, there is a calculated but largely tacit effort on the part of teachers to socialize the child to a world different from that of the home. The attempt is made to socialize without the warm emotional identification which is characteristic of the home.

Experiences in the home teach the child to function effectively in face-to-face relationships with significant others, in particular, how to communicate with them in order to share a common world. The school, however, is intended to provide a different kind of learning which pertains to a world quite different from that of face-to-face relationships. It does not

*Like the actor in the life-world, the phenomenological sociologist engages in *Verstehen* of the subjective purposes of the other. As a detached scientist, however, he objectivizes his understanding by setting it in a frame of reference organized around objective concepts such as "social role." Roles are thereby objectivized as containing the element of the subjective purposes of the actor.

overstate the case to say that the principal intent of schooling is to socialize the child to the objective world, which, as previously noted, is the third-person world of political life.

Prior to school experience, the child lives in what Jean Piaget describes as an "egocentric world."[19] Schooling is an attempt to force him into awareness of a larger world. He is thereby prevented from living his life on the level of the common-sense, recipe knowledge which is taken for granted in the world of primary socialization. He is forced to objectivize, that is, to put distance between himself and the world in order to see it from a reflected perspective. Thus, schooling alters the emotional climate of the home in order to induct the young person into the political world of third persons, that is, the world of others with whom one is not in dialogue.

Contrary to Paul Goodman's famous dictum, however, the process of schooling is not accurately described as one of "brainwashing."[20] In most instances little attempt is made at radical revision or alteration of the orientation given in the home. If schools attempted such brainwashing they would expect to lose the support of parents upon which their continuance depends. But parents generally welcome the exposure of their children to the reality of the objective, political world. They consider that part of their success as parents depends upon their children's ability to function effectively in that world.

The child leaves the home and enters school as a stranger to the objective world for which schooling serves as a rite of initiation. The child is not typically regarded as coming as a stranger to the school, either by his teachers or by other adults. The process of moving from home to school seems so natural to adults that typically they do not question the lack of continuity between the two. Only the child is aware of the trauma of the transition, but since it occurs at an early stage in his cognitive development, he does not think beyond the conventional wisdom which regards the abrupt shift as natural. A person can be an unrecognized stranger, however, as Albert Camus illustrates with his famous novel.[21]

In his discussion of the stranger as an ideal type,* Schütz confines his analysis to the adult trying to gain acceptance or tolerance from a group he approaches.[22] Since adults generally lack empathy for young children in the kind of situations which came too early in their own experience for them to recall, it is instructive to construct an analogy between the stranger as described by Schütz and the child entering school.

One of the clearest indications that the child enters the school as a stranger

*Schütz says of Weber's sociological category, the ideal type, that it is a means of introducing objectivity into the social scientist's understanding of actors in the social world. Each is typed apart from his unique personal characteristics, his individuality, and is regarded anonymously as always the same and homogeneous. No matter how many specific people are subsumed under the type, it corresponds to no one in particular. It is in this sense that Weber labelled such types "ideal."

can be seen in his position as an outsider in relationship to teachers as a group. Berger and Luckman make the observation about institutional life generally that, "outsiders have to be kept out" by means such that the legitimacy of the institution itself is not questioned by those excluded. They indicate several techniques by which this is done, including "intimidation," "mystification," and "manipulation of prestige symbols," and add that, "insiders, on the other hand, have to be kept in."[23] In just this way the majority of teachers want their students to be mystified, and want their colleagues to join with them in an effort to maintain the mystification. They fear that those colleagues who relax discipline in the classroom weaken their own position as authorities.

The beginning teacher, too, enters the school as a stranger whose loyalty is doubtful. But his route to admission to the in-group is clear; in contrast to the student, he loses his status as stranger as soon as he is able to internalize his membership in the community of teachers. This requires distancing himself from students.*

No matter how sincerely he wishes to join the in-group of teachers, therefore, the student retains his status as stranger throughout his school career. He remains in preparation for admission to adult culture—which the teacher represents—until commencement.

As in Schütz's analysis, the stranger is a person who, from the standpoint of the approached group, is a person without a history.[24] From the point of view of his personal biography, the student's knowledge of history is limited to the cultural pattern of his home group. The school's contribution is an introduction to objective history, which bears only a slight resemblance to the history he has known in the family group.

The child has learned about school in the home prior to his arrival there. But despite the parents' first-hand knowledge of school, their efforts to prepare the child for schooling resemble nothing so much as the manner in which members of a secret society describe the initiation process to those seeking admission. Schooling is something they have passed through, but they are vague about those details which would convey the effect of the experience. If they feel that they were successful in school, they expect a similar result for their child; if they feel that they failed at schooling, they fear his similar failure. In either event, however, they have little concrete advice to give him to aid his adjustment to the radically new environment.

The situation is analogous to that of the stranger who has been given a picture of the foreign group by members of his home group. The picture is inadequate, as Schütz observes, because it "serves merely as a handy scheme

---

*Jonathan Kozol reports that, as a beginning teacher, he did not do more to help students he felt were victimized by the school because he was more concerned with the judgments of his fellow teachers, who cautioned him not to become "too close" to his students. See *Death at an Early Age* (New York: Bantam, 1966).

for interpreting the foreign group and not as a guide for interaction between the two groups."[25] As a result, his confidence in his knowledge gained at home is shaken. He comes to feel that a new point of orientation is needed in order to comprehend his new social environment. He is a "border case," and therefore, "no longer permitted to consider himself at the center of his social environment."[26]

Schütz's analysis of the stranger was not written with the school child in mind. Yet nothing so characterizes the experience of schooling for the individual as the pressure he feels to give up the egocentric orientation to the world in which he has lived, unchallenged, in the home. The world he encounters from its periphery on entering school seems vast and impersonal by comparison.

The cultural pattern taught in the schools, which for educated adults represents a consistent whole, falls to pieces in the initial experience of the child. He is faced with isolated parts of a world which in many cases cannot be translated into elements of his own previous experience. He is a long way from being able to consider his interpretation of adult culture as accurate, since he does not experience it from the inside. Before he is able to do so, he may have abandoned the task as one reserved for intellectuals.

For the child, life in the home has come to be lived on the basis of recipe knowledge, that is, in most social situations the child is aware of the appropriate response, simply through force of habit. The cultural pattern of the home provides recipes for typical solutions to typical problems, involving typical actors. In such situations the subjective purposes of other actors need not be understood by the child in order for him to obtain his desired results. He need only conduct himself in the manner of the anonymous type.[27] To be fed, for example, he need only behave in the typical way which the type "parent" expects of the type "hungry child." The scheme is available for common use, regardless of characteristics peculiar to the individuals involved.

Contrast with this the child's difficulties in adjusting to the regimented eating policies of the school. Again Schütz's description of the stranger applies to the situation of the child in school. Since he "has not brought within his grasp the whole system of the cultural pattern," he finds himself "puzzled by its inconsistency, incoherence, and lack of clarity."[28] For the child, the cultural pattern of the school is, as is that of the approached group for the stranger, "not a shelter but a field of adventure, . . .not an instrument for disentangling problematic situations but a problematic situation itself and one hard to master."[29]

One result of this situation for the student, as stranger, is that his loyalty remains in doubt throughout the course of his schooling. The student, like the stranger, remains a "marginal man," "a cultural hybrid on the verge of two different patterns of group life, not knowing to which of them he belongs."[30] To members of the in-group, his teachers, he seems ungrateful to the extent that "he refuses to acknowledge that the cultural pattern offered to him grants him shelter and protection." From the standpoint of the student, however, the culture of the school will not become a shelter until he has completed his schooling and is regarded as an adult. For the present, school is " a labyrinth in which he has lost all sense of his bearings."[31] As much as he would like to trust the teacher as a guide, he typically finds that the teacher does not trust him. His feeling of disorientation is regarded by the teacher as a willful refusal to acknowledge what the school has to offer.

There is, however, a positive side to the student's being placed in the position of a stranger. Since the cultural pattern of the school constitutes a problematic situation for the child, in contrast to life in the home, it forces him to become objective in his understanding of the culture of the school. By bitter experience he learns the limits of "thinking as usual." He is tacitly aware of what Schütz himself experienced as a stranger, that "a man may lose his status, his rules of guidance, and even his history" when he ventures beyond his home group; and that, therefore, there is no guarantee attached to what he comes to consider "the normal way of life.[32]

As a professor in a German university when the Nazis came to power, Schütz faced the task of making a new life for himself in America, where university positions were difficult to find.* By reflecting upon these extreme circumstances Schütz became aware of the kind of lesson faced by all strangers, one to which we willingly submit our children at a time when they have relatively much less to lose in terms of status and history. Schütz is aware that the forced objectivity of the stranger is a part of all genuinely educative experiences. He notes that "strangeness and familiarity are not limited to the social field but are general categories of our interpretation of the world."[33] One's sense of strangeness invites inquiry, which goes forward until a feeling of familiarity with one's surroundings is restored.†

Because he stops short of tracing the social origins of this process of inquiry, however, Schütz makes no reference to the role of schooling in initiating the use of the method of inquiry. Yet it is in the schools that most people experience for the first time the kind and degree of strangeness which must be dealt with, which cannot be avoided by hiding under mother's apron. Nevertheless, it would seem the case that many of those who attend schools never learn to adapt successfully when placed in the position of a stranger and therefore do not engage in the type of problem-solving which John Dewey sees as central to education.

In many cases the student is never able to understand what is expected of

---

*In New York, Schütz eventually joined the faculty of the University in Exile, which consisted primarily of refugees from German universities, and which later became the nucleus for the Graduate Faculty of the New School for Social Research.

†Schütz's theory of inquiry, stated here in capsule form, bears considerable resemblance to that developed by John Dewey in *How We Think* (New York: Heath, 1910; rev. ed. 1933).

him in school. Instead, he comes to view his status as an outsider as the result of some personal failing on his part, or the result of his membership in a group commonly stereotyped as inferior. In such cases the student's experience of strangeness leads not to objectivity, but to frustration and defeat. We need, therefore, as clear an understanding as possible of the desirable function performed by the student's experience of strangeness.

The student is, in Schütz's terminology, a stranger, but a special type of stranger whose closest analogue is a person undergoing initiation. Most initiation rituals appear ludicrous to those not engaged in the ritual. In a similar way, schooling is often ridiculed by nonparticipants, even by those who have experienced the initiation and would not think of denying it to their own children. Similarly, most initiation rituals are justified as instructive to the novice—the chief value of the instruction being that, when effective, it results in the novice putting positive value on membership in the group to which he aspires. What adults want from the young is for them to recognize the value of the established culture. The surest means to achieve this is by an elaborate process of initiation.

Since the child is not given the choice of aspiring to membership in adult culture, the initiation aspects of schooling are left tacit, and emphasis is placed instead on the benefit to be derived by the student from schooling. It would be impossible, however, for the student to make sense of his schooling experience if he operated exclusively on the assumption that it is for his benefit. It does not take the student long to realize this, but it leaves him in doubt as to the actual nature of the role he is expected to perform. His sense of strangeness in the school impels him to objective analysis of his social surroundings, which is a necessary condition for gaining awareness of his freedom to transcend the role. Unfortunately, the suppression of awareness of the actual nature of the role on the part of teachers and parents often results in their failure to support the freedom of the individual in this regard.

There are two possible undesirable results of schooling where there is failure to understand the nature of the student's expected role: anti-intellectualism and conformist intellectualism. In the first case the student may reject the culture of the school as irrelevant to the basic realities of life, contributing further to the anti-intellectualism prevalent in American society among those who have had unsuccessful experiences in school. In the second case, the student may become a conformist to traditional intellectualism. His desire to make himself acceptable to the point where the school becomes a haven may cause him to avoid directing criticism toward his own experiences in school, with the result that he is unable to make a creative contribution.

EDUCATION FOR FREEDOM

The social reality of the school is a political one, since instruction is almost invariably carried on in groups of three or more. In this respect school serves as a means of inducting the young into political life, i.e., to life in groups in which one has no effective dialogue with many of the others to whom he must relate.

From the perspective of the individual student, however, the quality of educational experience is likely to depend on what he considers to be his dialogic relationship to the teacher. It is useful to recall Schütz's contention that the face-to-face dialogue forms the prototype for all social relationships. As a consequence, removal from the dialogue with significant others serves as a source of motivation to the individual to try to recreate the conditions for dialogue.

It is therefore advantageous for the teacher in a group setting to maintain the possibility of dialogue with each individual in the group. Should the teacher evidently focus in dialogue on a single student in front of the other students, the latter are likely to feel excluded, or even that the dialogue is at their expense as third parties.* If, on the other hand, the teacher reveals to the group privileged information he has gained in dialogue with an individual student, he incurs the enmity of that student, who is not in position to make as effective political use of the prior dialogue between him and the teacher.

Successful dialogue necessarily excludes all third parties, except where it occurs in ritualized form in group settings. Examples of this, however, are not actual dialogues, and might better be referred to as Dionysian experiences. One of the most effective means of teaching is the creation by the teacher of such a "Dionysian relationship" among members of the class.† The term "Dionysian" derives from the ancient Greek tragedies dedicated to the god Dionysos. Dionysian events are those which, like the tragedies, are ritualized, religious or quasi-religious,†† group experiences. As in most group religious worship, a liturgy is followed. In the case of the contemporary theatre, for example, there is a ritual in which the audience oscillates between silent attention to the players and applause for the performance at points of conclusion.

The teacher who makes use of techniques taken from the drama can establish a similar liturgy of class participation. He can at times involve students as performers, or at other times give what amounts to a solo performance. The ritual of dramatic performances catches the individuals up in a we-feeling which somewhat resembles that of the dialogue. The we-feeling is sustained by the imaginative creation of a fourth-person-as-common-outsider; that is, the other who is absent from the event and, therefore, left out of the mystery experienced by those involved. To the

---

*This is Jean-Paul Sartre's theme in his play, *No Exit.*

†Good examples of the Dionysian approach to teaching are found in David Denton's *Existential Reflections on Teaching* (North Quincy, Mass.: Christopher, 1972).

††I regard the category "quasi-religious" very broadly as including such events as the theatre, football games, or sensitivity groups.

extent that a teacher succeeds in creating a Dionysian relationship among members of a class, the students' sense of strangeness is reduced.

By means of ritual, the Dionysian group avoids fragmenting into dialogues which will create political tensions and destroy the we-feeling of the group. The participant in the Dionysian experience gives up his individuality, therefore, and engages in a typical ritualized performance. The experience of the Dionysian event is educative, providing the example of an effective mode of political life (given the presence of a charismatic leader). The loss of self-individuation entailed is typically balanced by emphasis on the Apollonian. In the manner of the oracle to Apollo at Delphi, the Apollonian outlook urges self-understanding upon the individual. Once again, it is the dialogue which is the prototype of social experience. In this case it is the social self which is created out of the elements of the dialogue.* By means of internalized dialogue, the individual stimulates his own articulation of purposes and plans, so that his stream of consciousness takes on a progressive dimension. It is by becoming a significant other in dialogue with the student that the teacher contributes to the student's self-awareness. There is the possibility, then, that a teacher can influence the education of a student on any of the three levels of reality of everyday life.

The highest purpose of education, however, is to be found neither in the individual's performance in dialogue, nor in either the Dionysian or the Apollonian modes. Education is the mode of living most conducive to the liberation of the individual. Liberation occurs when the individual becomes aware that the world is many, as well as one. His experience as a stranger in the school is the first step in this direction, providing that his awareness is encouraged and not simply frustrated.

Teachers can facilitate the student's awareness that his life-world consists of the interpenetration of multiple realities tied together by the symbols of his own biography. It is the freedom of movement from one level of reality to another which enables the individual to avoid coercion, by other people or by institutions, at any single level of reality. The individual has the freedom to join or to leave the Dionysian group; to engage in or disengage from dialogue with another; or to live at will in his stream of consciousness.

The maximum contribution the school can make to the education of the individual is that, once having challenged him with the primal experience of strangeness upon his induction into the political group, it can reverse the perspective from the political sphere to that of the subjectivity of the individual. Institutionalization provides means for avoiding awareness of the subjectivity, and hence the radical otherness, of the other, by focusing exclusively on the objective roles people perform within the institution. Thus, it is important to preserve dialogue within the institution, since it is in dialogue alone that a person can, without threat, be aware of the radical otherness of the other.

*See note 13.

REFERENCES

1. P. L. Berger and T. Luckman, *The Social Construction of Reality: A Treatise on the Sociology of Knowledge* (Garden City, N.Y.: Doubleday, 1966).
2. A. Schütz, , *Collected Papers,* I (The Hague: Martinus Nijhoff, 1962); II (1964); III (1966).
3. Schütz, "The Stranger: An Essay in Social Psychology," *op. cit.,* II, 91-105.
4. W. James, *Principles of Psychology,* II (New York: W. W. Norton, 1890), ch. 21, 293.
5. Schütz, "On Multiple Realities," *op. cit.,* I, 207-259.
6. M. Buber, *I and Thou* (New York: Charles Scribner's Sons, 1960; German edition, 1923) R.G. Smith, tr.
7. Plato, *Protagoras,* 348, B. Jowett, tr.
8. E. Albee, *Who's Afraid of Virginia Woolf?* (New York: Atheneum, 1962).
9. Buber, *Between Man and Man* (New York: Macmillan, 1965), R. G. Smith tr., ch. III.
10. This theory of the ontogenesis of mind and self, along with the term "significant other," is taken from G.H. Mead, *Mind, Self, and Society* (Chicago: University of Chicago Press, 1934).
11. Schütz, "The Homecomer," *op. cit.,* II, 106-119.
12. Mead, *op. cit.,* particularly the section on the self.
13. See particularly Schütz, *The Phenomenology of the Social World,* G. Walsh and F. Lehnert, trs. (Evanston and Chicago: Northwestern University Press, 1967).
14. Schütz, "The Homecomer," *op. cit.*
15. For Schütz's use of Weber's concept of *Verstehen* see particularly, "Concept and Theory Formation in the Social Sciences," *Collected Papers,* I, 48-66.
16. Berger and Luckman, *op. cit.,* p. 89.
17. Cf. Berger and Luckman, *op. cit.,* pp. 138 ff.
18. *Ibid.,* p. 143.
19. J. Piaget, *The Origin of Intelligence in the Child* (London: Routledge and Kegan Paul, 1953).
20. P. Goodman, *Compulsory Miseducation* (New York: Vintage, 1962), p. 67.
21. Camus, *The Stranger,* S. Gilbert, tr. (New York: Vintage, 1946).
22. Schütz, "The Stranger," *op. cit.,* p. 91.
23. Berger and Luckman, *op. cit.,* p. 87.
24. Schütz, "The Stranger," *op. cit.,* p. 97.
25. *Ibid.,* p. 98.
26. *Ibid.,* p. 99.
27. *Ibid.,* p. 102.
28. *Ibid.,* p. 103.
29. *Ibid.,* p. 104.
30. *Idem.*
31. *Ibid.,* p. 105.
32. *Ibid.,* p. 104.
33. *Ibid.,* p. 105.

ASPECT D

Aspect D is the last surface of the configuartion explored in this work. Here, the techniques of existentialism and phenomenology focus sharply on two questions having immediate relevance, that of time in the context of schooling and that of educational research and theory. Professor Troutner's "Time and Education" presents a description of time as it is typically thought of in schools, that is, as clock or mathematical or objective time; the contrast is drawn between that conception, time orientation of different cultures, and the student's own sense of time. Troutner, then, does a phenomenology of time, basing his work primarily, though not exclusively, on Heidegger. His exploration of school time illustrates the practical bearings which can result from phenomenological description and explication of educational phenomena.

9 | Time and Education

LEROY TROUTNER

I

Time is one of the most important ingredients in the education of a person, yet there has been very little research, either philosophical or sociological, on the general topic of time and education. Why this is so may not be too difficult to understand. Perhaps it is so close to us that we cannot see it. As the late Professor Quillen often reflected, "If fish were social scientists the last thing they would discover would be water." That which is the closest is the farthest away, and nothing is closer to us than time: in fact, man is time. Or perhaps we are simply too busy to take the time to examine time. When we are young and healthy, we seem to possess a surfeit of time; much like air, there is so much of it we do not notice it. It is only in extremity, so it seems, when we have little time left, that we realize how important time is. Whatever the reason, or more accurately, whatever the excuse, now that the existential phenomenologist has rendered explicit the basic structure of lived time, I think it is high time for us to examine the significance of time for education.

A glimpse into history tells us that it is also high time to discuss the connection between time and education. There is considerable evidence from Paleolithic culture to suggest that from early times man has always experienced some time sense.[1] For example, it is reasonable to inter that the making of tools presupposes some sort of primordial understanding of the three temporal moments; past, present, and future. We see the primitive toolmaker, instead of indulging himself in the leisure of the present, fashioning the hand ax or the arrowhead, according to his past experience with such objects, with the intention of using them on some future occasion. An even more significant piece of evidence of the time consciousness of Early Man can be seen in his cave art. Much of the wonderful fresco work found in the Pyrenees and in the Dordogne illustrates Cro-Magnon man's "disposition for intelligent planning, involving as it does, anticipation of the future in the light of the past and the application of present effort to future ends."[2] Also, there is that intimate and omnipresent knowledge of birth and death that invests the life of each individual with a temporal significance. After all, man is mortal and each individual can see the termination of his life no matter how far in the future he may hope it to be. Awareness of a time sense, then, involving the three temporal moments has always been a built-in characteristic of man's lived reality.

Still, though man, by virtue of being human, seems always to have possessed a temporal awareness, his attitude toward time down through the ages has not remained constant. Any inquiry into the nature of time cannot be separated from the many forms of its interpretation throughout the history of thought. As with all other of man's ideas and attitudes, our contemporary conception of time is the product of a long intellectual and social development. And it is one of the major theses of this essay that our contemporary attitude toward time is significantly different than it was, say, 200 years ago. Moreover, it is because of this difference in attitude that we need to make a thorough investigation into the contemporary meaning of time. I am referring to our ever-increasing tendency to live time in what Heidegger would call the inauthentic mode. In its simplest formulation this means living time as a succession of now moments, a temporal mode that is best illustrated by the movements of the clock, at the same time assuming that this kind of "objective" or "standard" time, rather than man's existential awareness of lived time with its three temporal moments, is the most primordial. Moreover, this contemporary attitude toward time, which is so prevalent in America, is intimately connected with the increasing atomization and fragmentation of life, a process which inevitably results in loss of significance and meaning. This, it seems to me, is one of the most important insights to be found in the existential phenomenological analysis of time.

Throughout the history of thought, particularly from the time of Plato down to the modern era, man has tended to see "reality," including his own, in terms of the being of a thing ("it *is*") rather than in terms of the being of man ("I *am*"). As a result, the being (or the to-be-ness) of man has come to be understood in terms of a substance, as a natural object like other natural objects or things. This same tendency, which, incidentally, Marx also detected in his study of capitalism,[3] can be seen in the way we comport ourselves in ordinary, everyday life. In average everydayness man tends to lose himself to the things he meets in the world. He tends to give himself away, to scatter himself among the many makings and doings of his world, so that he literally finds himself "out-there" among the multifarious things he has created and with which he is so busy. As he comports himself in average everydayness, modern man tends to be taken over by his world, to become a part of the world of things. Basic to this thing-world is the clock. "The invention of the mechanical clock was one of the most important turning points in the history of science and technology, indeed of all human art and culture."[4] What I am suggesting is that man has been taken over by the world of technique and machines, a world which, for the most part, is based upon clock time. In modern society, with its continual "augmentation of the world of *It*," and with the willingness, even eagerness, on the part of some thinkers to view man as a "technology of behavior," the following language takes on an uncanny, almost terrifying dimension. Buckminister Fuller writes, "A human being is such a beautiful technology . . ." "You and I are very extraordinary, self-re building television sets. . .";[5] the man in the street is wont to say, "You sure turn me on!" "I have only three minutes to give you, but you can take five." Today we not only live clock time, but some of us talk as though we were clocks.

THE TASK

Now that the existential phenomenologist has rendered explicit the hitherto largely implicit sense and structure of lived time, and in general helped the Western thinker realize that man lived time before he ever invented a machine to measure it, we are in a position to begin to wrestle with two very important temporal questions, questions which imply a significant connection between time and education: "How do we learn to live time?" and "What kind of time should we live?"

In order to open up the possibility of a meaningful connection between time and education, and also to limit our topic, the first thing we need to do is to describe those dimensions of education that show promise of temporal relevance. What aspects of education suggest a temporal dimension?

As we have indicated earlier in this book, the full range of educational meaning extant today is much broader than it was, say, fifty years ago. It includes not only the conservative view of education as the transmission of culture, and the liberal-pragmatic concern for providing the proper social-cultural conditions for the development of the child, but also a view of education which emphasizes, among other things, the child's "becoming." Many schools still concentrate on the subject matter to be taught, while others have become more liberal and pragmatic by adding a concern for proper environmental conditions to the importance of subject matter. But the more recent "radical" view of education,* which is the most difficult to classify, often shows little or no concern for the traditional educational aims of transmitting the culture and developing intellectual skills. Rather, the radical educator often prefers to concentrate his energies on the psychological dimensions of the child. He tries to look at the world through the eyes of the child and catch the "reality-child" in the act of seeing, imagining, playing, temporalizing, specializing, and becoming aware of and developing a self. In short, the focus is on the child's "becoming."

The way in which time is relevant to these three approaches to education is not difficult to discern. The teaching and learning of subject matter takes time, but how much time should it take? With today's mounting education costs, we often hear strident pleas to teach courses more efficiently, which often means in a shorter period of time. Another temporal consideration especially important to the conservative educator, because of his interest in preserving the culture, has to do with change. With the accelerated rate of change in American society the question is often heard, "Is education as the transmission of culture still a viable and meaningful educational project?" How can one transmit "the culture" when culture is changing so rapidly? The liberal-pragmatic educator, who also subscribes to many of the conservative educational aims, shares these temporal concerns, but in addition, he may also inquire into the temporal patterning of the social-cultural environment. The mode of temporality employed in the classroom is determined, for the most part, by the culture of which the classroom is a part; furthermore, the temporal style found in the classroom is going to have an effect upon the student's conception of time. Whereas the conservative might concern himself with, say, the relevance of time and change to teaching, the liberal-pragmatic educator would, in addition, look to the temporal pattern of our social environment in order to try to discover how time is learned. This, in turn, opens the door to the normative question, "What kind of time should be learned?"

But what does time have to do with the becoming of a person? The answer, as the word "becoming" suggests, is: everything. Man, including the child, is a temporal being; he is a becoming with a peculiar and unique integration of the three temporal moments of past, present, and future. The radical educator, with his concern for the becoming of a person would ask, if he were a philosopher, "How does the child live time?" not in the sense of what kind of temporal configuration the child lives, but rather, how it is possible to live time at all. What are the conditions of being human that make it possible for man to live time? What kind of structure do we find in human existence that makes temporality possible? For the most part the problem of time is an

---

*"Radical education" here refers to the educational perspective of many of the educational romantics such as Dennison and Holt, and some of the humanistic psychologists such as Maslow and Rogers.

"anthropological problem," that is, it is intimately and inextricably joined with the human condition.*

"HOW" DOES THE CHILD LIVE TIME?

Analyses of time, among contemporary philosophers, "tend to become polarized around two radically different kinds of temporality.[6] Some have referred to the distinction as that between human and cosmic time, others, more crudely, as that between psychological and physical time. Bergson, however, expressed this polarization in his distinction between clock time and real duration. But the existential phenomenological thinker who more than anyone else has opened up this whole area of how man lives time and how this living of time differs from the ordinary understanding of "objective time" is Martin Heidegger.† It is Heidegger's analysis of temporality, as well as his implied distinction between existential time and "objective" clock time, that we will be using, for the most part, to open up for discussion, and ultimately description, the phenomenon of the child's becoming.

In their deliberations on time most philosophers traditionally begin by addressing themselves to the question "What is time?" and then, within the context of their answer to this question, they try to handle the question of how man lives time. In answer to the first question philosophers for the most part have seen time as a flow of "now" moments, much like a clock. This conception goes back to Aristotle, who viewed time as an infinite succession of "nows" which follow each other in a definite order of coming to be and passing away. Time from this perspective, involving as it does an unending succession of "now" moments, is in principle objective and measurable. All attempts to start with objective time and then include an analysis of human time within the "larger" objective category have ended in failure, however; if one starts with the idea of objective time as a succession of "now" moments,

---

*This is not to say that all time is "subjective." It means rather that although there exists a great variety of temporal phenomena independent of man, "the only being on earth with an awareness of time, a being for whom the problem of time is not merely one of theory but one which is intimately related to the conduct of his life," is man himself. Kümmel explains further, "Man, unlike other beings, is not merely chained to time; he is the one being who can determine the order and content of his time. Freedom means to him essentially freedom to dispose of his time. The indeterminate and unformed time which lies before him appears to him as an unbounded possibility. Yet it is also time that gives him the sharpest sense of his own limitation. In this double consciousness of the power as well as of the impotence in respect to time man apprehends a challenge he must overcome." (See F. Kümmel, "Time as Succession and the Problem of Duration," F. Ganoa, tr., in Fraser, *The Voice of Time,* p. 32.)

† Heidegger, of course, would be very unhappy if he knew that he was being called an "existential phenomenological thinker." He has emphatically stated that, "My philosophical tendencies cannot be classed as *Existenz-philosophie.* . . The question which concerns me is not that of man's existence; it is that of Being in its totality and as such." (As quoted in R. Grimsley, *Existentialist Thought* [Cardiff: University of Wales Press, 1955], p. 39.)

each preceded and followed by an empty before and after, it is impossible to explain duration or lived time. The conception of succession, which in effect denies the past and the future, is incapable of accommodating existential time, which necessarily entails all three temporal moments of past, present, and future. When time is viewed as a succession of "now" moments the future becomes "a time which 'not yet' is but which will sometime come into being" and the past becomes "a time which, already having been 'no longer' exists."[7] Thus, in this conception, where the reality of both future and past are essentially denied, the only real time that remains is the transitory present. The basic structure of lived time, on the other hand, necessarily involves all three temporal moments simultaneously. In experienced time the past and future are inherent in the present. Even a cursory investigation into lived time reveals the coexistence of the past and the future in the present. At this present moment I am my past experience and my future possibilities. To start with succession is to miss duration (lived time).

Heidegger avoids this mistake in his analysis of temporality by reversing the process. Instead of starting with the ordinary understanding of time as succession in his discussion of time, Heidegger starts with an analysis of how man lives time, that is, how man lives the interpenetration of past, present, and future; then as a part of the analysis Heidegger shows how "now" time, which is based upon time as succession, is a derived modality of the more primordial existential time.

It is in Heidegger's description of lived time that we find, at least in part, a description of the child's becoming. But before proceeding, we need to point out more precisely how Heidegger describes this becoming. His analysis will not provide us with an ontic description of how time is lived, that is, a psychological description of how time is lived by the individual. Instead it will provide us with a description of the ontological conditions that make it possible for the individual to behave temporally. Barrett has pointed out that on the surface Heidegger's discussion of temporality closely resembles Dewey's belief that all thinking should involve a looking ahead to the consequences of one's actions. But the fact is that Heidegger's analysis, though superficially similar to Dewey's is really concerned with describing the ontological basis (the "within-which") that the pragmatic theory presupposes but does not make explicit.[8] It is, of course, important to see situations in terms of antecedents and consequences. It is wise to look ahead to the consequences of one's actions, but this is a description of the ontic rather than the ontological. Heidegger is directing his investigation to a different level of inquiry. He is concerned with explicating how man can think in terms of antecedents and consequences in the first place. What are the conditions that make such a temporal viewing possible? What is the structure of human existence that makes the measurement of time possible? What is the basic structure of our pre-thematic awareness of time? Dewey describes ends-in-view. Heidegger tries to describe "how man must a priori be in order to be capable of conceiving something like an end or aim at all.[9] So when we say Heidegger describes how Johnny lives time we are saying that he describes how it is possible—in the sense of what conditions make it possible—that Johnny experiences time. We will start with Heidegger's description of the basic structure of human existence as Care.

Heidegger concludes the first part of his *Dasein* analysis by describing the Being of *Dasein* as Care. As such, *Dasein,* or human existence, consists of three constitutive elements: existentiality, being-ahead-of-itself; facticity, already-having-been; and *Verfallen,* being-alongside entities in the world and being-with others.[10] This can be transcribed into less formal language by saying "I am a being who already has been (and that 'has been,' or past, is a part of my being), who exists alongside things and with people (thus making them present), and who is ahead of himself as possibility—toward which he exists (and that "toward which" is a part of my being).[11] On the basis of this threefold nature of human existence as Care, Heidegger, in Part Two of *Being and Time,* discusses temporality. It is significant, as we shall see later, that his analysis of time begins with a detailed analysis of *Dasein*'s being-toward-death.

For Heidegger, temporality, which is the meaning of Care, is not a "thing"; rather, temporality "temporalizes itself." "*Temporality is the primordial 'outside-of-itself' in and for itself.*"[12] Human existence is temporal; man *is* time. Time is not something outside man that he somehow appropriates unto himself. There is, of course, a sense in which man lives *in* time; that is to say, man does, in one sense, live in the flow of historical time, in the seemingly unending linear flow of befores and afters. But what Heidegger is at pains to point out in his analysis is that more primordially, man exists *as* time, as a temporalizing being who somehow lives the interpenetration of past, present, and future. But how is all this possible? What are the conditions that make it possible for the child to experience time?

For one thing, man exists as time because he is finite. We have already noted that the traditional conception views time as an *infinite* succession of "nows" which follow each other in a definite order of coming to be and passing away. The existential-phenomenological interpretation of lived time, which is the time of human concern as immediately experienced, directly challenges such an interpretation. At the very basis of the existential objection is the conviction that to view time as an infinite, quantitative, objective succession of instantaneous "nows" is to falsify it. Time to the existentialist refers to the finite time of immediate experience. Here, at the outset, we find one of the primary differences in our distinction, viz., the infinitude of objective time with its endless succession of "now" moments, without beginning or end, and the finitude of existential time, which is the time of human concern cast within the temporal horizon of birth and death.

Any description of man's lived time must of necessity include man's finitude. Man is mortal; he is born to die.

> Care is Being-towards-death. . . . In such Being-towards-its-end, Dasein exists in a way which is authentically whole as that entity which it can be when 'thrown into death.' This entity does not have an end at which it just stops, but it *exists finitely*. The authentic future is temporalized primarily by that temporality which makes up the meaning of anticipatory resoluteness; it thus reveals itself as *finite*.[13]

Man is finite, and any discussion of time should start with concrete human finitude rather than with any derived abstract idea about objective time: "only because primordial time is finite can the 'derived' time temporalize itself as infinite."[14] Equally important is the fact that man's finitude provides the ontological basis or ground for human futurity.

In his description of the authentic interpenetration of past, present, and future, Heidegger gives priority to the future: the "ecstatico-horizontal temporality temporalizes itself primarily in terms of the future."[15] It is the "future which makes present in the process of having-been." In the way time is ordinarily understood, as a succession of "now" moments representing what Heidegger calls the inauthentic mode of temporality, the basic phenomenon of time is seen in the "now."[16] As we have already seen, the only real time of succession is the transitory present. But in the authentic mode of temporality, which is ultimately based upon honestly appropriating one's own death into one's life, the temporal emphasis is on the future.* In thus giving priority to the future, Heidegger is emphasizing the importance of possibility to an authentic temporal stance. In honestly facing one's own death man stands before his "ownmost," "uttermost" possibility; for the possibility which is in issue here is nothing less than his own being-in-the-world. Death reveals the "possibility of no longer being-able-to-be-there."[17] Thus it is the facing of death that provides the ultimate horizon of all man's activities; it unifies his possibilities within the context of his finitude.[18]

So it is the living of our mortality authentically, appropriating our death into our life in anticipatory resolution, that ultimately grounds our futurity. This kind of anticipatory resoluteness can be seen as the prototype of all "future as coming towards."

> Anticipatory resoluteness, when taken formally and existentially. . . is Being towards one's ownmost, distinctive potentiality-for-Being. This sort of thing is possible only in that Dasein can, indeed, come towards itself in its ownmost possibility, and that it can put up with the possibility as a possibility in thus letting itself come towards itself—in other words, that it exists. This letting itself-come-towards-itself in that distinctive possibility which it puts up with, is the primordial phenomenon of the future as coming towards.[19]

---

*The sequence of events is from birth to death. It is because of this fact that the flow of time is irreversible.

When we pursue some definite aim or goal in anticipation of the future, we do not experience it as a fact, as "something that a man already is or has."[20] Instead, an aim or possibility is something man has before him or ahead of him which he anticipates with varying degrees of resolution.

Magda King describes such a situation:

> When a man sets himself a specific aim, for instance, of climbing Mount Everest, he conceives it as a possibility which he may or may not achieve sometime in the future. Until then, he lets this possibility in advance determine all the steps he takes here and now: he undergoes most rigorous training, exposes himself to hardship and danger, bends his energies toward organizing his expedition, collecting the equipment, etc.—and all this for the sake of a possibility which may never be realized and on whose outcome he stakes his life.[21]

No matter how remarkable such an achievement of an aim may be, to Heidegger the most remarkable thing is how the structure of human existence must be in order to conceive of an aim at all. King continues:

> For this, he must be able to throw himself forward into a future, to discover as yet completely "nonexistent" things and events and take his direction from them for what should be done "here and now." Above all, he must be able to understand himself not only in what *I am,* but in the possibility that *I can be* (e.g., I can be the Mount Everest climber), and thus come toward himself, so to speak, clad in his possibilities. In other words, man must be able to transcend, to go out beyond himself as he already is to the *possibilities* of his being.[22]

A more mundane example might be more appropriate since human existence always involves being-ahead-of-itself whether one is climbing Mount Everest or merely walking into one's office. As I walked into my office this morning there was spread out in front of me a futurity that both constituted and grounded my present perception. I was ahead-of-myself, coming toward myself in anticipation. All those papers, manuscripts, pencils, and books, laid out before me in incredible disarray on tables, chairs, and floor, were spread out in an open futurity as I moved toward myself in anticipation of writing. This futural temporal spread represents the condition, the "within-which," that makes it possible for me to move across the room, sit in the chair, and begin to write. This continual being-ahead-of-myself, this field of openness to the future, represents "that realm of the open out of which man temporalizes—that is, establishes himself meaningfully within time."[23]

The phenomenon of being-ahead-of and coming-toward is not a separate aspect of temporality; it is only one part of a single temporalizing synthesis. As Barrett describes it, "this spread toward future likewise takes into itself the spread backwards into the past."[24] All those papers, manuscripts, pencils, books, spread out before me in futurity as I entered the room, exist conjointly with and are dependent upon all the others in my past.

Temporality temporalizes itself as a "future which makes present in the process of having been."[25] Being-ahead is only possible within a context of having been. *Dasein* is continuously ahead-of-itself in possibilities; but these same possibilities can only be made present in the process of having been. I am my future possibilities, but my future possibilities can only be made present on the basis of my past experiences. I am not only what-I-can-be (but am not yet); I am also what I am as having-been.

The most distinctive feature of the finite time of human concern is, as Heidegger describes it, its ecstatic character:

> Temporalizing does not signify that ecstasies come in a "succession." The future is *not later* than having been, and having been is *not earlier* than the Present. Temporality temporalizes itself as a future which makes present in the process of having been.[26]

Existential time is always found in an ecstatic unity in which the three temporal moments, past, present, and future, are lived conjointly as inseparable phases of human existence. In this unity the past is never simply "past," nor the future simply "not yet," but somehow both are contained and integrated in the present. This coexistence and integration of the three moments, however, does not exclude the idea of succession; for the "three times" are not lived simultaneously. There is a sense in which the three moments, "*future* which makes *present* in the process of *having been*," do follow one another, but also they are all at the same time conjointly present. Man exists retentionally into his past as well as protentionally into his future, while, at the same time, he is always confronted with present choices.

Imagine a mother who has been in the hospital for weeks with a serious illness, but who has now apparently partly recovered, being presented with the opportunity of going home to be with her children for a day or two before reentering the hospital to continue with more tests and the possibility of a compete cure. Should she stay in the hospital, thus losing out on the joy of seeing but also avoiding the sadness of leaving her children, or should she take the risk and go home? Here we see in somewhat exaggerated form the ecstatic unity of existential time where both the past and the future bite into the present moment of choice by giving it breadth and thickness.[27] Here we see the "now" experienced as a living present which reaches back into the past while at the same time expanding into the future.

The mother's past illness is very much a part of her present moment of choice. She has been living in a world of sickness and suffering for many weeks. She knows the effect of illness upon the body and the spirit, and it is very much a part of her present. Unlike objective time where it is appropriate to speak of now moments as having "gone by," in existential time the past "has been" but has not "gone by" because the past continues to invade the present and play an essential part in our everyday decisions. It continues to nourish the present and provide it with repeatable possibilities. Having experienced a serious illness is to know what contingency is all about. It is to know the future is indeed uncertain. To know serious illness is to know the possibility of complete cure, partial cure, as well as lingering illness and eventual death. It is to know that being-unto-death is an integral part of life. In the process of "having been," all of these possibilities, which are now a part of both her past and her future, are made present in this moment of choice. But the woman's "having been" includes more than just the experience of serious illness. It also includes the experience of being a mother. And this facet of her "having been" also provides repeatable possibilities for the future. Having been a mother, she knows the joys of being with her children; hence, the future possibility of being united with her children is made present through the process of having been.*

The possibility of seeing her children, which also involves the possibility of experiencing the despair of leaving her children, maybe for the last time—both possibilities resulting from the process of having been—weighs heavily upon her present moment of choice. There are two basic attitudes open to the woman as she faces this moment, because there exist two primary possibilities of living time. One can choose to live time authentically by choosing one's possibilities in anticipatory resolve; or one can choose to live time inauthentically by choosing to live time as a succession of "now" moments.† In the authentic mode man chooses to become himself, or as Kierkegaard would say, "catch up with himself," through appropriating his own future in the process of having been, by decisive choice. Here man assumes the over-all responsibility for his own becoming. In the inauthentic mode, on the other hand, man chooses to forfeit this responsibility by becoming one with the things of his world, by becoming a unit in the Crowd, and instead of choosing in anticipatory resolve, he waits for the future to happen just as a clock waits for the next minute. This is the "now-time" of which Heidegger speaks. When we look at the clock and regulate ourselves accordingly, "we are essentially saying 'now'."[28] One mode of living time leads to integration while the other leads to fragmentation of the self. Owned (authentic) temporality "is a temporality of openness and resoluteness whereas disowned (inauthentic) time passively passes as if the human subject were not in a time of his own making."[29] Owned temporality is structured in a projection based upon repeatable and future possibilities, whereas disowned time "is telescoped and fragmented into isolated moments."[30] The woman

---

*"No act of man is possible with reference solely to past or solely to the future, but is always dependent on the interaction." See Kümmel, *op. cit.*, p. 50.

† In Heidegger's analysis there are authentic and inauthentic modes for each of the three temporal moments. Heidegger calls the ecstasies of authentic temporality "anticipation," "moment of vision," and "repetition," while the inauthentic future has the character of "awaiting," the inauthentic present "making present" and the inauthentic past "having-forgotten." "The *awaiting which forgets and makes present* is an ecstatical unity in its own right, in accordance with which inauthentic understanding temporalizes itself with regard to its temporality." (Heidegger, *Being and Time,* p. 389.)

can wait for the future to happen or she can appropriate the future into the present through a resolute decision. In living time in the mode of objective "now" time, the future is simply an item of "calculative awaiting." In authentic existential time the future is experienced as an anticipatory goal of human existence. Rather than awaiting what the future may bring, in the moment of decision the mother grabs hold of the future in anticipation and resolve, thus making it a part of her present.

This ecstatic unity of time with its accompanying modal options also illustrates the basic structure of the child's becoming. Taking into account a slight variation because of his age, the child will live his temporality just like the mother.[31] That is, the basic conditions that make temporality possible are the same in both cases. Just like her, the child's future is made present in the process of having been.

II

Having described the basic conditions of temporality, our next questions are: How does the child learn time? What kind of temporality does he learn? What are some of the consequences of the kind of temporality he will learn? It is to primarily sociological considerations of time that we must now turn.

HOW DOES THE CHILD LEARN TIME?
WHAT KIND OF TIME DOES HE LEARN?

All men are mortal; all live in the interpenetration of the three temporal moments with modal options. But within these conditions all men learn a particular temporal style with a distinctive rhythm and temporal emphasis according to the culture and era in which they live. Anthropological studies describing the different temporal orientations of different cultures abound. For example, in an in-depth study of a community near Gallop, New Mexico, where five different cultural traditions (Zuñi, Navaho, Mormon, Catholic Spanish-American, and Protestant American homesteader) were found living together, one of the most notable findings was the different temporal perspectives among the groups. The Spanish-American Catholics were primarily present-oriented, with an attitude bordering on fatalism. This temporal orientation was seen to be reflected in the afternoon siesta and the drama, color, and spontaneity of the fiesta. Homesteading Texans, on the other hand, had a very different temporal perspective. To them the future was important, and like typical Americans, they saw a world that was open to the future, a world which they themselves wanted to have a hand in shaping. The Mormons tended to be much like the Texans, while the Zuñi and the Navaho lived in the present, but also tended to look more to the past than the others, "to a glorious past in mythological time when their ancestors came out of the wombs of the earth to settle down and form the heritage of a way of life revered and kept distinct by ritual and belief to the present time."[32]

One can also see, by studying the ideational history of the Western world, that man's conception of time varies considerably from period to period. Compare, for example, the cyclical time of the ancients with the linear historical time of the Christians and moderns.

Given the temporal variation from culture to culture, and the fact that what kind of time a child learns will be determined, to a large extent, by the culture in which he is reared, we must consider American temporal patterning in order to answer the "how" and the "what" of the child's learning of time. An essay of this type is not the place for a lengthy examination of all the extant studies of the American temporal patterning. What I want to point out and discuss is the startling degree to which American culture reflects the kind of temporal patterning described by Heidegger as "now-time." To an inordinate extent, Americans seem to follow the lead of clock "now-time," which is based upon succession, rather than authentic lived time.

It may be because we are so concerned with efficiency, organization, or just getting things done, but whatever the reason, the fact is that in America we tend to look to the clock to tell us what to do. We use objective time as the master organizer of our lives. We do everything by the clock: we get up by the clock, we eat by the clock, we work by the clock, we play by the clock, we have cocktails by the clock, we go to bed by the clock. We meet deadlines by the clock. We have so many minutes left in this day with which to write this paper. We have so many class hours we must accumulate in order to get a degree. Lest we think that this is the way everybody lives, we need only note that primitive societies do not even have clocks. But even in other Western societies, for example in Greece, most people pride themselves on not allowing the clock to tell them what to do. They get up in the morning, go to work, eat, leave work, go to bed, not when the clock tells them to, but when they themselves are ready.[33]

Much like the radio and television people, we generally see time in an infinite succession of "now" moments that need to be filled. We carve up each day, week, month, and even year into so many time slots or units which are then to be filled with activity in the most efficient way possible. Every moment must be filled with activity, for in America, time must not be wasted. It is a precious commodity that must be used wisely. When we "have time on our hands," i.e., time that is not filled, we become bored and often nervous. (There is an interesting parallel here between this description of the inauthentic mode of living time and Heidegger's description of the inauthentic mode of living language, i.e., speech. Just as we try to fill every temporal moment with activity, so we also try to fill every speaking moment with idle chatter. In this mode silence is *verboten.*)

Meyeroff explains this modern temporal attitude by pointing out how, in modern industrial technological societies, time has become a commodity. Time has become precious because it is "the indispensable instrument for the production of goods in an ever expanding market"; being an indispensible instrument it has come to be looked upon as a commodity itself. Thus we equate time with money. Meyerhoff continues his explanation by showing how the modern world of time differs from the Greek and medieval conceptions.

> This concept of time as a *commodity* has prevailed in the modern world. In contrast to the ancient and Medieval outlook, time in the modern world has become more and more an instrument serving no other function than to produce goods for consumption and profit— hence the changed conception of *ransoming* time through ceaseless activity, production, and profit, in contrast to the Greek idea of ransoming time through contemplation of eternal verities and values, or the Medieval conception of ransoming time through membership in the City of God and attainment of eternal salvation.[34]

In the modern world time is seen as a unit to be used and the clock is there to tell us the exact amount of consumption. This predisposition to see time as a commodity to be used as efficiently as possible helps to set the dominant temporal rhythm of American society, a rhythm that can best be described as a nervous staccato. We race to the accented rhythm of the clock. Every moment counts. Early in the morning in order to be turned on and tuned in to this temporal rhythm, all one has to do is turn on the radio, and the rhythmic beat of the music, the jolly, gay, raucous laughter, the fast talk, as well as the repeated announcement of the time, will get one ready for the day. After having been thus launched on the clock-time treadmill, the rest of the day will take care of itself; for every activity has its appointed time. If perchance one finds that he cannot get everything done in the allotted time, there are time-saving machines, or time-organization specialists.

Our businessmen speak of time as money. Parents and teachers admonish their children not to waste time. Workers punch time clocks. Radio and television advertisers sell time on the air. Idlers and the bored try to find ways to "kill time." Most of us go about "spending our time" foolishly or wisely, "having" or "not having" time. But all of us in this culture, whether we buy it or sell it, save it or waste it, spend, do, bide, or kill it, seem to assume that time is an objective, measurable flow of "befores" and "afters" interspersed with the transient "now." For the most part we have forgotten the meaning of authentic existential time in America.

Where is this temporal perspective learned, and what are some of the consequences of this perspective for human development? Much of this temporal patterning is learned in the home, particularly with our growing addiction to television watching which has greatly increased the importance of the hour and half-hour time slots.* Nevertheless, the schools have greatly

---

*Some of my students tell me that although they no longer watch television nearly so regularly as when younger, they still find themselves waiting for a particular half hour or hour time slot before going to bed.

reinforced the learning of this temporal rhythm, because the master organizer of the school is also the clock. When a teacher comes in to school in the morning and when he leaves at night, he must check in, dutifully noting time of arrival and time of departure. If a student is late for class or has been absent he must go to the office to get an excuse. He must give an account of the clock time that he has missed. When he leaves his class for some special reason, the time is duly noted on his pass, and when he arrives at his destination the teacher checks to see that he has not wasted any time. The school day itself is cut into time slots. As a result of this continual monitoring of clock time, the child learns to identify time with the clock, and soon we see him cutting his own day into measurable time slots and then filling them as efficiently as possible. Thus the young are enculturated into the dominant temporal mode of American life.

If one lives in the typical American mode of "now-time," rather than in a temporal pattern that recognizes the primordiality of existential time, there is grave danger that one may live one's whole life without ever finding the time to face the great implacables. When we allow the clock and the schedule to tell us what to do we rarely find time for such questions as: "What's it all about?" "Why is there something rather than nothing?" "What is the meaning and the purpose of life in general and my life in particular?" I believe this is what Barnaby Keeny was talking about when he said:

> I think the greatest defect in American collegiate education is that the men graduate and get involved in their work, and the women get involved in other things. Then when they are about forty or fifty they suddenly wonder what is going on and they can't get back into it. I would like to find some way of stimulating people in all stages of their career to remain active intellectually.[35]

To remain active intellectually and philosophically is to understand that existential time is more primordial than clock time, and to understand existential time in such a way as to live it. Existence entails temporality. Some would even say the essence of existence is time.

III

CHANGE, THE DEPRECIATION OF THE PAST, AND TEACHING

The third and perhaps most serious consequence of living in the American temporal mode is the tendency to neglect the importance of the past. In order to realize the full impact of this consequence, it is necessary to discuss briefly some of the temporally related technological developments of the 45 years since Heidegger first described clock "now-time." For if the clock has influenced our perception of time, as Heidegger suggests, what about the effect of some of the more recent developments in electronic technology, such as the computer, upon our temporal perception?

It is commonplace these days to note that American society is changing at an ever-increasing rate, but what has not been given sufficient notice is the effect of this phenomenon upon some of the most important basic life processes. This speeding up of the rate of change in American society is probably more responsible than anything else for what is popularly called the "generation gap." With society changing so rapidly we find the child brought up in a significantly different environment with significantly different values than his parents. As a result, parent and child often find it difficult to share a common world of discourse and meaning. Although this problem may not yet have deteriorated to the point where there is a real separation between generations, it is a very serious problem indeed; in a very real sense the whole business of life, that is its continuance on human terms, depends upon communication between generations. Human life can be seen as a compact between age and youth where parents are willing to give of themselves to rear, feed, protect, and educate their young. Edmund Burke went so far as to define society as a partnership between generations, "a partnership in all science, in all art, in every virtue and in all perfection not only between those who are living, but between those who are dead, and those who are to be born."[36] If this partnership is now in the process of being dissolved, if this compact between age and youth no longer exists, then the days of civilization as we have known it are limited. As one might expect, this problem is becoming increasingly critical in our schools. Because of the ever-increasing rate of change in America, many educators, particularly conservative educators, who seem to be more concerned than most with "transmitting the culture," are being forced to ask some very serious questions, like: "What culture shall we teach?" or, more directly, "Do we have an American culture that can be taught?" This phenomenon has also forced to the surface that perennial question, "What knowledge shall be taught?" With the accelerated rate of change in beliefs, ways of doing things, and knowledge itself, many educators eventually claim that the only safe thing to teach the child today is how to cope with change itself. And the best way to cope with change, it is argued, is to learn how to learn and how to solve problems. This kind of educational program makes eminent sense in a world where the speed of change threatens to render the future unrecognizable.

While many conservative educators are now beginning to question the wisdom of concentrating exclusively on the past, we can see, at the same time, a number of the more radical educators who recommend that we jettison the past completely and instead concentrate on trying to help fashion a new, more human culture. Their logic, at least on the surface, seems plausible. Having accepted the acceleration of change as an inevitable fact of modern life, they then conclude that since it is impossible to maintain any real continuity but with one's own immediate past, there is no point in teaching students about what has gone before. Thus, the best curriculum is no curriculum, at least in the traditional sense. Rather, let us start from the present and try our best to define what the future will bring.

This attitude and approach has been greatly abetted recently by the increased use of the computer as well as in increasing interest in futurology, or futuristics. Quentin Fiore, of McLuhan and Fiore fame, describes the influence of the computer on our sense of time as follows:

> Very high electronic speeds have made predictive techniques of amazing accuracy possible. Sophisticated probing tools such as correlation, sampling, and simulation now permit us to learn from *projected* experience without having to suffer the possible consequences of these experiences. The rapid information movement of computer technology transforms the future into the present, and, in an environment envisaged by some physicists, TIME may have little meaning—there may very well be no such thing as "before" and "after."
>
> It is in this very disturbing and highly perplexing environment of accelerated change that a wholly new psychic situation of "future-presents," of time mixes, is beginning to emerge. It is a wholly new environment, which is forcing us to entertain some very new notions about ourselves and about most of our institutions.[37]

This alleged shift in time perception from "now" to "now-future" has prompted some educators to recommend that courses in the "now-future" become an integral part of every curriculum in the land. For example, as long ago as 1945, Ossip K. Flechtheim was advocating such a plan.

> If we fail. . . to make the future an essential part of the integration of the past, our interpretation of human culture will be neither complete nor meaningful. Any synopsis neglecting the impact of the days to come upon the days gone by would prove fragmentary or scholastic at best. . . Even more important than physical chemistry or Old English grammar to the present-day student, whose life span may well stretch into the twenty-first century, should be a knowledge of what is in store for him . . . he has a right to know what to expect, what will be the causes of his troubles, and what are their place and meaning in the chain of unfolding events.
>
> A course with the future as its subject matter . . . would have to be taught by a truly creative scholar with a wide sociocultural background and a vital interest in the forces of our age. He would have to possess strong scientific discipline in order to rid himself and his students of prejudice and to force them to part with many of their most cherished hopes and illusions. Though an active participant in the life of his century, he would have to be, for the purposes and the duration of this course, a dispassionate and disinterested observer of things future.[38]

With science being capable of telling us what the future will be like, apparently one will no longer need to select a future. As Fiore has suggested, with modern sophisticated techniques "we can learn from *projected* experience *without having to suffer the consequences of these experiences*" (second italics mine). In such a situation, choice, at least choice as risk, will be a thing of the past. To make a decision, all one will have to do is go to the computer. It is almost as though contingency has been eradicated from being human! This is yet another illustration of man's tendency to forfeit his responsibility for his own becoming by getting lost in the world of things. In any case, anyone who believes that we are now living or should live in the present-future orientation will probably consider a study of the past a wholesale waste of time.

Many of the technological developments in the communications media have also greatly stimulated and encouraged the living of now-time. For example, with the increasing use of satellite telecasting, one can be in Karachi, Vietnam, the North Pole, and at home almost simultaneously, right now, by merely turning a switch. One is reminded here of the curious connection between pleasure, change, and the *now* that Kierkegaard noted over a hundred years ago in his theory of the three stages of human existence. The predominant style of life on the lowest level of existence, which Kierkegaard calls the aesthetic level, consists of subordinating oneself to the pleasures of the moment. Here we see the temporal mode of the present being dispersed over as many different pleasurable activities as possible. Observe the aesthetician, Kierkegaard writes:

> See him in his season of pleasure: did he not crave for one pleasure after another, variety his watchword? Is variety, then, the willing of one thing that abides the same? Nay, rather it is the willing of something that must never be the same. But that is just to will the manifold, and a man with such a will is not only doubleminded but all at variance with himself, for he wills one thing and immediately after the opposite, because oneness of pleasure is disappointment and illusion, and it is the variety of pleasures that he wills. Change was what he was crying out for when pleasure pandered to him, change, change![39]

We are always hurrying things along so we can consume at an ever-accelerating rate. It's not the quality but the quantity of the experiences that counts. In history, events occur and become continuous with other events in the inexorable flow of historical time. But in now-time, we do not allow events to unfold slowly, duly noting interconnections with past and future. Rather, we package tiny little pieces of history for man's consumption *now;* then, after having momentarily sated our curiosity, we throw them away in the scrap heap. It is almost as though the past, seen as a used-up present, is completely worthless.

This attitude toward the past, as Meyerhoff explains it, presents us with a curious paradox.

The barriers of the past have been pushed back as never before; our knowledge of the history of man and the universe has been enlarged on a scale and to a degree not dreamed of by previous generations. At the same time, the sense of identity and continuity with the past, whether our own history or history's, has gradually and steadily declined. Previous generations *knew* much less about the past than we do, but perhaps *felt* a much greater sense of identity and continuity with it because of the fixity, stability, and relative permanence of their social structure. Despite the enormous knowledge we have accumulated about the past, the temporal perspective in the lives of individuals has become so foreshortened in our age as to condemn them to live in a perpetual present—not the experiential, qualitative, co-presence of all the elements constituting their own past recaptured by memory, but the qualitative units of the present as defined by the consumption of goods, news, and the instrumental use of human beings themselves.[40]

Living time inauthentically means, among other things, forgetting one's past, disregarding the call of conscience, and being generally indifferent to one's responsibility for one's own becoming. To concentrate on one's consuming pleasure *now* greatly facilitates all of these dimensions of the inauthentic. It means depreciating the past, waiting for rather than appropriating the future, and generally forfeiting one's responsibility for one's becoming to the They.

The accelerated rate of change with its inevitable depreciation of the past, in conjunction with our predisposition to live in clock now-time, not only threatens to break continuity between past generations, but also threatens to break continuity in individual lives. It is becoming increasingly difficult "to keep in touch with the past, to reconstruct one's own personal biography according to a coherent, unified, and significant pattern."[41] The essence of existence is temporal; and anything that threatens to upset the delicate balance between the three temporal moments at the same time threatens existence itself. To tamper with the ecstatic unity of time is to tamper with the very center of life, that is, significance and meaning. Kümmel describes the interpenetration of past, present, and future as an open circle.

No act of man is possible with reference solely to the past or solely to the future, but is always dependent on their interaction. Thus, for example, the future may be considered as the horizon against which plans are made, the past provides the means for their realization, while the present mediates and actualizes both. Generally, the future represents the possibility, and the past the basis, of a free life in the present. Both are always found intertwined with the present: in the *open circle* of future and past there exists no possibility which is not made concrete by real conditions, nor any realization which does not bring with it new possibilities. This interrelation of reciprocal conditions is a historical process in which the past never assumes a final shape nor the future ever shuts its doors. Their essential interdependence also means, however, that there can be no progress without a retreat into the past in search of a deeper foundation.[42]

This interpenetration of past, present, and future in lived reality must remain open and circular. To live time with a foreshortened past, or with an inauthentic orientation to the future—that is, one conceived without contingency—is to grievously threaten this temporal structure.

What can we do in the schools to alleviate some of the more serious consequences for human development of our American temporal patterning? We can help our students understand the potential threat to meaning when living in a society where we assume as fact that the *new* is always better than the *old* and where the rate of change is increasing. The real threat is not change; societies and individuals have always been able to accommodate themselves to slow, gradual change. As Robert Oppenheimer has observed, "what is written today deploring change, or welcoming it, has its parallel in almost every decade for the last four hundred years"[43] We can find this sentiment in Newton, in the dying Galileo, and in John Donne who in 1611 wrote:

> And new Philosophy calls all in doubt,
> The Element of fire is quite put out;
> The Sun is lost, and th' earth, and no mans wit
> Can well direct him where to looke for it.
> And freely men confesse that this world's spent,
> When the Planets, and the Firmament
> They seeke so many new; then see that this
> Is crumbled out againe to his Atomies.
> 'Tis all in peeces, all cohaerence gone;
> All just supply, and all Relation.[44]

A constant acceleration of change is another matter.

We must help students understand the importance of the past. The young person has a built-in temporal limitation. He is not yet able to see himself in history. He seems not to be able to realize the importance of the past for continuity and identity. We must teach our students to relate to their heritage so that they do not become either resentful or adoring slaves to their past. We must somehow instruct our students in the past so they internalize it and then build upon it.

Finally, I think that we must instruct our students in the difference between living time inauthentically as an ever-accelerating succession of now moments, and living time authentically in an anticipatory resolute futurity made meaningfully present through the process of having been. There is every indication, as Heidegger claims, that modern man has become lost in his world of things. He has become one with the multifarious things of the world where motors and machines talk like human beings and human beings talk like television sets and clocks. Modern man—at least some modern men—go to great lengths to try to conceptualize *homo sapiens* mechanically replete with inputs and outputs. Others talk longingly of developing a "technology of behavior" beyond freedom and dignity. But we should never forget that man was here before the clock, the television, and the computer. Man lived time before he built a machine to measure time. In point of fact, man still lives his own existential time, albeit for the most part inauthentically, even though he may be unaware of it. Moreover, he has the right, even the responsibility, to respect, guard, and use *his* time as his own, for man's existential time is his life. Maybe if we could instill this idea in the youth of the nation, we would be able to take that first step toward reasserting man's supremacy over his machines, toward starting to control the system rather than allowing the system to continue to control him. With a real understanding of the importance of living existential time authentically, this modern generation might even begin to think about how to control this accelerated rate of change which poses such a grave threat to the very stuff of life.

We have seen *how* the child lives time, that is, the conditions within which he temporalizes temporality. Man is a finite being who temporalizes a future made present in the process of having been. We have also noted that within these conditions there exist significant variations in temporal configurations from culture to culture, and that the child for the most part learns the time of the culture within which he is raised. But one must never forget that from the perspective of the existential phenomenologist man is a choosing being. The child may "pick up" the temporal configuration of his culture, but man has the power to choose within any given situation what style of temporality to live. *Dasein* can temporalize temporality in different ways. The "basic possibilities of existence, the authenticity and inauthenticity of *Dasein*, are grounded ontologically in possible temporalizations of temporality.[45] In any situation, then, temporality can temporalize itself authentically or inauthentically. But it should not be forgotten that both these modes are constituent elements of human existence. It is not a question of ridding oneself of inauthentic temporality, but of living the tension between the two, ever cognizant of the fact that authentic temporality is the more primordial of the two, and that the inauthentic constitutes a levelling off of the more primordial authentic. One of the most serious drawbacks of living time inauthentically is the tendency to assume that clock now-time is original rather than derived time. *Dasein* can choose an integrative temporality in which he assumes responsibility for his own becoming, or he can choose a fragmenting temporality in which he chooses to become one with the comforting but distracting world of things.

This intimate connection between time and choice is especially important for education. It means that the time that we live is not determined by circumstance, but depends, at least in part, upon our own freedom and choice. This fact opens the door for the question of what time the child *should* learn. It is of course true that since time is so close to us ("that which is closest is the farthest away"), to think of teaching for a certain style of temporality would seem to be, at best, a very remote possibility. But a possibility it is nonetheless, because the existential phenomenologist has now opened up for all to see *how man lives time*. This is what happens when the philosopher renders the implicit explicit. Being able to see how man lives time, we are now in a position to ask, "What kind of temporality *should* we live?" It seems appropriate to conclude with an echo from the introduction: "It is high time we take the time to think about time and education."

REFERENCES

1. See S. G. F. Brandon, "Time and the Destiny of Man," *The Voice of Time: A Cooperative Study of Man's Views of Time as Expressed by the Sciences and by the Humanities*, J. T. Fraser, ed. (New York: Braziller, 1966), pp. 140-162.
2. *Ibid.*, p. 142.
3. See A. W. Levi, "Existentialism and the Alienation of Man," *Phenomenology and Existentialism*, E. N. Lee and M. Mandelbaum, eds. (Baltimore: The Johns Hopkins Press, 1967), pp. 243-265. In his translation of Marx, Levi calls this process the "Thingification of Man."
4. J. Needham, F. R. S., "Time and Knowledge in China and the West," in Fraser, *op. cit.*, p. 106.
5. Buckminster Fuller, in a discussion with Neil Hickey, *TV Guide*, February 6, 1971, p. 12. The entire statement reads: "So it could be that when you and I have a thought, we may be getting 10-million-year-old signals into our television studio. Young people have been very much misled about technology: a human being is such a beautiful technology, and the sort we've been producing ourselves is so crude by comparison. You and I are very extraordinary self-rebuilding television sets *through* which we talk."
6. W. Barrett, "The Flow of Time," *The Philosophy of Time; A Collection of Essays*, R. M. Gale, ed. (Garden City, N.Y.: Doubleday, 1967), p. 354.
7. F. Kümmel, "Time as Succession and the Problem of Duration," F. Ganoa, tr., in Fraser, *op. cit.*, p. 43.
8. *Ibid.*, p. 358.
9. M. King, *Heidegger's Philosophy. A Guide to His Basic Thought* (New York: Macmillan, 1964), p. 43.
10. M. Heidegger, *Being and Time*, J. Macquarrie and E. Robinson, trs., (New York: Harper & Row, 1962), p. 237.
11. P. T. Brockelman, "A Phenomenological Analysis of Time" (Dissertation, Northwestern University, 1970), p. 53.
12. Heidegger, *op. cit.*, p. 377.
13. *Ibid.*, p. 378.
14. *Ibid.*, p. 379.
15. *Ibid.*, p. 479.
16. *Ibid.*, p. 473.

17. *Ibid.*, p. 294.
18. J. F. Irvine, "Martin Heidegger, Discourse and Education" (Thesis, University of California, Davis).
19. Heidegger, *op. cit.*, p. 372.
20. King, *op. cit.*, p. 43.
21. *Ibid.*, pp. 43-44.
22. *Ibid.*, p. 44.
23. Barrett, *op. cit.*, p. 358.
24. *Ibid.*, p. 355.
25. Heidegger, *op. cit.*, p. 401.
26. *Ibid.*
27. C. O. Schrag, *Experience and Being: Prolegomena to a Future Ontology* (Evanston and Chicago: Northwestern University Press, 1969), p. 56.
28. Heidegger, *op. cit.*, p. 469.
29. H. Alderman, "Heidegger on Being Human," *Philosophy Today* (Carthagena, Ohio: Society of the Precious Blood) XV (Spring 1971), p. 24.
30. See R. Guardini's *Die Lebensalter; Thre Ethische und Pädagogische Bedeutung* (6th in *Weltbild und Erziehung* series, Würzburg: Werkbund-Verlag, 5th ed., 1959) as interpreted by D. Vandenberg in *Being and Education: An Essay in Existential Phenomenology* (Englewood Cliffs, N.J.: Prentice-Hall, 1971), p. 27.
31. *Ibid.*, pp. 44-45.
32. G. D. Spindler, *Education and Culture* (New York: Holt, Rinehart, and Winston, 1963), p. 21.
33. D. Lee, *Freedom and Culture* (Englewood Cliffs, N.J.: Prentice-Hall, 1959), pp. 141-153.
34. H. Meyerhoff, *Time and Literature* (Berkeley: University of California Press, 1960), p. 107.
35. "A Salty Spokesman for the Humanities," *Life*, LXI (September 16, 1966), 53-58.
36. E. Burke, *Reflection on the French Revolution* (London: J. M. Dent, 1910), p. 93.
37. Q. Fiore, "The Future of the Book," *The Future of Time*, H. Yaker, H. Osmond, and F. Cheek, eds. (Garden City, N.Y.: Doubleday, 1972), p. 488.
38. O.K. Flechtheim, "Teaching the Future," Yaker, Osmond, and Cheek, *op. cit.*, pp. 504-505.
39. S. Kierkegaard, as quoted in R. Jolivet, *Introduction to Kierkegaard* (New York: E. P. Dutton, 1946), p. 142.
40. Meyerhoff, *op. cit.*, pp. 109-110.
41. *Ibid.*, p. 109.
42. Kümmel, *op. cit.*, p. 50.
43. R. Oppenheimer, "Perspectives in Modern Physics," *Perspectives in Modern Physics*, R. E. Marshak, ed., (New York: Interscience, 1966), p. 3.
44. J. Donne, as quoted in Oppenheimer, *op. cit.*, p. 3.
45. Heidegger, *op. cit.*, pp. 351-352.

In his earlier work, Donald Vandenberg concerned himself with the question of educational research, specifically the ontological grounding, or lack of it, in such research. In "Phenomenology and Educational Research," Vandenberg moves beyond his earlier writings. First he explicates the problem of educational research and then, recognizing that the problem must be grasped at the more fundamental level of theory, he inquires into the nature of educational theory itself. From this, he sets forth a major original contribution to philosophy of education under the heading of "Fundamental Educational Theory." In drawing on his own translations of the educational writings of such Europeans as Otto Bollnow and Martinus Langeveld, Vandenberg brings new insights to his sources.

10 | Phenomenology and Educational Research

DONALD VANDENBERG

Educational research is the factual and theoretical investigation of educational practice. Research investigates what is, rather than what should be, but unexamined values will remain operative in practice unless normative inquiry is also included in research. To confine research to existing educational practice restricts it to an extremely varied set of phenomena, not all of which are of equal worth, to research or to the student or to society. If research is confined to what is, it is not clear how its findings could be applied to improve practice, for from statements about what is there follow merely statements about what is. The preliminary definition of educational research can be expanded to make a more useful application possible. Educational research is the factual, theoretical, and normative investigation of the reality of education, that is of educating.*

Not every educational inquiry, of course, can be factual, theoretical, and normative at once. Various kinds of inquiry belong within the scope of the study of education. The focus upon the practical art of educating suggests, however, that not all instances of educational practice (i.e., schooling) are of

*Charles Brauner's main thesis in his critical history, *American Educational Theory* (Englewood Cliffs, N. J.: Prentice-Hall, 1964), is that practice has been the context of most research and theory of education in the United States.

equal interest to research. If instances of educating, of pedagogic action that does in fact educate, can be distinguished theoretically, then a normative perspective can be built into educational research at the beginning. Although many researchers rightfully protest this beginning with a normative perspective because when the researcher lets his own values confuse his "findings" the result is rather unsuccessful research, what has been said in no way implies that the researcher's own values or his normative perspective should influence the investigation of educating. Nor is there any suggestion that some philosopher of education should assume the role of legislator of possible research. The problem is of much larger magnitude and lies wholly on a different plane.

THE SCOPE OF EDUCATIONAL THEORY

The Problem

The major problem of the study of education as a discipline concerns the horizontal integration of numerous findings from a great variety of approaches and the vertical, explicit connection of these to the act of educating. All the sciences of man (psychology, sociology, anthropology, economics, political science, etc., and their respective sub-fields) and all the normative sciences (logic, philosophy of science, ethics, social and political philosophy, etc., and their respective sub-fields) and a great number of "empirical," or quantitative, studies do in fact bear upon the concrete problems of educational practice, but how?

This problem has been approached through the development of the intermediary disciplines—psychology of education, philosophy of education, sociology of education, and so on—but its solution seems as remote as ever, especially to the more sophisticated researchers in these areas. A philosopher of education, for example, can recommend a particular version of the democratic classroom, but what if its long-range effect is to promote the development of the authoritarian personality? A psychologist of education can recommend either a Skinnerian or Rogerian learning model for application to the classroom, but not both, or not both at the same time. When use which?

This problem was confronted honestly in philosophy of education in the "implications" literature when it was discovered that different applications of the same philosophical beliefs resulted in different "implications" for educational practice. Different philosophical beliefs, too, occasionally led to the same educational "implication."[1] Some poor logicians then proceeded to eliminate either the philosophical beliefs or the educational "implications" for non-logical reasons. The problem is much more complex than this extreme solution suggests, for it exists in the application of any part of any of the disciplines to any instance of educational practice. If some minor miracle resolved this problem, furthermore, the other problem of the integration between these disciplines as they applied to education would remain untouched.

Hirst's Solution

The recent, widely read attempt by Hirst seems to have accomplished the essential task of "application" simply by suggesting that a body of educational principles that are justified by reasons related to the findings of the factual, theoretical, and normative disciplines, but that are logically independent of these sciences, should be called educational theory.[2] More precisely, educational theorizing is the activity of justifying a body of educational principles by reasons from the foundational disciplines. The principles that become constitutive of educational theory are not derived by logical deduction, or direct application, of any of the relevant behavioral, social, or normative sciences, or from quantitative research.[3] Rather, they depend upon the latter in a contextual manner. For example, principles concerning punishment or non-punishment in schooling have their own being but are formulated and justified by reasons from moral and social philosophy, psychological and sociological theory, and quantitative research. All of these are necessary for the adequacy of the educational principles. This makes educational theory autonomous from other disciplines, though dependent upon them; as simple or as complicated an undertaking as one might wish; and focused primarily upon the practical art of educating, thereby deserving of the name "educational theory." This last point, particularly, makes Hirst's view a felicitous point of departure.

Hirst's extremely important discovery of the realm of educational principles, educational theory, and pedagogy warrants closer examination. Hirst claims that conceiving of educational theory as educational principles connected in one direction to the more abstract, special sciences and in the other direction to the more concrete situations of practice, but in either case connected merely by an open-textured, informal, contextual logic, creates an autonomous realm, a real space or province of meaning, in which to place educational theory.[4] This realm, in turn, allows the concrete situation of educational practice to emerge in its wholeness, unreduced by the methods of inquiry of the special sciences. It lets education—and educating—appear. This is the prerequisite for the development of the study of education as a discipline in its own right.

Criteria of Educational Theory

The shortcoming of Hirst's view, and of approaches similar to his, is the extreme open-endedness of the "body" of educational principles. Presumably the same open-textured logic operates between the principles themselves, between the principles and the practical situations, and between various practitioners and theorists. This open-endedness leaves educational theory completely amorphous.* Hirst seems to think that this is necessarily the case because educational concepts (rather than disciplinary concepts) mark out the area of concern but of themselves have no particular logical form or conceptual structure.[5] The main reason for the latter is that educational concepts have emerged from the practical activities of educating. Educational theory is consequently a practical, not a scientific, theory. It is concerned with a practical, not a mechanical, art.

Hirst conceived educational theory on a practical rather than scientific model because the latter involves conceptualization rigorous enough to permit hypotheses to be deduced and tested in experimental conditions, making the theory inapplicable to the domain of practice. Practice is implicated in a concrete, uncontrolled, goal-directed context that requires value judgments, to which many non-scientific factors are highly pertinent.[6] He also conceived educational theory on a practical rather than "philosophical" model (as these have come down to us) because the latter involves a synthesis of the special sciences to obtain, for example, the most valid generalizations about man and society. The form of the latter is compatible with educating as a practical activity, but its formulation involves many nonphilosophical elements.[7] Scientific and "philosophical" (hereinafter called "macrocosmic") models of theory would cause educational theory to commit reductionisms by not allowing sufficient room for philosophical analysis of its normative elements or for empirical inquiry concerning its factual elements, respectively.[8] Hirst's recommendation, however, substantively approximates the macrocosmic model. The collective justification of educational principles by various specialists simply replaces what the individual macrocosmic theorist previously attempted single-handedly in a long overdue application of the principle of the division of labor.

This does not eliminate the problem, however, because he established no criteria of coherence to unify the educational principles and no criteria of relevance for selecting resources from psychology, philosophy, sociology, etc. Without explicit intersubjectively valid criteria of coherence and relevance, any educational principle whatsoever can be "justified" by any knowledge or theory whatsoever. He seems to assume that such criteria will function in theory of education, but without their explicit articulation and justification, the door he thought he was closing is not merely ajar but wide open.

---

*"Educational principles are justified entirely by direct appeal to knowledge from a variety of forms, scientific, philosophical, historical, etc. Beyond these it requires no theoretical synthesis." Hirst, "Educational Theory," p. 55.

The solution lies in fuller characterization of the nature of educational theory in the realm Hirst discovered, for it seems he has basically resolved, if not solved, the problem of applying the special sciences to educational practice. Full articulation of the nature of educational theory in the location uncovered by Hirst will resolve the problem of their horizontal integration as well. Hirst's criticisms of the alternatives, by no means original with him, have been well-documented by various scholars representing various points of view.* They seem to be the basis from which educational theory must now proceed. The task is to characterize educational theory so that it can in fact unify findings from the various factual, theoretical, and normative sciences and enable their application to practice in legitimatized ways.

The major clue lies in Hirst's claim that educational concepts have no logical characteristics of their own that permit the conception of educational theory as a coherent, articulated, intellectual context, that is, as a theory. Of course not. And the recognition of Hirst's claim becomes the starting point for the construction of a scholarly educational theory. It is not a question of examining the logical characteristics that educational concepts may or may not already have, as if these concepts existed autonomously in a Platonic realm of ideas independently of someone's having them in mind, but rather a matter of finding educational phenomena (or facts) about which one will subsequently formulate a theory with concepts that in fact do have the requisite logical—and ontological—characteristics. But after Hirst this still must mean formulating educational theory without snagging upon the Scylla of a scientific model or sliding into the Charybdis of the macrocosmic model.

The other literature on the nature of educational theory offers a few suggestions. In his "Preface to a Logic" Butler said that he was searching for a logic accountable to the flow of human existence that would treat human existence more as poetry and fiction do, "in the same key as human living."[9] Although he cited Bultmann, Heidegger, and Tillich as sources for his notion, he makes no reference to Dilthey, who also sought a humanistic logic for humanistic studies and whose method heavily influenced them. Dilthey's method, too, was developed in opposition to the methods of the natural sciences, which he thought inappropriate to the study of man.[10] A parallel notion from a very different quarter is Gowin's suggestion for criteria for educational theory. After a profound and knowledgeable exposition of scientific canons of theoretical adequacy, which he found inappropriate for educational theory, Gowin said that because educating was an act performed in a personal relation upon another person, the theory would have to account for a morally responsible, goal-directed, interpersonal act of educating. The "object" of this theory was the person being educated, as contrasted with the thing that is the object of scientific and engineering theories.[11] McClellan,

*Among the earliest is Foster McMurray's "Preface to an Autonomous Discipline of Education," *Educational Theory*, V (July 1955), 129-140. Appropriately cited by Hirst.

too, has said that the "anthropomorphic" way of considering man is the proper educational way.[12]

Levels of Reality and Theory of Education

If educational theory is to be a humanistic theory, formulated by a method of the humanities, it cannot be the older, macrocosmic theory that was correctly rejected by Hirst and countless others, nor can it replace the justification of educational principles as recommended by Hirst. It cannot be located "between" the principles, or their justification by knowledge from the special sciences would lack point, nor can it exist alongside them. It must subsist underneath them as a conscious formulation of the elements that would function to establish coherence and relevance wherever the theorizing that Hirst recommends occurs.

The word "underneath," however, suggests levels of reality. The approach to educational theory exemplified by Hirst in fact presupposes a conception of levels of reality, and the structure of the levels presupposed by Hirst's view are to be rejected or fundamental educational theory becomes one of the macrocosmic theories. The first level in Hirst's view is the concrete situation of practice. This requires pedagogic judgment within the horizons of the particulars of practice and educational principles. The second level is the realm of educational principles, formulated within the horizons of the practical situation in general and the special disciplines. At the third level the philosopher, the psychologist, the sociologist, etc., look for philosophical, psychological, sociological, etc., elements underlying practice. This occurs within the horizons of the general features of the educational situation from the vantage point of the parent discipline. It is closer to the parent discipline and returns to the second level if and only if something directly contributory to the justification of educational principles is forthcoming. When these theorists lose sight of the educational situation altogether and explore issues in the parent discipline in their own right, they are at the fourth level. The levels presupposed by Hirst—as well as by Plato—are the apparent reason for the amorphous open-endedness of the "body" of educational principles. In the absence of explicit criteria of coherence and relevance, the third level is not close enough to the first level to allow for the return to the "cave" of educational practice once the beauteous forms have been glimpsed on the fourth level of the "parent" field.

These levels therefore have to be reconstructed before formulating the humanistic educational theory underlying the educational principles. The interrelations have to occur in totally different dimensions. Hirst's suggestion that the intervening space of educational principles creates a previously unnoticed domain of theoretical discussion insufficiently notices the domain of educational practice thereby opened to theory. This domain is not investigated by the methods of the special sciences when applied to schooling practice because of the reductionism necessarily entailed by their modes of inquiry. In the domain Hirst disclosed, educational phenomena that had become hidden and invisible by the reductionism of prevailing modes of inquiry are again made accessible to research. This point requires considerable explication, particularly to the extent it is valid, because of the doubt occasionally expressed concerning the existence of distinctly educational phenomena and facts.*

It is commonly thought that educational facts are reducible to psychological facts, for example. Psychologists, however, abstract things from the living, concrete situation of the classroom and do not deal with "the pupil-in-relation-to-the-teacher as an educational fact."[13] As Broudy suggested, it is literally impossible for the teacher to chop up the living child into the modes of abstraction created by the various disciplines, and this confrontation of the "whole child" by the teacher creates the educational facts that an educational theory is designed to explicate or explain. Hirst's view, of course, prevents psychologizing, sociologizing, or philosophizing the concrete, particular child away. It prevents psychologizing the pedagogic relation (and thereby educational phenomena) away. Within the pedagogic perspective, and only within the pedagogic bracketing, the child appears as this-child-in-need-of-educating. This most fundamental need has never appeared among "psychological," etc., needs that have been attributed to children by the special disciplines, because this primordial educational phenomena is simply not visible within any other than the pedagogic, educating perspective. The task of educational theory is the restoration of the wholeness of educational phenomena as they appear within the educating perspective.

Modes of Educational Theorizing

The question of reconstructing the levels of theory, then, requires the juxtaposition of the humanistically formulated educational theory and educational practice to retain this pedagogic perspective and to maintain visibility of educational phenomena as such. Three modes of educational theory are thus indicated. The first mode is that of the practitioner himself as he comes to understand concrete situations of practice, and educational facts within them, through experience in the pedagogic relation. The second is that of educational principles and their justification by knowledge from the special sciences as delineated by Hirst. The third is the philosophical explication and elucidation of the prescientific, pre-theoretical understanding attained in the first mode and unconsciously presupposed in the second

*Scheffler, for example, in "Is Education a Discipline?" in *The Discipline of Education,* reprinted in his *Philosophy and Education.*

mode. Three interpenetrating, equiprimordial modes of theorizing are required, as depicted graphically below:

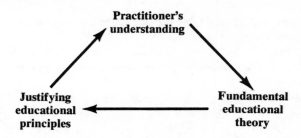

Of these, only the area on the left demarcated by Hirst's view should be called "educational theory." The practitioner's understanding of education as developed through experience is for the most part a "tacit knowing" (Polanyi). It is a pre-theoretical, pre-philosophical understanding, not articulated in conscious thought, for the most part. Teachers, for example, occasionally possessed great pedagogic wisdom before pedagogy became an object of university research. This is a non-thematic understanding that is acquired through the buffetings of experience in the classroom. "Experience" is used here in the same sense that it is used in the phrases "the experienced horseman," "the experienced mechanic," or "the experienced doctor."[14] This "implicit" theory is pedagogic "horse sense,"* which is no longer "common" sense in an age of pluralism and/or societal disintegration, and which therefore requires supplementation by the other two modes of theory. When the practitioner's pre-theoretical understanding is rigorously explicated by an immanent reflection, i.e., by an interpretive hermaneutic, it becomes fundamental educational theory.[15] The latter, as will be seen later, requires concretization by educational theory in Hirst's sense to regain applicability to given, historical, societal circumstances. If fundamental educational theory is merely the scholarly explication of the "tacit knowing" of the practitioner, it introduces no philosophical, theological, or ideological doctrine of its own (thus staying within Hirst's strictures), but it does tap an extremely rich resource of knowledge that has hardly been explored previously.[16] It also retains the bond to practice that can furnish the criteria of coherence and relevance so obviously lacking in Hirst's view. It is no depreciation of his brilliant formulation to indicate that he apparently lacked knowledge of the

---

*Philip G. Smith also suggested that experienced practitioners in any area having a long history may be doing much better than they know, i.e., than they can consciously articulate, and suggests that this operational understanding might be articulated by theoreticians. (*OISE*, pp. 44, 57.) Rather than calling this kind of knowledge the effect of custom, common sense, or folklore, as does Scheffler (*op. cit.*, p. 73), it can be thought of as sedimented meanings (Merleau-Ponty) to render it accessible to conscious articulation.

mode of philosophizing that merely explicates pre-philosophical understanding, that he was apparently unaware of the phenomenological, hermeneutical interpretation of what is pre-given in experience that had its origin in Dilthey and has been subsequently extended in scope by Husserl, Heidegger, and then scores of others, and that is in fact the philosophical but experiential (radically empirical in William James's sense), humanistic but rigorous method that is required to establish the study of education largely independent of other disciplines, including philosophy.[17]

The practitioner's inchoate understanding with its unself-conscious, uncritical, contextual criteria of coherence and relevance underlies any attempt to engage in educational theory, in Hirst's sense at any rate. The addition of the proposed fundamental educational theory merely enables a more complete self-understanding of educational theory; this in turn thwarts the tendency toward Platonizing inherent in Hirst's view and insures that educational theory remains theory of education. This can be indicated by completion of the previous diagram:

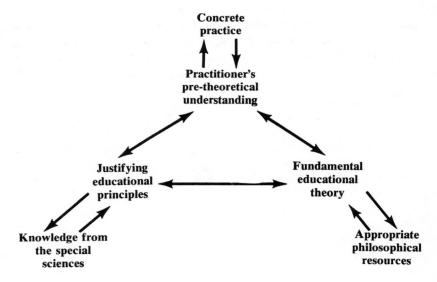

The three interpenetrating modes of educational theorizing form a quasi-unity, but each is dependent upon resources that fall outside of the theoretical circuit. Under Hirst's view, practice and its understanding are unable to affect the formation of its own principles in a direct, explicit way because of lack of sufficient intellectual "clout," which it can obtain through transformation into fundamental educational theory. Analogously, the impact of the factual, theoretical, and normative sciences upon the formation of educational principles prevents fundamental educational theory from affecting practice directly and from within a closed horizon of understanding. Similarly, the impact of fundamental educational theory upon the justification of educational principles prevents its educational theorists from becoming lost in the parent field by supplying the context of relevance. Each of the three outside resources necessary for the three modes of theorizing discourages the distortion of educational theory by the other theoretical modes by serving as a counterbalance.

Before this can be taken up in detail, it is necessary to discuss the nature of fundamental educational theory, prior to which its method must be expanded in some detail.

THE HERMANEUTIC OF EDUCATION

The Problem

In order to grasp the problems of formulating fundamental educational theory by a phenomenological, hermeneutical interpretation of the pre-philosophical understanding of educating, the concepts of "phenomenology," "hermeneutic," and "interpretation" require examination. "Phenomenology," of course, refers to Husserl's attempt to describe the stream of consciousness, as well as to his legitimate progeny.[18] The magnitude, preëminence, and place in intellectual history of his work suggests that the word is now used improperly to refer to the work of Aristotle, Kant, Hegel, or his contemporary, Cassirer. They did not have access to the method of phenomenological bracketing as it was developed by Husserl: they did not really have access to consciousness as such. At any rate, the present reference is to post-Husserlian phenomenology.

"Post-Husserlian phenomenology," however, includes a great variety of approaches, not all of which may be equally promising for fundamental educational theory. The variety is exemplified by Husserl himself, for the "late Husserl" of *The Crisis of European Sciences and Transcendental Phenomenology*[19] is more like the existential phenomenologies of Heidegger, Sartre, and Merleau-Ponty than like the pure phenomenologies growing out of the "early Husserl."[20] For instance, the approach to the lived-world of the *Crisis* parallels Heidegger's attempt to explicate human existence as the being-in-the-world of everyday existence.[21] Whereas Husserl's project was to gain access to consciousness as such through the phenomenological bracketing, even in *The Crisis*, Heidegger's project was to perform a descriptive hermeneutic to allow phenomena to emerge from their hiddenness, i.e., to let them appear, to let them be.[22] Because Heidegger's reinterpretation of the concept of hermeneutic (taken from Dilthey but referring to his own way of employing the method of phenomenology adopted from Husserl) is closer to the method herein advocated for fundamental educational theory than are other versions of phenomenology, the task of this section is to explain how to do a hermeneutic of education.

The phenomenon upon which Heidegger performed a hermeneutic in *Being and Time*, human existence, is less important for the present point than is his method. His explication was guided by the pre-philosophical understanding of this phenomenon, and the neologisms were necessary to make the everyday-ness of human existence emerge from the hiddenness it undergoes simply by being so much with us.* It is this kind of phenomenological hermeneutic that is necessary to obtain fundamental educational theory because its phenomena are likewise hidden as a result of their great familiarity.†

For two reasons, it is entirely appropriate, furthermore, to indicate that this theory will be an interpretive rather than explanatory or speculative one. One reason will emerge slowly in the following discussion. The other reason is to distinguish it sharply from scientific, explanatory, deductive, speculative, and macrocosmic models of theory, and in this way avoid unseemly cognitive claims. An interpretation is always open to revision, and a phenomenon can always be reinterpreted. The reference to "interpretation," however, does not deny its own kind of cognitive validity and in no way posits freedom to make any claims whatsoever. The phrase, "phenomenological, interpretive herme-neutic of education," rather, means that the elucidation of the pre-philosoph-ical understanding of education can be as rigorous as Husserl's phenomen-ology or Heidegger's hermeneutics, if need be. Some educational phenomena can be examined adequately only with this kind of rigor; only rigor enables one to change his mind, i.e., conduct genuine, fundamental inquiry. Without sufficient rigor, fundamental educational theory would not be achieved, macrocosmic theory would result, and the criticisms represented by Hirst would be in order.

Philological Hermeneutics

The term "hermeneutic" has its roots in classical antiquity. Aristotle's treatise on logic was entitled *Peri Hermeneias*, which would be translated *On Interpretation*, or *Hermeneutic*, which suggested to Ricoeur that language itself was interpretation according to the Greeks.[23] Palmer indicates the relation to *hermeios*, the word for the priest at the Delphic oracle, and to *Hermes*, the messenger of the gods and bringer of language and writing.[24] As

---

*Cf. "The phenomenology of Dasein is a *hermeneutic* in the primordial signification of this word, where it designates this business of interpreting." (Heidegger, *Being and Time*, p. 62, emphasis his.) For pre-philosophical (pre-ontological) understanding, see pp. 32, 36-38; for the hiddenness of everydayness, see p. 69. For a readable account of the role of hermeneutics in Heidegger's work as a whole, see Palmer, *Hermeneutics; Interpretation Theory in Schleiermacher, Dilthey, Heidegger, and Gadamer*, chs. 9 and 10.

† For example, there could be no thought of applying either a Skinnerian or Rogerian learning model to the classroom were not educating as a phenomenon "hidden."

revitalized by Dilthey, hermeneutical method was an attempt to obtain a humanistic methodology for the study of human life through the humane sciences in opposition to the growing application of the methods of the natural sciences to the study of man at the end of the nineteenth century. His quest was basically one in philosophy of science, or theory of knowledge: How can we learn about human life? With Dilthey, hermeneutical method focused upon the study of historical documents and literary texts, but it was sharply distinguished from standard philological hermeneutics. The latter involves the clarification of obscure expressions, phrases, and passages in a sympathetic attempt to make their meaning clear, and an exigesis to reveal the deep and/or "hidden" meaning of the text, resulting in a "reading" of the text.[25] For example, Samuel Johnson, Coleridge, and Bradley gave different "readings" of *Othello*, varying in their interpretation of Iago's motivation. In drama, too, one might refer to Olivier's interpretation of Hamlet, his "reading" of Hamlet. Dilthey's revision of philological hermeneutics required a deeply felt experience with the text, within the horizons of which the subsequent interpretation of the text occured. The hermeneutic then focused on the text to enable the reliving of the original experience that produced the text, thus making a greater understanding of life possible. The penetrating elucidation of the text was also reflexive, assisting the reader in understanding his own life.[26]

The latter is the source of Dilthey's distinction between philological hermeneutics and general hermeneutic. With Dilthey the former became the method to understand the literary text, the methodology of this understanding, and the methodology of the understanding of life as it occurs through understanding the text. The next step is philosophical or general hermeneutic, the methodology of understanding *qua* understanding.[27] Before the latter is explored, it should be noted that philological hermeneutics has been developed in two directions since Dilthey. One is the use made by Bultmann and subsequent biblical scholars in his line in their "demythologizing" of Scriptures as mentioned by Butler (cited above).[28] The other development occurred in literary criticism as an outgrowth of the New Criticism.[29] Philological hermeneutics possesses great merit in the study of the great educational theories of the past—Plato, Rousseau, Pestalozzi, Dewey, for example—for these can make explicit the student's pre-conceptual understanding of education as it has already been formed through his own experience of it. They can serve to yield visibility of educational phenomena as such if approached accordingly.*

Descriptive/Normative Definitions

Although philological hermeneutics is not to the primary point, it can, as

---

*This point is not dissimilar to J. R. Burnett's, "The Interpretative Function of Metaphysics in the Education of Teachers," *Proceedings of the 22nd Annual Meeting of the Philosophy of Education Society* (1966), pp. 42-49).

Bollnow suggested, furnish criteria of procedure. The hermeneutic of educating requires a text. To parallel Heidegger's turn to general hermeneutics within the criteria of philological hermeneutics, the "text" can be the pre-philosophical understanding of educating. To be true to Dilthey's method, however, this pre-theoretical understanding of educating has to be acquired in deeply felt experiences, i.e., within teaching experience in the public school. Only a disturbance or dislocation in this practice prompts reflection upon the immediate experience.[30] The priority of practice, incidentally, parallels Dewey's view of the relation of theory to practice, but it does not assume that all immanent reflection should conform to one model. In this respect, hermeneutics is more like Dewey's practice in his own theorizing than his theory of practice. The insistence upon the priority of practice so that there is a "text" to interpret depends upon a different conception of experience than Dewey's. In this view, experience, at least much of experience, is the result of things over which one has little or no control. It is a slow assimilation of many things that are not thematically reflected upon that slowly develops one's pre-theoretical understanding. Palmer's exposition of Gadamer on this point uses the illustration of a person who deals with people most of his working life, gaining a great understanding of people that he can not explicate.[31] This is the experience of the experienced mechanic, etc., cited above. When unexpected things happen to one, there is nothing to do but try to understand them in a subsequent interpretation, immanently, hermeneutically. Within the horizons of educational practice, this analysis of the pre-given (of the "text" of the pre-understanding) discerns meanings that have been only incompletely realized in the educational reality (as philological hermeneutics recognizes meanings that were incompletely realized in the first reading). The elucidation of the pre-given then generates a descriptive/normative definition (i.e., a more complete reading of the text). Dewey's description of the social elements of society parallels this: his discernment of the incomplete realization of the possible sharing of numerous and varied interests in the society he saw resulted in the descriptive/normative definition of democracy associated with his name.[32] Any analysis of any kind is without point unless the clarifying process discriminates significant elements, extracting the "ought" from the "is" in the delineation of the phenomenon. The very criteria of the analysis, or of the method of analysis, function to make the interpretation descriptive and normative at once. This kind of effort is often avoided in the interest of methodological purity, but in the educational realm the alternatives are less desirable.[33]

If the difficulties of practice have temporal priority, the question is how the subsequent reflection can come to a solution of the practical problem merely by interpretation of its elements. If this interpretation results in a descriptive/normative definition, how does this result in fundamental educational theory rather than mere opinionatedness? Criticisms of attempts to obtain descriptive/normative definitions have their point, but the question concerns the cognitive validity, or truth value, of such definitions. The rigor of orthodox phenomenology plays its crucial role at this point, because it yields the methodology whereby the individual investigator can avoid certain well-known errors. Because of his recognized place in the phenomenological movement, Strasser's attempt to supply criteria for formulating fundamental educational theory will be followed. Strasser suggested that the correct grasp of phenomenology's concepts of "describing," "phenomenon," and "essence" was necessary for fundamental educational theory to be philosophically responsible.[34] After their exposition, the discussion will return to their relation to philological hermeneutic and suggest concrete procedures for the hermeneutic phenomenology of education.

The Dialogic Principle

Strasser distinguished two generic modes of phenomenological description from among those developed since Husserl: the least rigorous, impressionism; and the most rigorous, dialogical.[35] Other views fall on the continuum between these (and thus this accounts for all of them). Any phenomenology seeks to be "presuppositionless" in its attempt to avoid prejudging the phenomenon being described and to allow it to appear, to let it be. If the idea of "presuppositionlessness" is not understood with sufficient depth, however, the result is "impressionistic" phenomenology. The attempt to avoid prejudging the phenomenon "ought primarily to mean that phenomenology is not based upon descriptions of scientific theories, hypotheses, preconceived meanings.[36] If there is a pre-theoretical understanding of a phenomenon that is explicated in the phenomenological description, then a prejudgment has already indeed been made and it is in fact the unconcealment of this prejudgment—or prejudice—that is the *raison d'ètre* of the hermeneutic.[37] The "presuppositionlessness" of phenomenology cannot mean that the phenomenologist's experience has built up no hidden assumptions. It means that the language of the description can contain none, which is why it means the rejection of scientific terms in order to describe purely.

If scientific terms are employed in describing a phenomenon, it is partly explained rather than described. For instance, perception can be explained scientifically by relating perceptual phenomena to their physiological bases, but the use of the terms that do this does not help describe perception as it is experienced. To the contrary. The phenomenology of perception cannot use this knowledge, or terms or concepts presupposing it, without covering up the phenomena it is trying to uncover.[38] Making all terms responsive to immediate experiencing, the primary datum of all theory, is phenomenology's radical empiricism. This refusal to employ received constructs is what is meant by "presuppositionlessness." The knowledge of the physiology of perception, however, cannot be ignored, forgotten, or repudiated by a phenomenology of perception: it is put into brackets, out of play, because the inquiry of the physiology of perception lies wholly on a different plane. The previous point, that prejudgments are accumulated non-thematically in experience, is a phenomenological finding. Its counterpart in the special sciences are the concepts of enculturation, conditioning, the relation of memory to brain traces, etc. The latter should suffice to prevent any phenomenologist from assuming that he can really start from the beginning in his description of perception. The first impression may suggest that, but further interpretation discovers the phenomenological counterpart of the physiology or sociology of perception in the matter of sedimented meanings and the fact that the world is always already there. Analogously in fundamental educational theory: it can make no use of the terms of the special sciences or it will hide the educational phenomena it should disclose, but it cannot ignore their findings. Interaction with educational theory in Hirst's sense remains necessary.

This means, ultimately, that no description can really be totally abstracted from its historical, societal, cultural, and religious circumstances.[39] It attempts to achieve this, but cannot assume complete success. In any and all cases, the prejudgments accumulated in experience "are the historical reality of one's being," and there can really be no such thing as presuppositionlessness.[40] To forget this results in impressionism, for the phenomenologist yields to whatever impression occurs to him. If he is "successful," he is in reality a literary artist, clever at arranging examples, telling anecdotes, using words, but his work is of secondary worth. An equally gifted writer could maintain the opposite.[41] The genuine merit of the work of an impressionist when he brilliantly articulates a profound insight is not of itself helpful in formulating fundamental educational theory.

To attempt to avoid prejudgment in the pejorative sense, but to recognize that this is an extremely difficult undertaking that is not fundamentally possible, one can employ the dialogical principle. The static intuition of the experienced reality of the impressionist is placed in the dynamic of the dialogue.[42] Dialogic phenomenology merely engages in real or imaginary dialogue with others. The multisided descriptions thus obtained include common insights that have public truth value. These are not empirical generalizations but descriptive judgments of necessary validity.[43] When using the dialogic principle, the description of the initial intuition is consciously converted into a thesis. Then its antithesis is formulated in an attempt to disprove the thesis. This technique is ordinarily designated as dialectical method, but the latter term conveys a great many historically accumulated meanings, including argumentativeness, that are not intended. The "antithesis" of the present concern, rather, is that which occurs in amiable conversation, at least imaginary. It enriches, corrects, and modifies the original "thesis" in the spirit of cooperative inquiry to obtain the most multifaceted perspective possible. The point is not to "prove" the initial thesis but to arrive at an adequate description of the phenomenon, which may very well have been hidden to the initial description (e.g., as "schooling" remains hidden to Illich's "phenomenology"). If each antithesis ultimately confirms the validity of the initial thesis through the dialogue, it becomes a descriptive judgment that is necessarily true.[44]

According to Strasser, the universally valid judgments of dialogic phenomenology can be obtained only in the realms of knowledge concerning human existence and interhuman relations.[45] This conforms to the aforementioned criteria and indicates a further characteristic of fundamental educational theory: it will consist of a finite number of necessary judgments that describe the essential features of educating as an interhuman, existential phenomenon. What these might resemble is apparent in Strasser's three examples. The initial intuition is that the child requires help. This is a descriptive judgment: the child appears as help-requiring. The "thesis" can be denied on the level of formal logic, if not in dialogue, but when one tries to imagine the phenomenon of the child without any characteristics of helplessness, the perceptual content of the description disappears. The child is no longer there, for he has ceased to be childlike. One could then describe nothing childlike; thus helplessness is an essential characteristic of being-child (as he appears). If this seems trivial, one might try explaining it as a thesis to the antithesis that would be forwarded by the romantic critics of the schools, or consider the second example. The initial description is that educating occurs in a restricted social and historical context. The opposite is that it occurs in a neutral milieu. When one attempts to describe educating that takes place "nowhere" and "at no time," however, the phenomenon disappears. That educating is historically and societally situated is an essential characteristic of the educational process (as it appears).[46] If this also seems trivial, try combining these two with the third example. Authority is involved in every pedagogic relation. If one attempts to perceive the phenomenon without the presence of authority, one sees the teacher perceiving the child as already grown up, the child remains as he is, and the teacher is through with his work as a teacher. The interaction becomes an amiable (or hostile) conversation between people of different ages, but the pedagogic relation disappears. Even in extreme progressive education—Rousseau, Neill—even in "free" schools, leading is manifested in one form or another, if only as a catalytic agent.[47] The most nonauthoritarian forms of the pedagogic relation manifest the presence of nonauthoritarian authority, which indicates the necessary validity of the initial description.

The dialogical principle is therefore the means to avoid subjectivism, for the *dialogue is the intersubjective test appropriate to a humanistic methodology.* All methodologies require an intersubjective test; in the natural sciences this is related to instruments and pointer readings; in a humanistic methodology it is dialogue. Dialogue amends and enlarges perception and makes it possible to distinguish the accidental and individual from the necessary and universal.[48]

The Experienced Phenomenon

The question then, is how a dialogic description can enlarge perception, for it would seem that perception of the phenomenon has to precede description. The examples indicate that the description of the initial intuition promotes further perception of the phenomenon, unconcealing it, through explicating the meanings in language as one lets the phenomenon address him. The description itself lets the phenomenon appear, as the examples begin to let the phenomenon of educating appear: educating is a relation between an adult and a child, who is to some degree helpless, in a given historical, societal context, and some measure of nonauthoritarian authority pervades the relation, perhaps constituting it. This description grasps a broader phenomenon than all three original "theses" added together, most noticeably in the fact that the "antithesis" contributed the insight that the authority necessarily present is at most nonauthoritarian. The non-thematic nature of pre-philosophical understanding allows the phenomenon to remain hidden until it becomes the theme of a phenomenological, hermeneutical description, which thematization enlarges explicit perception. There is a danger of letting the description escape into pure abstraction in a separation of discursive thought from the originally intuited phenomenon, but this can be counteracted by an adequate understanding of the phenomenological conception of "phenomenon."

Strasser's example of the second concept, "phenomenon," that must be adadequately understood for fundamental theory to be philosophically responsible, is heat. What one feels in front of an open fire, on a sweltering day in August, in a hot shower, etc., is the real phenomenon of heat. This appearance of heat in the lived-world as it is experienced prior to any reductionism by sophisticated modes of inquiry is the real thing. It is the heat itself. The conceptions of the physicist or engineer deal with secondary (if more precise, according to one hierarchy) aspects of the phenomenon. Heat is primordially experienced in the lived-world as the heat we feel. This statement does not deny the cognitive validity of the physicist's interpretation of the phenomenon in his second order experiencing, nor does it deny him greater cognitive "objectivity" concerning the highly reduced phenomenon that he has made more precise through his methods of inquiry. But the heat one feels before an open oven is more objective because it is the whole phenomenon, which is irreducible to the "heat" of the physicist. The "phenomenon" referred to by the phenomenologist, at any rate, is the experiential, prescientific, pre-theoretical lived-phenomenon, behind which lies no *Ding an sich*. The heat one feels is not the subjective appearance of the "object" studied by the physicist, but the reverse (i.e., phenomenology reverses the claims of phenomenalism).[49] And so on, *mutatis mutandis*, for all other phenomenal regions (as suggested above in respect to education).

Conversely, just as the appearance of heat in the lived-world is not really hidden at all but can become concealed through the dominance of the phenomenalism of the natural sciences (heat may not be a felicitous example), so too are educational phenomena not primarily hidden. They are immediately recognizable and can be readily distinguished from occupational, political, religious, artistic, and scientific activities, even upon first visit to an alien culture. Specific situations, relations, and activities are immediately recognizable as educational situations, relations, and actions. This depends upon the pre-philosophical understanding of them, acquired in experience, but it does not depend upon explicit, intellectual understanding of education or educational theory. It makes that theory possible.[50] This intuitive apprehension of educating as it appears prior to any explication is as essential to the validity of fundamental educational theory as employment of the dialogical principle, and may be possessed most strongly by the impressionistic phenomenologist. This, however, is but another way of asserting the temporal priority of practice.

Essential Characteristics

The third concept necessary to establish the legitimacy of fundamental educational theory according to Strasser is that of "essence." Perhaps it is better to speak of the "essential characteristics" of educating. The word "essence" carries such a heavy load of accretions that a rejection of these accumulations can result in a rejection of the word itself, all the more reason for stressing its importance to indicate the kind of objectivity and rigor necessary for fundamental educational inquiry. Among the reasons "essence" may be overlooked in some quarters is acceptance of Sartre's slogan, "Existence precedes essence."[51] When one says "Existence precedes essence," he means man makes himself. Explaining the slogan in conversation requires one to say that each person has to decide for himself who he is and who he will become in concrete situations, or its equivalent. This shows the formula is false, for explaining it makes generic claims about human existence in order to refute the claim that such claims can be made. The slogan did not prevent Sartre himself from describing essential features of human existence. The use of the dialogue principle thus confirms that phenomenological description deals with essential characteristics. Heidegger also rejected traditional conceptions of the essence of man, but his contention was that they considered man with categories appropriate to nonhuman entities and thereby overlooked man's temporality, historicality, and existence, which are, for Heidegger, his essential characteristics.[52] Heidegger, that is, maintained explicitly that the essence of man lies in his existence.[53] Analogously, claiming that the hermeneutic of educating will have to disclose the essential features of educating to be philosophically responsible presents no major difficulty: the necessary descriptions obtained by the dialogic principle grasp essential characteristics when the dialogue is thorough.

Not merely the dialogic principle, but every process of description presupposes selection of elements sufficiently significant to the description for inclusion in the description, i.e., that are also essential to the description. To seek the "essence" in a description is the essence of description. Then to say that phenomenological description seeks the constitutive features of the phenomenon merely raises into self-consciousness a procedure belonging to any descriptive process. The reference to the concept of "essence" points to a disposition of the phenomenologist to be as fully aware of the process of describing as possible. Rather than representing truth claims, which may always be premature, it means that the phenomenologist has to strive to attend to the essence of the phenomenon he is describing as it appears in the lived-world. But presupposing that the purpose of a description is to grasp the essence of a phenomenon in no way insures that it does. The utilization of the dialogical principle does that. Strasser's example illustrates. If no entity appeared to possess essential characteristics, the world appearing to man would consist of a vast number of incomparable, unique, and isolated entities. Nothing would be knowable in such a world, and there could be no talk of or about educating.[54] To claim that this view is absurd (and it is, technically) does not deny the "experience of the absurd," nor does it depreciate the view that maintains that general concepts help little in understanding particular entities in their particularity. But the world in which things would appear to be absolutely incomparable is the world that was experienced in pre-historic days, before the development of language, before the caveman, who understood caves to be alike in certain essential respects.

In the educational area, the thesis is that there are essential features of educational phenomena. One of its antitheses would be that every child is absolutely unique. To say that every child is a unique, incomparable being makes a statement about every child, a generic statement about one essential characteristic of being-child. This is at least a necessary, essential, and universal claim that is extended whenever someone says that every child is unique. The antithesis confirms the thesis even though it complicates it immensely.[55]

Procedural Recommendation

The "orthodox" interpretation of the concepts of "describing," "phenomenon," and "essence" as delineated by Strasser are probably not necessary criteria for every published contribution to fundamental educational theory. They are suggestive of the manner by which the hermeneutic of the pre-understanding of the phenomena of educating can be articulated with the rigor necessary to: build a cooperative, continuing community of investigators; enable acceptance of individual contributions by that community and, in this sense to become permanent contributions to fundamental educational theory upon which other researchers can build; through this cooperative inquiry, establish a body of literature that encompasses the entire range of educational phenomena, and thus, constitute a comprehensive educational theory; furnish a basis for concrete, controlled, quantitative, experimental research of the pure phenomena of education; interact with, and underlie, educational theory in Hirst's sense; establish the foundation for, and interact with, concrete pedagogics; make possible the founding of education as a discipline in its own right in considerable independence of other disciplines by furnishing the basic concepts necessary to establish the study of education within a distinct form of knowledge.

To establish these things, fundamental educational theory does have to arrive at the "proto-evident," necessarily true, descriptive judgments called for by Strasser, but there is also need for numerous intervening studies, which, because phenomenology is an empirical method, would be positive contributions in the same sense that quantitative and historical studies are positive. Such preliminary studies are not fundamental educational theory, however, and their role would be either to enter into educational theory in Hirst's sense on a par with the findings of the other special sciences and analytic philosophy as suggested by Hirst, or to become further refined and transformed into fundamental educational theory.

The foregoing discussion of the methodology of fundamental educational theory has not been patterned on a chronological procedure except in a rough way. Bollnow's suggestions are much to this point. He suggests three basic, not wholly separable, procedures: linguistic analysis, phenomenological description, and categorial analysis.[56]

The first phase parallels Anglo-American linguistic analysis but is not its equivalent. One begins with words as they are used in ordinary language in talk about a particular educational phenomena, thereby yielding the requisite priority to practice. This means the "text" of the hermeneutic of education is the linguistic usages that embody the pre-theoretical understanding of educational phenomena. This is supplemented by extraordinary usages such as newly emergent words, testimonials, maxims, the words of the poet, philosophical statements, and so on.[57] As the linguistic interpretation becomes richer and more integrated and differentiated, so does the phenomenon that it discloses, and the hermeneutic of the linguistic usage passes gradually into the phenomenological description of the phenomenon disclosed. The second phase of the phenomenological description employs transcendental language and the criteria suggested by Strasser. It ends with a definite, phenomenologically interpreted concept. This concept, finally, is employed in the third phase to classify the particular phenomenon in respect to others, locating it in the structural context of the whole province of education.[58]

To follow Bollnow's procedural recommendation would allow a kind of collaborative research among a broader community of researchers in philosophy of education than previously suggested. The analysis of educational concepts carried out by methods of ordinary language analysis by non-phenomenological philosophers of education (e.g., Komisar) is in fact a hermeneutical process, and analyses completed by this method might very well be useful for the first phase of fundamental educational theory. When the methodology of fundamental educational theory proceeds from an examination of language to phenomenological description utilizing the criteria recommended by Strasser, it is appropriately designated the *hermeneutic phenomenology of education.**

FUNDAMENTAL EDUCATIONAL THEORY

It is now necessary to discuss the nature of fundamental educational theory in bold outline in order to proceed to the methodological aspects of the utilization of philosophical resources in its development and thus to return to the main argument concerning the interpenetration of the three modes of educational theorizing in the following section.

The Aim of Educating

The concept most crucial to outlining the phenomena of educating is that of the aim. If the aim can be ascertained, then whatever promotes it is educating, and whatever hinders it is not educative. The view that emerged from American pragmatism that an abstraction such as education cannot have an aim because only people have aims need not be rehearsed here because it has been implicated from the beginning in the concern for educating. Educating, the phenomenon in the lived-world, must have an aim. As a practical activity, it is goal-directed. An aim is an essential, i.e., constitutive, characteristic of the phenomenon. Different instances of educating have different aims, of course, but these are immediate objectives, which are justified by intermediate objectives, which are justified by long-range goals,

---

*This term is used by Ihde to designate the work of the later Ricoeur, for similar reasons, to distinguish it from the structural or existential phenomenologies of Heidegger, Sartre, Merleau-Ponty, etc., thereby retaining the connotation of philological hermeneutic to accentuate the first phase of language analysis, added to the connotations of the word "phenomenology" as discussed in the text, but not excluding existential phenomenology.

which are justified by the aim of educating. The latter may not always be within the horizons of the teacher within particular acts of educating, however, and questions must be asked.

Is there one such principal goal underlying all particular instances of educating, justifying objectives and other goals? Could such a goal be utilized as a criterion for distinguishing educative from miseducative instances of schooling, and thus yield the normative perspective that is required to apply any research findings to practice? Finally, is there a pre-philosophical understanding of this aim among experienced practitioners?

The last question is of singular significance in the present context, for an affirmative answer would support the previous claim that fundamental educational theory introduces no new doctrine or biased ideology of its own, that it is in fact presupposed by the justification of educational principles in the activity of educational theorizing in Hirst's conception, and that it can be explicated by a hermeneutic of education as herein proposed. If educating occurs within a relationship between an adult and a child in need of help that is constituted as a distinctly pedagogic relation by the presence of nonauthoritarian authority, a number of things can occur to prevent the relation from being pedagogic and thus to end educating.

If the authority that constitutes the pedagogic relation is nonauthoritarian, it is noncoercive. When the child does not enter into the pedagogic relation freely and freely acknowledge the authoritativeness of the teacher, there is no educating. There may be schooling, training, and even learning, but not educating.

The child acknowledges the authoritativeness of the teacher when he perceives that he requires help and that the teacher is able to help him. It is unnecessary to discuss the details of the various kinds of help the child needs and understands that he needs to indicate that when a child perceives, or believes, that a particular teacher can no longer help him, the pedagogic relation is broken. When either the teacher seems unhelpful or the child no longer requires the kind of help obtainable from him, there is no basis for ascribing the kind of authoritativeness that is constitutive of the pedagogic relation. Considered on the larger scale of the entire developmental course, when the youth, rightly or wrongly, thinks he no longer needs help, educating is ended.

Under optimal circumstances, the cessation of the youth's need for help and his perception of the termination of this need coincide at the end of educating. The scope of educating is thus demarcated by the essential characteristic of the help-requiringness of the person being educated. As the point of any help is to enable the recipient to do without help and in this sense to put an end to helping, so too is the aim of educating to put an end to itself. In contrast to Dewey, for whom the aim of education was more education, the aim of educating is "no more" educating. The general aim underlying all acts of educating is to completely eliminate the need for further educating.

Previous discussions of the aim of education have often referred to the end of education, but they have employed the word "end" in the sense of purpose, cause, or reason, as in the Aristotelian "final end" of education, or as in the usage in the wornout and by now certain to be misunderstood phrase from the heritage of philosophy, "the end of man." What is the end of man? To what end? Why? The present use of "end" instead of "aim," to the contrary, is intended quite literally. The aim of educating is to be able to stop educating. The underlying purpose of all specific acts of educating is to cumulatively make it possible to put an end to educating, to enable youth to finally leave the pedagogic relation entirely and for good. The aim of educating is the development of the adult who exists independently of any pedagogic relation, that is, the independent adult.

The simplicity of this statement should not disguise its theoretical force. The corroboration from the pre-philosophical understanding shows this. First, one of the standard themes of graduation exercises is, "You are now on your own." Its banality is the point. The pre-philosophical understanding of audiences of commencement addresses is that the aim of schooling is to enable an adequate commencement in life upon leaving school, without further parental or adult guidance. Second, many parents and youth feel that schooling has failed the youth, is "irrelevant," if it does not prepare them to cope as adults with life in an adult society. Even if these views falsely equate schooling and educating, they manifest an understanding that the aim of schooling is the independently functioning adult. They express a concern that schooling should be educating, as defined above. The third corroboration comes from noticing that educating emerges from the parental relation to the child as part of child rearing. As the culture of a society becomes too complex to be transmitted through informal means of educating, schools are established to transmit it through formal education, but schooling remains an extension of the rearing of the child by the parents that allows the child to take his place in society as an independent adult on a par with his parents.

This third point indicates that the aim of educating stated above is cross-culturally valid. Educating in any society is understood as the rearing of the child to adulthood as the latter is defined within a particular culture: the purpose of educating is to allow the youth to leave the parental home and begin life on his own, however this may be defined in the particular circumstances; the schooling process may vary accordingly.

These points indicate that the optimal conditions under which educating comes to an end disclose the aim of educating. The description of the phenomenon of educating yielded the descriptive/normative definition of educating as simply helping another person to become an independently functioning adult (in a given societal, historical situation), which was corroborated with brief examples of the pre-philosophical understanding of this aim to show that the formulation discloses educating as it occurs in the lived-world. It can also be subjected to the dialogic principle. One might claim, at least on the level of formal logic, that it is desirable to prolong dependence upon the parents into adulthood, but the adult who remains dependent upon his parents appears to be childlike. Where this dependence occurs, the "adult" disappears from perception and is replaced by the childish "adult" who seems to require further educational help (or psychotherapy). Independence in this sense is an essential, necessary characteristic of adulthood. A second antithesis would assert that because of the fact of the interdependence of men, as established by the social sciences, the aim of education is the complete socialization of the individual that assimilates the person into society and societal roles, rather than the individualistic matter of helping him become an independent adult. When one tries to imagine the adult who accepts civic, moral, familial, vocational, and perhaps religious responsibilities as defined by societal roles, however, he finds at the core of these roles a social-moral being who is able to fulfill these role expectations responsibly, i.e., the independently functioning adult. Without someone at the core of the roles to accept responsibility for them, the content of the perception disappears. The initial thesis is again corroborated.

The aim of educating, furthermore, can be restated from the child's point of view to allow for a statement of the nature of education. When the pre-schooler plays with toys, he is consciously exploring their possibilities, i.e., the possibilities of the world within his horizons. At the other end, the independently functioning adult is sufficiently aware of the possibilities of the social-historical world to assume responsibility for himself in the situations in which he finds himself. The transition from the former to the latter occurs through the exploration of the world, beginning with the physical world immediately surrounding the child and the people of his intimate acquaintance, and going through a gradual transformation to the exploration of the intellectual-historical world. This world furnishes insights into the possibilities of the social-historical world that the person will dwell in as an adult. The exploration and discovery of the possibilities of the world is the educative process; help in this exploration and disclosure of the possibilities of the world is the educating process. Just as under optimal conditions the child wants to explore the world, so too does he want to become adult. His perception of "bigger" children, whether in play or in the grades ahead of him in school, makes him want to become "bigger," like these older children. As his horizons stretch out through his explorations of the world, he gradually, and more and more, wants to become adult.

The child's wanting to explore the world, his wanting to become "bigger," and his wanting to become adult can be restated as his wanting to become someone, which again can be respecified as his wanting to be independently, or, simply, his having to be. These various formulations describe the phenomenon at various levels, and they indicate that stating that the aim of educating has its end in the independently functioning adult has an effect upon fundamental educational theory similar to the effect of the point of the slogan, "existence precedes essence." Traditional statements of the aim of education were based upon a definition of the essence of man: if the essence of man is his rational intellect, then the aim of education is perfection of intellect, and the process of education is conceived accordingly. When the aim of education is said to be adult existence, this is an essential description of the aim as it occurs within human existence. It discloses the essence of education because both aim and process depend upon the pupil's wanting to be someone himself, upon his having his being to be. They depend upon the pupil's desire to be because he will explore the world, discover its possibilities, require pedagogic help in this exploration and in the disclosure of possibilities, enter into the pedagogic relation, let the teacher disclose possibilities of the world that are otherwise inaccessible, and eventually reach the end of educating under the aforementioned optimal conditions if but only if his fundamental desire to be someone himself is not frustrated.

Philosophical Resources

This brief attempt to specify the essential nature of education is a hermeneutic of parental pre-philosophical understanding of education.* It has required the use of transcendental language ("possibilities," "world," "horizons," "disclosure") to proceed from the analysis in ordinary language to the description of the phenomenon appearing in the lived-world. This two-fold origin of the explication means that reference to the child's desire to be someone himself is equiprimordially based upon the appearance of the child (or youth) from within the pedagogic perspective, and upon the general features of human existence as they have been disclosed through the transcendental language of previous descriptions of the lived-world by existential phenomenologists.

But does this impose the preconceptions of philosophy upon educational phenomena? If so, fundamental educational theory is merely a new name for the old macrocosmic theory, which would make Hirst's view superior without supplementation. Is fundamental educational theory merely a deductive application of philosophic doctrine to a context foreign to it? Further consideration of the method involved will indicate the way in which philosophical resources can be legitimately implicated in the explication of

---

*Neither the "overprotective" nor "underprotective" parent has this understanding because neither sees the child as existing in his own right as a child. Further development of this point would require the elucidation of parental love, the necessary existential condition of the pre-philosophical understanding referred to in the text.

the pre-theoretical understanding of educational phenomena that results in fundamental educational theory.

In Heidegger's hermeneutic of the pre-philosophical understanding of human existence, the structures of human temporality and historicity are based upon the fundamental existentialia of understanding, moodedness (or having-a-mood) and projection into possibilities.* By "understanding" he means the primary understanding of one's own existence (implicit or explicit, obscure or lucid) that one has at any moment. His designation of this understanding as an "existentiale" (one "member" of the "class" of existentialia) indicates his judgment that it is one of the fundamental "categories" that are definitive of human existence. No other existing thing has it. This understanding, furthermore, always exists within some underlying mood or state of being (i.e., equanimity, elation, boredom, dread). Both understanding and the state of being are dynamically interrelated with a projection into the world and future.

If Heidegger's description is adequate, then human existence is always projecting into some possibilities in the world and future, this projection is understood, and the understanding of the project of being is permeated with personal concern such that it is never moodless. This mooded understanding of moving open-endedly into the future is an awareness of having one's being to be. It is understood prephilosophically as being responsible for one's own actions and one's own life, whether or not this responsibility is clearly understood and taken over. "It's *your* life." "It's *my* life." Although Heidegger's elaboration of the existentialia was accomplished with the rigor appropriate to fundamental ontology, there is no doubt that an adequate understanding of his thought requires not merely a first-rate intelligence but also an existential understanding.† One has to come to understand his own existence by means of, or through, or in struggle with Heidegger's words. One has to have the existential understanding beforehand, pre-philosophically. It is not that his words have to be comprehended but that the phenomena have to be seen.

The point of this illustration with Heidegger is that if the phenomena of human existence are at least partially disclosed by the descriptions of a particular philosopher, then a different theorist can subsequently proceed to describe the "same" phenomena that are now visible to him with words and meanings available to him. That some of the words he uses are the "same words" as those employed by the original philosopher (his transcendental language) does not mean that he is utilizing deductive logic to impose the meanings of a formal system of symbols upon an unknown phenomenon. It

---

*There are more existentialia, but these three suffice for the present point. For their principal explication, see Heidegger, *Being and Time*, section 31.

†"Unless we have an existential [personal] understanding, all analysis of existentiality will remain groundless." Heidegger, *Being and Time*, p. 360. See also p. 33.

means, rather, that the original descriptions have a degree of intersubjective validity proportional to their genuine disclosing power, which in turn depends upon the adequacy of the original intuition into the real, experienced phenomenon. Thus having one's being to be, or, more simply, having to be, is descriptive of human existence as it appears in the lived-world. Marcel, Sartre, and others have also written about "having to be." Human existence *is* a "not yet," for it is lacking the kind of substantive content in its futural, worldly dimension that could take this responsibility away from it: "Any Dasein always exists in just such a manner that its 'not-yet' belongs to it."[59] One has to be this being that he is not yet. He has his being to be.*

The "transposition" to the educational realm is simply this. The child as he appears in the lived-world (as he appears to ordinary parents and older brothers and sisters) already appears as a "not-yet."[60] The pre-philosophical perception of the child is partially constituted by the perceived fact that he is not yet talking, not yet walking, not yet going to school, not yet dating, not yet financially independent, and so on. The dialogic principle can also be employed. If one tries to perceive the child without the characteristic of the "not yet," the childlike, youthlike content of the perception disappears. The not-yet is an essential characteristic of being-child. The appearance of the child as a not-yet is a "special case" of the "general case" of the appearance of man as a not-yet. The subsequent use of philosophical resources occurs with the use of the transcendental (i.e., nonobjectifying) language to further describe and make explicit what is *already given* to *pre*-philosophical understanding concerning the special case of the child. If all human existence appears as having its being to be, so does childlike existence, only much more emphatically so.

The not-yet of the child, furthermore, is something that he, too, is emphatically aware of. The more he is aware of larger children, older youth, and adults, the more he is aware that he is not yet like them, that he cannot yet do what they do, is not yet as big as they are, is not yet in junior high school, is not yet a high school senior, all of which, as they come into his horizons, he becomes aware of as his possibilities that he not yet is. Because he also ascribes status and prestige (or, better, *value*) to being what he is not yet, because he sees these not as roles or possibilities but as what he will become, it is more appropriate to phrase the fundamental motivation of having one's being to be implicitly understood by the child himself as his wanting to be someone, too. Part of this appropriateness is due to the very attempt to describe the "having to be" at the phase of life of educating, before the end of educating is attained. At its end, the "pupil" is someone, too.

There is a parallel to this use of the transcendental language of the

---

*This can be called the existential imperative. See Vandenberg, *Being and Education* (Englewood Cliffs, N. J.: Prentice-Hall, 1971), pp. 66, 167.

philosophical resources of existential phenomenology that may be illuminating. Various non-phenomenological philosophers have spoken of the necessity to "unpack" an obscure concept. Sometimes they have spoken as if it were the major task of philosophy to engage in "unpacking" confused concepts, tending to assume that the elaboration can unpack the meanings that already lie hidden within the concept. This unpacking, however, seems to be merely the explication of the pre-philosophical understanding of the concept. Analogously, the use of language from the philosophical resources of fundamental educational theory serves to unpack the intuition of the educational phenomenon at hand. In this way the perception of the child's not-yet unfolds into his wanting to be someone himself and the latter unfolds into having his being to be. Describing the aim of educating as its end in the independently existing adult is likewise a concretization of having one's being to be, but taken over responsibly. This result was not obtained deductively from the philosophical literature, however, but explicated from the pre-philosophical understanding of the phenomenon of educating as it was already given in the lived-world.

The legitimate use of philosophical resources in the formulation of fundamental educational theory, then, occurs after the "intuition" of the educational phenomenon in order to supply the language necessary for its presuppositionless (in the aforementioned sense) phenomenological description in the second phase of Bollnow's procedural recommendation. To say that it occurs after the intuition of the educational phenomenon merely means that its use must be guided by the pre-philosophical understanding of the experienced practitioner, or by macrocosmic, rather than fundamental, theory results.

The Task

Because transcendental language furnishes the means to locate educational concepts in the lived-world, which is the context of the logic involved in Hirst's view of educational theory, it also makes the coherence of fundamental educational theory possible. This coherence, it should be clear, is not that which is found in the transcendental language as it is established in the philosophical resources. It must be established anew in the descriptions of particular educational phenomena that comprise fundamental educational theory as each concept is related to the structural context in the *third* phase of Bollnow's recommendation. Thus the brief articulation of educating, of the concept of the pedagogic relation, was put into the context of the aim of educating above. The aim of educating delimits the structural context of the entire educational process, within which all educational phenomena can be conceptually ordered subsequent to their phenomenological description. The normative descriptions of these phenomena in the context of a unitary life establishes the coherence of fundamental educational theory. The task of fundamental educational theory, consequently, is to describe all basic educational phenomena and to show how they are interrelated in the context of an integral human life.

This means that fundamental educational theory is the anthropology of education, the theory of the anthropogenesis of man.[61] If it investigates how the child becomes adult through educating, it inquires how man becomes man *sub species educationes,* under the aspect of education. Its initial premise is that man is the educable animal.[62] Fundamental educational theory indicates how man can become a human being through educating by articulating the basic phenomena of education in the structural context demarcated by the aim of educating. Because man is the only animal that educates, it finds its own coherence in the logos of man, in the structures of human existence that make education possible.[63] For example, the help-requiringness of the child is generically different from that of young animals, due to the child's conscious existence and to our (parents, teachers) conscious awareness of his conscious existence, which occurs within our conscious existence, including our self-awareness of our own efforts to help him. This makes educative help—as distinguished from training—possible. Extensive phenomenological descriptions of the various kinds of help required by the child in order to reach the end of educating are basic to fundamental educational theory; a conceptual ordering of the modes of help in "developmental" perspective can ground this aspect of fundamental educational theory in the structures of human existence. Various modes of nonauthoritarian authority accompanying various kinds of help require similar elaboration and conceptual ordering vis-à-vis the *logos* of man to ground fundamental educational theory in the being of man by articulating the framework of educating as helping the person to gradually assume responsibility for his own being so that he can reach the end of educating.

Hirst's view of educational theory is "anthropological" only by accident. He did not explicitly notice that the findings of the various factual and normative disciplines study man. Every finding by any of the resources implicated by his view is a finding out about man. Research in the special sciences was historically possible, moreover, only when inherited theological and metaphysical doctrines about man no longer sufficed to understand him and to account for human action, i.e., only when man became an open question. The factual and normative sciences of man necessarily presuppose that man is an open question,[64] i.e., that he is a being who is in question in his being, who has his being to be. The findings of these specialized ways of studying man are therefore partial answers to this open question of who man is and can become, and any effort to unify the partial findings of various of the separate disciplines is by definition anthropological. When this effort is made in an orientation toward education, as through the media of educational principles as advocated by Hirst, it is substantively an effort in the anthropology of education. It is an implicit, inchoate theory of the anthropogenesis of man.

Hirst's view of educational theory, furthermore, arises in the anthropological dimension. It arises only when the macrocosmic theories of the education of man evaporate consequent upon the collapse of their ideological components, for then not just man, but his education to become man, becomes problematic and questionworthy for the first time. Because Hirst—and any view similar to his—fails to recognize the anthropological context, it follows as a matter of course that the resulting body of educational principles is without coherence. It is without a means of coherence other than the pre-theoretical understanding of man that is presupposed in its theorizing. Hirst was right to "throw out" any and all "logic," any static method of symbol manipulation, to furnish coherence between educational concepts and principles, but the operative criterion of coherence in the open-textured logic that he advocated to connect the special sciences, including philosophy, to the educational principles would be the pre-philosophical understanding of man possessed by the theorizer.* But this implicit view of man cannot come into explicit consciousness in his view because of its own strictures. Similarly, the operative criterion in the open-textured logic that connects the educational principles to practice is the practitioner's pre-philosophical understanding of the educability of man, but this, too, cannot come into explicit awareness within the strictures of Hirst's view. In either case the contextual logic is guided by the inarticulate meanings (tacit knowings) emergent from experienced phenomena that require, on principle, a hermeneutical phenomenological description for their uncovering. They cannot be seen through the language employed in the mode of theorizing advocated by Hirst, for it is purposively (and fruitfully) abstracted from the lived-world.

It is of the utmost importance to notice that views such as Hirst's, and it should be recalled that Hirst's view is selected here because it represents widespread practice in the application of the special sciences to education, deal with findings and concepts that are neither educational nor explicitly anthropological. This practice therefore prevents the emergence of the specifically anthropological dimension of educational theory.[65] It therefore prevents the emergence of the study of education as a discipline, for each of the separate disciplines of man emerges as a separate discipline with the establishment of a unique anthropological claim.

Two such claims have been extended herein. The claim that the aim of educating is its own end is such an anthropological claim definitive of the

---

*For example, the choice between applying a Rogerian or Skinnerian model of learning to be the formation of educational principles rests upon a compatibility between the implicit view of man of the theorizer and that underlying the model.

scope of the study of education. If the end of education is the independent adult, this means that the adult himself says who he is. He who can say for himself who he is and accept full responsibility for himself is adult, and in no need of pedagogic help. This rests upon the anthropological claim that is definitive of philosophical anthropology, i.e., that man is an open question, an entity who has his being to be, which is therefore validated by philosophical anthropology rather than by educational theory.[66] Claiming that the aim of educating is the independently functioning adult, however, is a claim of educational theory that has to be made by educational theory the moment that the theological, philosophical, and ideological doctrines of macrocosmic educational theory become untenable and the moment that the geographical and historical relativity of every particular form of man becomes apparent through the research of the factual sciences of man. As soon as the factual sciences of man are recognized as positive sciences, in other words, man emerges as the open question and the educator confronts the human being directly.[67] Who is this child? What will become of this youth? What are his possibilities? The emergence of the open question determines that the aim of educating is the independent adult who is responsible for his being because more determinant expressions of the aim take away from the pupil that task which belongs to (and defines) his educational process—finding out who he is and can become.

The anthropological claim concerning the aim of educating allows educational phenomena to become visible. It thereby supports the assertion of the primary anthropological claim that man is the educable animal. It is this ontological claim that establishes education as a field of study in its own right and gives the privileged position to fundamental educational theory. The latter remains within the practitioner's perspective in order to confront the human being in his educability directly. The direct access to "man" in his being and possibilities afforded to fundamental educational theory enables it to investigate man in his essential characteristic of requiring educating to become man because everything that man is able to do or be that is distinctly human is due to his having been educated. For the present, however, it suffices to indicate that the accessibility of "man" in his educability that is afforded to fundamental educational theory, when the latter is a hermeneutic phenomenology in the sense herein defined, yields the distinctly educational phenomena that furnish the distinct object of research that is studied by no other discipline, thereby creating the possibility of a discipline of education.

INTERRELATIONS OF THE THREE MODES

Once it is recognized that, because the resultant educational principles become determinants of what man will become, views such as Hirst's recommendation are normative educational anthropologies, the strength of his suggestion for the horizontal integration of the innumerable and varied forms of research in their application to education becomes apparent. The direct application to education of any single finding or concept of any of the separate disciplines immediately becomes recognizable as lying ipso facto in the realm of normative anthropology. It is programmatic, and, as Scheffler has indicated, the validity of the programmatic use of the concepts of the separate sciences in no way depends upon the validity of the concepts in their own domain, but must be evaluated in terms of the program conveyed,[68] that is, in terms of the effect upon the child's life in determining who he will become. Because the sociologist sees man as the social animal, the political scientist sees him as the political animal, the economist sees him as the economic animal, and so on, the direct application of concepts from these separate disciplines to educational practice has the effect of making him become the social, political, economic, and so on, animal. A thorough and complete application of one of the special sciences, for instance, political science, with no applications of the other sciences, would turn man into a political animal and alter human existence radically. This program can be evaluated on the basis of the form of human existence it would promote—one in which the political dimension of life dominates every other dimension, an obviously inhuman life. The strength of Hirst's view is that the horizontal integration of the special sciences it facilitates would prevent this kind of reductionism from occurring.

But all this is not visible within the horizons of researchers and theorists involved in the mode of theorizing represented by Hirst, for they are specialists, totally occupied with the examination of philosophical, sociological, psychological, and so forth, questions and issues underlying practice from within the frame of reference of one of the special sciences.[69] The individual theorists are predominantly restricted to the investigation of educational problems from within one of the forms of knowledge of one of the parent or sister disciplines, in reality functioning within a branch of this mode of theorizing. Actual integration of the resources occurs for the most part by chance. The incoherence of this mode requires the counterbalance of fundamental educational theory.

It can now be seen why fundamental educational theory furnishes the context of relevance so essential to Hirst's view. The universal judgments of necessary validity resulting from adequate employment of the dialogic principle are, or should be, tacitly presupposed by every educational principle.[70] Established on the ontological level, they necessarily underlie every principle that can be established by Hirst's view on the ontic level. Thus the ideal and regulative goal of both modes of inquiry is the production of mutually complementary, parallel bodies of theory, one on the ontological-normative level in the form of a unified system of concepts expressed in terms of necessary judgments, the other on the ontic-prescriptive level in the form of a unified body of educational principles justified in terms of the forms of knowledge of the special factual and normative disciplines. Neither mode, however, can attain this goal without the interpenetration by the other mode.

It has already been sufficiently noticed that Hirst's mode cannot reach this goal without the criteria of relevance and coherence that can only be supplied by fundamental educational theory. It may not be so obvious that the latter requires the assistance of the former to reach its goal. Briefly, all hermeneutic remains within a closed horizon of understanding because it merely explicates the pre-given. Some novelty is required to enable it to break through the closed world of the hermeneutical circle.[71] This novelty can come from two sources: the irruptions of practice or the findings of empirical research. That is to say that the novelty essential to the health of the hermeneutic of education comes from the resources of the other two modes of educational theory. These place the previous understanding in question and force it to a new interpretation to deal with the new phenomenon. Hermeneutic arises of its own accord only when some novelty breaks through existing understandings as one attempts to come to an interpretive understanding of the upsetting circumstance.[72] The disturbances of practice and the new results of empirical research are necessary to provide the dynamic of fundamental educational theory.

It is absolutely crucial to notice that the resources of the other two modes of educational theory have this role to play in the shaping of fundamental educational theory because the latter has the task of laying the foundation for the entire discipline of education, which would wrongly seem imperious if the mutual interpenetration and interdependence were not noticed. If fundamental educational theory can furnish essential descriptions of educational phenomena, then its hermeneutic furnishes the foundation for all possible modes of theory and research in education. Empirical researchers, particularly, would resist such a guardianship, and rightly so.[73] All empirical research, however, requires a hermeneutical interpretation of the phenomena to be investigated before the inquiry can begin, and if this is not accomplished through a phenomenological laying of the foundation, it occurs through the interpretations of common sense, macrocosmic theory of education, or through the conceptualizations of a parent or sister discipline, in which case the result is a contribution to the other discipline. Secondly, the understanding of the results of empirical research in other than the original context is at bottom a hermeneutical affair, as Hirst correctly but unknowingly points out. Third, the claim that fundamental educational theory receives priority insofar as it establishes the foundation upon which experimental research into the pure phenomena of education can be conducted is in fact balanced by the preceding statement of its partial dependence upon experimental findings for its own stimulation. This obliges it to maintain an openness to new knowledge and to the counterclaims coming from experimental research. This reciprocal interaction creates a tension without which the study of education becomes barren. Sterility for both parties results when either the "philosophical" or the "empirical" tendency gains ascendency or when the two tendencies become separate from each other.[74]

The necessity of the two modes is to be found in the realm of application as well as in the domain of investigation. If fundamental educational theory is normative but not prescriptive, it is because it is too general to apply directly. It requires concretization by the factual and normative disciplines.[75] For instance, the statement that the child is help-requiring is thoroughly descriptive of how the child appears, and it is normative because it outlines a desirable attitude toward the child: it is not analytic, or formal in the Kantian sense.[76] Nor is it prescriptive, because it does not say how the child should be helped. It applies equally to the mentally retarded and the gifted child, for example, and must be concretized by the factual sciences to become concretely applicable to these cases. Precisely what help ought be given, furthermore, to the mentally retarded or gifted child cannot be derived directly from the factual sciences, for they merely indicate what help can be given. The normative disciplines of ethics and social philosophy are needed to obtain the prescription and to weigh the claims of the retarded child against those of the gifted child, to weigh the claims of both against those of the normal child, etc. The statements of fundamental educational theory are substantive, but the generality necessitated by the attempt to encompass the essential characteristics of educational phenomena makes them substantively-poor, lacking in richness of concrete content. They are likewise normative, but goal-poor, lacking in the specificity of immediate objectives. To fill these lacks, interaction with the mode of theorizing advocated by Hirst is necessary.

The latter also needs interaction with fundamental educational theory for the addition of transcendental language, i.e., the child's wanting to be someone himself, his project of being, his projection into possibilities of the world, and whatever else becomes necessary to talk about conscious learnings. This transcendental language is necessary to allow educational theory to conform to the criteria indicated by Butler (that it be formulated in a logic that is responsive to the flux of human existence) and by Gowin (that it account for the fact that educating is a morally responsible, goal-directed act of educating). Although Gowin does not suggest that educational theory requires the use of transcendental language, he does say that it should not consider the person being educated as a thing but as a human being. This requires the corresponding kind of language, which is that of the philosophical resources utilized for fundamental educational theory by definition. Butler suggested that its language must be in the same key as human living, but the point here follows Derbolav. Derbolav indicates that because every educating act has the anthropogenesis of the child as its goal, and because the task of the anthropogenesis of the child is increasingly taken over by the child himself as he grows older, the "propositional" structure of educational theory has to preserve, among other things, the character of the "Thou-relatedness" of the act of educating.[77] This is similar to Broudy's point, but it is transferred to the nature of educational theory. According to Derbolav, the terms of educational theory have to be such that they can enter into actual pedagogic conversation with the pupil himself without destroying the conditions of dialogue. This means that the necessity for interaction with the practitioner's theorizing requires the addition of transcendental language so that the pupil is not objectified by the teacher through the intrusion of an inappropriate language when pedagogic conversation has the occasion to turn toward the topic of the nature of education. The object-categorizing language of the factual sciences involved in Hirst's mode does not meet this criterion, for they consider the child as an "It" and intrusion of this language into the pedagogic relation would prevent that relation from achieving the reciprocity of dialogue. Reciprocal interaction of the three modes of theorizing about education is as necessary in application as in investigation.

Continuous and open-ended interpenetration of the three modes of theorizing will of itself serve to integrate all the various resources of educational theory and all the specific inquiries that bear upon educational problems. The integration begins with fundamental educational theory and occurs within the research itself. As each phenomenon is described and located in the structural context of human existence, the concepts become interwoven as the categories become visible. The more phenomena that are described, the more the integration of the concepts occurs of itself, because the structures of the phenomena bring the theorizer to coherence.[78] As the hermeneutic phenomenology of education proceeds, it will come to disclose an entire phenomenal region.[79] It will supply a regional ontology of education. The essential features of this region can then furnish the means to integrate the entire discipline of education through the reciprocal interaction with the other modes of educational theorizing.

REFERENCES

1. Originally by J. R. Burnett, "Analysis of Some Philosophical and Theological Approaches to Formation of Educational Theory and Practice," in *Proceedings of the 17th Annual Meeting of the Philosophy of Education Society* (1961); and in his "Observations on the Logical Implications of Philosophic Theory for Educational Theory and Practice," *Educational Theory*, XI (April 1961), 65-70. See also H. W. Burns, "The Logic of Educational Implication," *Educational Theory*, XII

(January 1962), 53-63; and R. S. Guttchen, "The Quest for Necessity," in *Proceedings of the 20th Annual Meeting of the Philosophy of Education Society* (1964), pp. 52-58.

2. P. H. Hirst, "Educational Theory," in *The Study of Education,* J. W. Tibble, ed. (London: Routledge and Kegan Paul, 1966), pp. 29-58. This is a revision of "Philosophy and Educational Theory," *British Journal of Educational Studies,* XII (November 1963), 51-64, which original version appears in *Philosophy and Education,* I. Scheffler, ed. (Boston: Allyn and Bacon, 1966), pp. 78-95; and in *What is Philosophy of Education?,* C. J. Lucas, ed. (New York: Macmillan, 1969), pp. 175-187. References are to the revision in Tibble's volume.

3. Hirst, *op. cit.,* pp. 35-36. Compare this to Scheffler's statement that teaching rules are based on "factual information," part of which comes from the experience of practice, and that these rules are not directly related to the scientific structure of scientific statements. (I. Scheffler, *The Language of Education* [Springfield, Ill.: Charles C Thomas, 1960], p. 73.)

4. Hirst, *op. cit.,* p. 33.

5. *Ibid.,* pp. 49, 53.

6. *Ibid.,* pp. 40-41, 56-57. According to Scheffler, scientific definitions are conterminuous with the scientific network of theory and evidence in their domain. Removal from that domain for application elsewhere makes them programmatic, and their status in their own domain lends little support for their programmatic use, which has to be evaluated in terms of the program conveyed. (Scheffler, *op. cit.,* pp. 12, 34.)

7. Hirst, *op. cit.,* pp. 33-34.

8. *Ibid.,* p. 41.

9. D. Butler, "Preface to a Logic," *Educational Theory,* XIV (October 1964), 229-254. See especially page 249.

10. O. Bollnow, "Der Wissenschaftscharakter der Pädagogik," *Erziehung in anthropologischer Sicht* (Zurich: Morgarteb Verlag, 1969), p. 23.

11. D. B. Gowin, "Can Educational Theory Guide Practice?" *Educational Theory,* XII (January 1963), 6-12. In Lucas, *op. cit.,* pp. 209-216.

12. In *The Discipline of Education,* J. Walton and J. L. Kuethe, eds. (Madison: University of Wisconsin Press, 1963), p. 70.

13. H. S. Broudy, in *Philosophy and Education: An International Seminar,* B. Crittenden, ed. (Toronto: Ontario Institute for the Study of Education, 1967), p. 153. Hereinafter this volume will be referred to as *OISE.*

14. Bollnow, *op. cit.,* pp. 30-31.

15. Bollnow, *op. cit.,* pp. 38-40. R. S. Peters' statement in a context generally supportive of Hirst's view can be taken from its specific context to support the present view: "Philosophy has an important contribution to make to practical wisdom; but it is no substitute for it." *OISE,* p. 19.

16. W. Loch, *Die anthropologische Dimension der Pädagogik* (Essen: Neue Deutsche Schule Verlagsgesellschaft, 1963), pp. 79-80; 80, n. 133.

17. The shortcoming is indicated by M. J. Langeveld, *Einführung in die theoretische Pädagogik* (Stuttgart: Ernst Klett Verlag, 1969), p. 208, n.

144. The last point in the text is the rejected goal of the original version of Hirst's paper. See the reprint in Scheffler, *Philosophy and Education*, p. 84.

18. See H. Spiegelberg, *The Phenomenological Movement* (The Hague: Martinus Nijhoff, 1960), two volumes.

19. E. Husserl, *The Crisis of European Sciences and Transcendental Phenomenology*, D. Carr, tr. (Evanston: Northwestern University Press, 1970).

20. Such as A. Gurwitsch, *The Field of Consciousness* (Pittsburgh: Duquesne University Press, 1964). For the general point, see J. Edie, "Transcendental Phenomenology and Existentialism," *Journal of Philosophy and Phenomenological Research*, XXV (September 1964), 52-63.

21. Compare paragraphs 40-41 of *The Crisis* with section 12 of Heidegger's *Being and Time*, J. Macquarrie and E. Robinson, trs. (New York: Harper & Row, 1962). Or compare Part III, A, of the former with Part One, Division One, III-V, of the latter. For a brief comparison of the two on the lived-world, see R. E. Palmer, *Hermeneutics; Interpretation Theory in Schleiermacher, Dilthey, Heidegger, and Gadamer* (Evanston and Chicago: Northwestern University Press, 1969), pp. 179-180.

22. Heidegger, *Being and Time*, section 7.

23. Cited by D. Ihde, *Hermeneutic Phenomenology; The Philosophy of Paul Ricoeur* (Evanston and Chicago: Northwestern University Press, 1971), p. 89. See Heidegger's explication of this point in *On the Way to Language*, P. D. Hertz, tr. (Harper & Row, 1971), pp. 28-36.

24. Palmer, *op. cit.*, pp. 12-13.

25. Ihde, *op. cit.*, p. 83.

26. Palmer, *op. cit.*, ch. 8.

27. *Ibid.*, pp. 46, 123.

28. *Ibid.*, ch. 4.

29. See E. D. Hirsch, *Validity in Interpretation* (New Haven: Yale University Press, 1967).

30. Bollnow, *op. cit.*, pp. 19-20.

31. Palmer, *op. cit.*, p. 195.

32. J. Dewey, *Democracy and Education* (New York: Macmillan, 1916), ch. 7.

33. Bollnow, *op. cit.*, pp. 19-20.

34. S. Strasser, *Erziehungswissenschaft-Erziehungsweisheit* (Munich: Kosel-Verlag, 1965), pp. 91-92.

35. *Ibid.*, p. 91.

36. *Ibid.*, p. 98.

37. See Bollnow, "Considerations on the Construction of a Philosophical Knowledge," *Universitas*, XIII (1971), 115-117.

38. Strasser, *op. cit.*, pp. 95-96.

39. *Ibid.*, p. 97.

40. Gadamer, quoted by Palmer, *op. cit.*, pp. 182-183.

41. Strasser, *op. cit.*, p. 98.

42. *Ibid.*, p. 98.

43. *Ibid.*, pp. 99-100.

44. *Ibid.*, p. 100.
45. *Ibid.*, p. 100.
46. *Ibid.*, p. 101.
47. *Ibid.*, pp. 101-102. See J. Kozol, "Free Schools, A Time for Candor," *Saturday Review* (March 4, 1972), p. 51-54.
48. Strasser, *op. cit.*, p. 103.
49. *Ibid.*, pp. 92-93.
50. *Ibid.*, p. 94.
51. Appearing in the highly popularized *Existentialism* (New York: Philosophical Library, 1947), p. 18.
52. Heidegger, *Being and Time*, pp. 37-39, 41-43, 70-71.
53. *Ibid.*, pp. 32-33, 67-68.
54. Strasser, *op. cit.*, pp. 103-104.
55. *Ibid.*, p. 104-105.
56. See Bollnow, "Encounter and Education," *Educational Forum*, XXXVI (March and May 1972), for an illustration of an application of this procedure.
57. Bollnow, *op. cit.*, p. 38.
58. *Ibid.*, pp. 39-40.
59. Heidegger, *Being and Time*, p. 287.
60. Langeveld, *Die Schule als Weg des Kindes* (Braunschweig: Westermann, 1966). p. 25.
61. J. Derbolav, "Das Selbstverstandnis der Erziehungswissenschaft," *Hermaneutik, Phänomenologie, Dialektik, Methodenkritik*, S. Oppolzer, ed. (Munich: Ehrenwirth Verlag, 1966), p. 120.
62. Loch, *op. cit.*, pp. 79, 92.
63. Langeveld, *Einführung in die theoretische Pädagogik*, p. 173.
64. Loch, *op. cit.*, p. 77.
65. *Ibid.*, pp. 75-76.
66. Strasser, *op. cit.*, p. 108.
67. Loch, *op. cit.*, pp. 73-74.
68. Scheffler, *op. cit.*, p. 34.
69. Hirst, *op. cit.*, pp. 55-56.
70. Strasser, *op. cit.*, p. 103.
71. Bollnow, "Der Wissenschaftscharakter der Pädagogik," p. 37.
72. *Ibid.*, p. 42.
73. *Ibid.*, p. 44.
74. *Ibid.*, p. 44.
75. Strasser, *op. cit.*, p. 112, citing Derbolav.
76. *Ibid.*, p. 107.
77. Derbolav, *op. cit.*, pp. 120, 123.
78. Loch, *op. cit.*, p. 103.
79. Bollnow, *op. cit.*, p. 48.

Biographical Notes

J. GORDON CHAMBERLIN

Educated at Cornell College (Iowa), Union Theological Seminary (New York), and Teachers College of Columbia University. Presently, Professor of Education, Pittsburgh Theological Seminary, and Adjunct Professor at the University of Pittsburgh. From 1951-1960, Minister of Education, The Riverside Church, New York. A Fellow in the Philosophy of Education Society, member of the Society for Phenomenology and Existential Philosophy, and President of the Latin America Foundation. Author of numerous articles and several books, the last four being *Parents and Religion* (1961), *Churches and the Campus* (1963), *Freedom and Faith* (1965), and *Toward a Phenomenology of Education* (1969).

CLINTON COLLINS

Educated at the University of Wisconsin, New School for Social Research, and Indiana University. Presently, Associate Professor of Philosophy of Education, University of Kentucky. At New School he studied social phenomenology with Alfred Schütz. A Fellow of the Philosophy of Education Society. His articles have appeared in *The Educational Forum* and *Philosophy of Education,* the most recent being, "On the Subjectivity of Toothaches and Teaching: An Application of the Phenomenological Sociology of Alfred Schütz."

DAVID E. DENTON

Educated at the University of Tennessee, he has done post-doctoral work in phenomenology with Erwin Straus. Presently, Associate Professor and Director of Graduate Studies, Department of Social and Philosophical Studies in Education, University of Kentucky. A Fellow of the Philosophy of Education Society, Past-President of the Ohio Valley Philosophy of Education Society, and member of the Society for Phenomenology and Existential Philosophy. Author of several articles, his related books include *The Philosophy of Albert Camus* (1967), *The Language of Ordinary Experience* (1970), and *Existential Reflections on Teaching* (1972).

MAXINE GREENE

Educated at Barnard College and New York University. Presently, Professor of English and Educational Philosophy, Teachers College. Past-President of the Philosophy of Education Society, currently President of the American Educational Research Association, and Executive Board member of the John Dewey Society. Has published over 65 articles in scholarly and professional journals, and is the author of *The Public School and the Private Vision* (1965), *Existential Encounters for Teachers* (1967), and *Teacher As Stranger: Educational Philosophy in the Modern Age* (1972).

EUGENE KAELIN

Educated at the University of Missouri, Université de Bordeaux, and the University of Illinois. Presently, Professor of Philosophy, Florida State University. Has published numerous works in existentialism, aesthetics, and art education, the most noted being *An Existentialist Aesthetic* (1962).

PHILIP PHENIX

Educated at Princeton, Union Theological Seminary (New York), and Columbia University. In 1967, he studied in Mexico, investigating philosophies of value in Latin American thought. Presently, Professor of Philosophy and Education, Teachers College. He is the Immediate Past-President of the Philosophy of Education Society. Author of numerous articles and books, his most recent books being *Philosophies of Education* (1961), *Education and the Common Good* (1961), *Realms of Meaning* (1964), *Man and His Becoming* (1964), and *Education and the Worship of God* (1966).

LEROY TROUTNER

Educated at San Jose State College and Stanford University. Presently Associate Professor of Education, University of California, Davis. A Fellow of the Philosophy of Education Society. His works on Heidegger and Dewey have appeared in *Philosophy of Education, Educational Theory, Harvard Educational Review,* and *The Personalist.*

DONALD VANDENBERG

Educated at Maryville College (Tennessee), and at the Universities of Wisconsin and Illinois. Presently, a Visiting Professor at the University of Calgary. A Fellow of the Philosophy of Education Society, member of the Society for Phenomenology and Existential Philosophy, and an Executive

Board member of the John Dewey Society. His articles have appeared in numerous journals, and he has published *Teaching and Learning* (1969), *Theory of Knowledge and Problems of Education* (1969), and *Being and Education: An Essay in Existential Phenomenology* (1971).